Praise for *The Lie*

"Claustrophobic, tense…a thrill-ride of a novel that keeps you guessing."
> —Elizabeth Haynes, author of *Into the Darkest Corner*

"A gripping and disturbing psychological thriller."
> —Clare Mackintosh, author of *I Let You Go*

"My heart was racing… Dark, creepy, and full of twists. I loved it."
> —Rowan Coleman, author of *The Day We Met* and *We Are All Made of Stars*

THE
LIE

C. L. TAYLOR

sourcebooks
landmark

Published by Sourcebooks Landmark, an imprint of Sourcebooks, Inc.
P.O. Box 4410, Naperville, Illinois 60567-4410
(630) 961-3900
Fax: (630) 961-2168
www.sourcebooks.com

Originally published in 2015 in the United Kingdom by Avon, an imprint of HarperCollins Publishers, UK.

Library of Congress Cataloging-in-Publication Data

Names: Taylor, C. L.
Title: The lie / C. L. Taylor.
Description: Naperville, Illinois : Sourcebooks Landmark, [2016] | ?2015
Identifiers: LCCN 2015041053 (pbk. : alk. paper)
Subjects: | GSAFD: Mystery fiction. | Suspense fiction.
Classification: LCC PR6120.A89 L54 2016 | DDC 823/.92--dc23 LC record available at http://lccn.loc.gov/2015041053

Printed and bound in the United States of America.
VP 10 9 8 7 6 5 4 3 2 1

To Laura B., Georgie D., and Minal S.

1

PRESENT DAY

I know he's trouble before he even sets foot in the building. I can tell by the way he slams the door of his 4×4 and storms across the parking lot without waiting to see if his short, bespectacled wife is following him. When he reaches the glass double doors to reception, I avert my gaze back to my computer screen. It's best to avoid direct eye contact with an aggressor. When you spend twelve hours a day with dangerous animals, you learn a lot about confrontation, fear, and hostility—and not just in relation to dogs.

The bell above the doors rings as the man enters the reception area, but I continue to enter the details of a seven-day evaluation into the computer database. A German shepherd named Tyson was brought in by an inspector a week ago. We've been evaluating him ever since, and I've identified behavioral issues with other dogs, cats, and humans—unsurprising in a former drug-den guard dog. Some people believe that a dog like Tyson should be put down for his own good, but I know we can rehabilitate him. Your past doesn't have to define your future.

"Where's my fucking dog?" The man rests his elbows on the reception counter and juts out his chin, contempt etched onto his thin, sunken face. His shoulders are narrow beneath an oversize leather jacket, and his jeans hang loosely from his hips. He can't be much older than late forties, early fifties tops, but he looks worn down by life. I suspect he's the sort to own a dangerous breed. Small man, big car. Big dog too. No wonder he wants him back. He's missing his canine penis extension.

"Can I help you?" I swivel around to face him and smile.

"I want my dog. One of my neighbors saw the inspector turn up when we was out. They took him out the backyard. I want him back."

"He's named Jack, he's a Staffordshire bull terrier, and he's five years old." His bespectacled wife puffs into the reception area, her black leggings sagging at the knees, her pink lipstick neatly applied, and her gray-streaked hair scraped back into a tight ponytail.

I look back at her husband. "And your name is?"

"Gary. Gary Fullerton," the man replies, ignoring his wife.

I know the dog they are talking about. Jack was brought in four days ago. His right eye was so swollen it was sealed shut, his lip was torn and bloody, and his left ear was so mangled the vet had to remove half of it. He'd been in a fight, but it clearly wasn't a one-off. You could tell that by the scars on his body and the wounds on his face. This owner's obviously fresh from the police station. On bail pending a hearing, probably.

My smile fades. "I'm afraid I can't help you."

"I know he's here," the man says. "You can't keep him. We haven't done anything wrong. He got into a fight in the park, that's all. We've got seven days to claim him. That's what my mate said."

I angle myself away from him so my shoulders are square on to the computer and we're no longer facing each other. "I'm sorry, but I can't discuss special cases."

"Oi!" He leans over the counter and reaches for the monitor, yanking it toward him. "I'm talking to you."

"Gary…" His wife touches his arm. He glares at her but lets go
of the monitor. "Please." She peers at my name badge. "Please,
Jane, we just want to see Jack, that's all, just to check he's okay.
We don't want any trouble; we just want to see our boy."

Her eyes mist with tears behind her glasses, but I don't feel
sorry for her. She must know Gary enters Jack into fights. She's
probably objected from time to time, maybe tried her best to clean
Jack up with a wet washcloth afterward, but ultimately, she's done
nothing to stop that dog from getting torn to bits.

"I'm sorry." I shake my head. "I really can't discuss indi-
vidual cases."

"What bloody case?" the man roars, but his hands hang loosely
at his sides. The fight's gone out of him. He knows he hasn't got
a leg to stand on, and the shouting's just for show. The worst
thing is he probably does love the dog. He was no doubt proud
of Jack when he won his first few fights. He probably gave him a
big handful of dried dog biscuits and sat next to him on the sofa
with his arm around him. But then Jack started to lose, and Gary
didn't like that; it knocked his pride, so he kept entering him into
competitions, kept waiting for his fighting spirit to return, kept
hoping his luck would change.

"Everything okay, Jane?" Sheila, my manager, strolls into
reception from the corridor to my right and puts a hand on my
shoulder. She smiles at Gary and his wife, but there's a tightness
around her lips that suggests she's heard every word.

"We're going." Gary slaps the counter with the palm of his
right hand. "But you haven't heard the last from us."

He turns and stalks toward the exit. His wife remains where
she is, fingers knotting in front of her, silently pleading with me.

"Come on, Carole," Gary snaps.

She hesitates, just for a second, her eyes still fixed on mine.

"Carole!" he says again, and she's off, trotting obediently at
his side.

The bell rings as they leave reception, and they cross the parking lot in single file, Gary leading, Carole following behind. If she glances back, I'll go after her. I'll make up an excuse to talk to her on her own. That look she just gave me…it wasn't just about the dog.

Look back, look back, Carole.

Lights flash as Gary points his key fob at the Range Rover, and he opens the door. Carole clambers into the passenger seat. Gary says something as she settles herself, and she takes off her glasses and rubs her eyes.

"Jane." Sheila gently squeezes my shoulder. "I think we should have a nice cup of tea, don't you?"

I get the subtext: Jack's your business, Carole's not.

She heads for the staff room, then stops suddenly. "Oh! I forgot to give you this." She hands me an envelope. My full name is handwritten on the front: *Jane Hughes, Green Fields Animal Shelter.* "A thank-you letter, I imagine."

I run my thumb under the seal and open the envelope as Sheila waits expectantly in the doorway. There's a single piece of paper inside, folded into four. I read it quickly, then fold it back up.

"Well?" Sheila asks.

"It's from Maisie's new owners. She's settled in well, and they're head over heels in love with her."

"Great." She gives an approving nod before continuing into the staff room.

I wait for the sound of her footsteps to fade away, then glance through the glass double doors to the parking lot beyond. There's an empty space where Carole and Gary's 4×4 was parked.

I unfold the piece of paper in my hands and read it again. There's a single sentence, written in the center of the page in blue ink:

I know your name's not really Jane Hughes.

Whoever sent it to me knows the truth. My real name is Emma Woolfe, and for the last five years, I've been pretending to be someone else.

2

FIVE YEARS EARLIER

Daisy doesn't say a word as I sit down opposite her at the table. Instead, she pushes a shot toward me, then glances away, distracted by a group of men squeezing their way through the pub to an empty table near the bathroom. One of the men at the back of the pack—a short, dark-haired guy with a paunch—does a double take. He nudges the man next to him, who pauses, glances back, and gives Daisy a nod of approval. She dismisses him with the arch of one eyebrow, then looks back at me.

"Drink!" she shouts and gestures toward the glass. "Talk afterward."

"Nice to see you too."

I don't ask what it's a shot of. I don't even sniff it. Instead, I knock it back, then reach for the glass of white wine that Daisy pushes toward me. I can barely taste it for the strong aftertaste of aniseed from the shot.

"You okay, darling?"

I shake my head and take another sip of wine.

"Geoff the Asshole giving you shit again?"

"Yeah."

"So quit."

"If only it were that easy."

"Of course it's that bloody easy, Emma." Daisy runs both hands through her blond hair, then flicks it over her shoulders so it cascades down her back. "You print out a resignation letter, you give it to him, and then you leave, middle-finger salute optional."

A man holding two pints knocks the side of my chair with his hip. Lager slops out of the glasses and soaks my left shoulder.

"Sorry," I say automatically. The man ignores me and continues onward, his mates in his sights.

Daisy rolls her eyes.

"Don't."

"What?" She gives me an innocent look.

"Don't give me shit for apologizing, and don't go after him."

"As if I would."

"You would."

She shrugs. "Yeah, well, someone's got to stand up for you. Want me to have a word with your boss for you too? Because I would, you know."

Her cell phone, on the table in front of her, bleeps, and she jabs it with a bitten-down fingernail. Daisy's eyeliner is deftly applied, her blond hair straightened and shiny, but her cuticles are ragged, her red nail polish chipped and flaking. Her nails are the one chink in her perfectly polished armor. She catches me looking and clenches her fingers into fists, burying them in her lap.

"He's a bully, Emma, pure and simple. He's been criticizing you and making you feel like shit since the day you started."

"I know, but there's a rumor he's going to take over the Manchester office."

"You've been saying that for three years."

"I can't just leave."

"Why? Because of your mom? Jesus Christ, Emma, you need to grow a pair. You're twenty-five years old. You only get one life; do what you want. Fuck your mom."

7

"Daisy!"

"What?" She tops up her glass and knocks it back. From the glazed look in her eyes, I suspect that this bottle of wine isn't her first of the night. "Someone's got to say it, and it might as well be me. You need to stop caring about her opinion and do what you want. It's getting boring, your obsession with what your bloody family thinks. You've been on about it since university and—"

"Sorry I've bored you. I thought we were supposed to be friends." I reach for my bag and stand up, but Daisy reaches across the table and grabs my wrist.

"Don't be like that. And stop bloody apologizing. Sit down, Emma."

I perch on the edge of my seat. I can't speak. If I do, I'll cry, and I hate crying in public.

Daisy keeps hold of my hand. "I'm not being a bitch. I just want you to be happy, that's all. You've already told me you've saved up enough money to stop work for three months."

"That's emergency money."

"And this is an emergency. You're miserable. Come work with me in the pub until you get something else. Ian would take you on in a heartbeat; he loves redheads."

"It's dyed."

"For God's sake, Emma—"

Her phone vibrates on the table, and the tinny sound of Rihanna and Eminem's "Love the Way You Lie" cuts through the chatter and hum in the pub.

Daisy holds up a hand to me, then snatches up her phone. "Leanne? You okay?" She puts a finger in one ear and frowns in concentration. "Okay. Yeah, we'll be there. Give us fifteen minutes to grab a cab. All right? Okay. See you in a bit."

She tucks her phone into the tiny clutch bag on the table, then looks across at me. There's concern in her blue eyes, but a sliver of excitement too.

"That was Leanne. She's in that new gay club, Malice, in Soho with Al. Al's on the hunt for Simone and her new girlfriend."

"Shit." I clutch my bag and reach around for my coat on the back of my chair.

"You okay if we go? I know we were talking about your job, but—"

"It's fine." I stand up. "Al needs us. Let's grab a cab."

~

We sit in silence as the taxi splashes through puddles and the bright lights of London's West End speed past us. The streets are unusually empty, the heavy rain forcing locals and tourists into already packed pubs, their windows misty with condensation.

Daisy looks up from her phone. "You know it's the anniversary of her brother's death, don't you?"

"Al's brother?"

"Yeah. I called her at lunchtime."

"How was she?"

"Drunk."

"Shit, at work?"

"No, playing hooky; she was in the pub."

"She's been doing that a lot recently."

"Yeah, when she's not stalking Simone," Daisy says, and we share a look.

It's been over a month since Al and Simone split up, but Al's behavior is becoming more and more erratic by the day. She's convinced that Simone left her because she met someone else, and she's determined to find out who it is. She spends hours on Google, looking for "clues," and she's created several false Facebook profiles to try to get access to Simone's page and the pages of anyone she's friends with. None of us had seen the split coming, not least Al, who'd been planning on proposing. She'd been saving up for months for a ring and a safari in Kenya so she could propose on an elephant ride—Simone's favorite animal.

"Here we are, ladies," the cab driver says over his shoulder as we pull up in front of the neon-pink Malice sign.

Daisy pokes a tenner through the glass partition, then opens the taxi door. "Let's go get Al."

~

"Excuse me, darling. Thank you. Excuse me."

Daisy elbows her way through the throng of bodies clogging up the stairs, and I follow in her wake. We've already squeezed our way across the dance floor on the ground level in search of Leanne and Al, but there is no sign of them. No sign of Simone either.

"Bathrooms!" Daisy twists back and waves her cell phone at me as she reaches the top of the stairs, then takes a left.

I struggle to push my way through the huge crowd of women drinking beer and hanging out outside the women's bathroom but finally manage to make my way inside.

"Oi!" A large woman wearing a Superdry T-shirt and oversize jeans shoots out a tattooed arm to bar my way as I attempt to squeeze past her. "There's a line."

"Sorry, I'm just looking for a friend."

"Emma, in here!" A stall door swings open, and Daisy waves at me through the gap. She makes an apologetic face at the woman in the line. "Sorry, we're dealing with a crisis in here."

"Bloody lesbians," the woman says. "Always a melodrama."

~

There's no room for me to squeeze inside the stall, so I hover outside and poke my head around the door. Al is sitting on the toilet with her head in her hands. Leanne and Daisy are pressed up against the walls on either side of her. Every couple of seconds, the main door into the bathroom opens, and pumping house music floods the entire space as women file in and out, grumbling as they squeeze past me to find an empty stall.

"Al, sweetie." Daisy hitches up her dress and squats down next to her friend. "Let's get you home."

Al shakes her head. The hems of her jeans are wet with rainwater, and the laces of one of her sneakers are untied. There's cellophane poking out from beneath the arm of her T-shirt. She's had another tattoo, but I can't make out what it is.

Leanne catches my eye as though noticing me for the first time. She's dyed her bangs pink since the last time I saw her. Her sharp black bob has always looked a bit severe, but with the pink streak and her new, thick-rimmed black "geek" specs dominating her thin face, she looks like she's wearing a motorbike helmet.

She shrugs and angles her arm toward me so I can read the time on her Mickey Mouse watch. It's midnight. She flashes her fingers at me, then holds up two more. Shit, Al's been drinking for twelve hours.

This isn't the first time Leanne's had to call Daisy and me to take Al home. At five foot six, about two hundred pounds, and bull-like in temperament, it takes all four of us to maneuver Al anywhere, especially when she's drunk. Simone used to manage it, but she had an advantage: Al was in love with her. She could always talk her into going home, no matter how much she'd had to drink.

Two of the girls washing their hands in the sink behind me start laughing, and Al looks up.

"Are they laughing at me? Are you fucking laughing at me?" She half rises, but Leanne presses down on her shoulder, and Daisy grips hold of her wrist so Al is rooted to the toilet.

I glance behind me. "They can't even see you."

"They know." Al runs a hand over her Mohawk. "Everyone knows. I'm a fucking laughingstock."

"No, you're not," Daisy says. "Relationships end all the time, Al. No one's judging you."

"Oh yeah? Then why did Jess at reception say 'Ticket for one?' when I came in?"

"Because you came alone?"

"Oh, fuck off, Daisy." She yanks her hand out of Daisy's grip. "What would you know? You haven't been dumped once in your whole life."

"Well, *I* have," I say, "and I know how much it hurts, especially if they leave you for someone else. I'd had my suspicions about Jake for a while, but then when he—"

"Emma!" Leanne makes a *stop talking* gesture with her finger across her throat.

"Not that Simone left you for someone else," I say, but it's too late. Al's on her feet and barging past me.

"If she's here with that fucking bitch, today of all days, I'm going to swing for her. I'll swing for both of them. Fucking baby dyke bitches."

"Al!" Daisy totters after her, reaching for her arm. "She's not worth it. Al!"

"Well done, Emma." Leanne glares up at me from behind her neon bangs. "I'd just talked her down, and you fired her up again."

"She didn't look very chilled to me."

"You didn't see her before. She was punching the stall walls. She nearly got us both thrown out."

"Sorry. I didn't mean to—"

She pushes past me. "You never do, Emma."

~

By the time I find the others, they're standing in the center of the dance floor downstairs with a circle of people surrounding them.

Al is in the middle, jabbing her finger at Simone and some other girl I don't recognize. Daisy and Leanne are on either side of her.

"I fucking knew it," Al says. "I knew you were sleeping with Gem."

"Actually"—Simone squares up to her, even though she's several inches shorter and several pounds lighter—"Gem and I got together after we split up, not that it's any of your business."

"I think you'll find it is." Al turns her attention to the other woman, who takes a step closer to Simone and slings a heavy arm around her shoulders. She's at least six feet tall, all sinew and muscle, with a heavy jaw and close-cropped hair. She's got a boxer's physique and the attitude to match.

"Think you're clever, do you?" Al asks. "Taking Simone off me?"

"I don't think anything."

"'Course you don't. Pig shit doesn't think."

Boxer Woman smirks. "Piss off, Al. No one's interested, least of all Simone. And for the record, I didn't take her off you. She came running."

"Bullshit. We were happy before you started sniffing around."

"Is that so? According to Sim, you're a possessive control freak who wouldn't let her out."

"Is that what you told her?" Al glares at Simone. "That I'm a control freak? After everything I did for you? When we met, you had nowhere to live. You had nothing, Simone, and I let you live with me rent free. I gave you money to go clubbing. I would have done anything for you."

"You smothered me."

Al's eyes mist with tears. "Then you should have told me, not run off with this bulldog."

"What did you call me?" Boxer Woman drops her arm from around Simone's shoulders and takes a step toward Al. "Say that again to my face, you fat bitch."

"Fuck you." Al half steps, half jumps forward and swings at the taller woman before Leanne or Daisy can stop her. Her fist makes contact with Gem's jaw, and Gem stumbles backward. Her foot slips on the beer-stained floor, and she tumbles to the ground. The crowd whoops with excitement, and out of the corner of my eye, I spot a male member of security, walkie-talkie pressed to his ear, striding toward us. Daisy sees him too and gestures for me to help Leanne, who's desperately shoving Al toward the door.

It doesn't take much persuasion to get her to leave now. She's so jubilant she practically skips out of the room.

"Fucking yeah!" She punches the air, then winces and hugs her right hand to her body. She glances behind us as we hurry her toward the exit. "Where's Daisy?"

Leanne and I exchange a look. "She'll be fine. She's chatting up the bouncer."

"Dirty slut." Al laughs all the way out of the building and into the waiting cab.

3

I t's the next morning, and I've only been at my desk for ten minutes when Geoff, my boss, wanders over. He lingers behind me, his hand on the back of my chair. I shuffle as far forward as I can, so I end up perched right on the very edge of the seat.

"Late again, Emma."

"Sorry." I keep my gaze fixed on the spreadsheet in front of me. "Tube was delayed."

It's a lie. We didn't get Al into bed until 2:00 a.m., and then I had to wait for a taxi to get me back to Wood Green. By the time I rolled into bed, it was after three.

"You'll have to make up the time. I want you here until seven."

"But I need to get to Clapham by then. My brother's in a play."

"You should have thought about that this morning and gotten up earlier. Now…" My chair creaks as he rests his full weight on it and leans around me so his mouth is inches from the side of my face. I can feel his breath, hot and sour in my ear. "I'm expecting that spreadsheet by lunchtime so I can look over it before I speak to the sales team this afternoon. Or should I expect that to be late too?"

I want to tell him to stick his spreadsheet up his ass. Instead, I curl my hands into fists and press my fingernails into the palms of my hands. "You'll get it."

~

I've been Geoff's assistant for three years. He's head of sales here at United Internet Solutions, a software, hosting, and search engine optimization company. I was only supposed to be here for three months—it was meant to be just another of the countless temping jobs I took after university—but he extended my contract and then offered me a five-grand pay raise and a permanent position. Daisy told me back then to turn it down and do something else, but the only thing I've ever really wanted to do is be a vet, and you can't do that with a business degree. And I couldn't face temping again.

I wait until Stephen Jones, Geoff's favorite salesman and self-proclaimed "top dog," strolls past us and into his office, closing the door behind him, and then I head for the ladies' bathroom, my cell phone hidden up my sleeve. I check the stalls to make sure that neither of the other two women who work for UIS are about, then I dial Mom's number. It's Tuesday, which means she should be at home. She works in the doctor's office she and Dad set up when they were newly married and still childless, but she only does Mondays, Wednesdays, and Fridays. The phone rings for several minutes before she finally picks up. She's had her cell phone for years but still hasn't worked out how to set up voice mail.

"Shouldn't you be at work?" That's how she greets me. No "Hello, Emma," no "Everything okay, darling?" just "Shouldn't you be at work?"

"I am at work."

"Should you be on the phone? You don't want to upset your boss, not after your recent appraisal."

"Mom, can you just... Never mind. Look, I can't make it to Henry's show tonight."

There's an audible intake of breath followed by an exaggerated sigh. "Oh, Emma."

There it is, her disappointed tone, the one perfectly pitched to make me feel like utter shit.

"I'm sorry, Mom. I really wanted to make it, but—"

"Henry will be disappointed. You know how much work he's put into his one-man show. Tonight's the night he's invited lots of agents along, and it's so important that the audience is on his side, and—"

"Mom, I know."

"He wants to take it to Edinburgh; you know that, don't you? We're ever so proud."

"Yes, I do know that, but Geoff—"

"Can't you ask him nicely? I'm sure he'd understand if you explain why."

"I have asked him. He said I have to work until seven because I was late this morning."

"Oh, for God's sake. So it's your own fault you can't come? Don't tell me you were out drinking until late with your friends again."

"Yes. No. We had to help Al. I've told you how upset she's been about Simone recently, and—"

"And that's what I should tell Henry, is it? That your friends are more important to you than your family?"

"That's not fair, Mom. I've been to all George's matches, and I was there when Isabella opened her dance studio."

I spent most of my childhood being dragged from one sibling event to another, a habit that has now become so ingrained that I start each day by checking the calendar in my kitchen to see who's doing what. Isabella is my oldest sibling. She's thirty-two, an ex-dancer, ridiculously beautiful, and married with a son. George is my older brother. He's twenty-eight and a golf pro. He lives in St. Andrews, and I rarely see him. Henry's the youngest; he's twenty-four and the next Eddie Izzard, if you believe my mother.

"Mom?"

There's a pause, a pause that stretches for one, two, three, four seconds.

"Mom? Are you still there?"

She sighs again. "You should get back to work. It sounds like you're in enough trouble as it is."

I swipe at my eyes with the heel of my hand. "Could you wish Henry good luck from me?"

"I will. I'll speak to you soon. You'd better get back to it. Work hard and make us proud."

The line goes dead before I can reply.

4

PRESENT DAY

'm sitting in the staff room, the letter in my hand, my messenger bag at my feet. It's been six hours since Sheila handed me the envelope, and I've lost count of the number of times I've examined it. There's my name, my assumed name—Jane Hughes—at the top, then Green Fields Animal Shelter, Bude, Nr Aberdare, Wales. There's a first-class stamp in the top right corner. It's been stamped, but it's too smudged to make out the town or date. The letter itself is written in blue ink in cursive handwriting. The words aren't large and bold and shouty. They're neatly written, punctuated and spelled correctly.

"You haven't stopped reading that since I gave it to you," Sheila says, taking a step toward me, hand outstretched. "Can I see?"

"It's nothing. Like I said, just a letter from Maisie's owners. Nothing important." I crumple the letter in my hand and throw it toward the trash before she can reach me. It hits the rim and bounces in.

Sheila stops short in the middle of the room. Her outstretched hand drops to her side, and she makes a small "oh" sound, but she doesn't retrieve the letter from the trash. Instead, she gives me a puzzled smile, then heads for the coat stand in the corner of the room. She pulls on her waterproof jacket, grabs her oversize handbag from one of the chairs, and hoists it over her shoulder.

"I'm off, then," she says. "Are you in tomorrow?"

"Yeah."

"Make sure all the gates are secured before you go. We don't want Mr. Four-by-Four and his mates attempting a dognap in the middle of the night, do we?"

"I will, don't worry."

"I won't." Her smile widens, and she raises a hand in good-bye, then heads for the door.

Thirty seconds later, the bell above the main doors tinkles as she leaves. I fish the letter out of the trash, tuck it back into its envelope, and put it in my back pocket. Then I pick up my messenger bag and take out my cell phone.

There are two texts and one missed call.

17:55—Text from Will:

You still on for dinner tonight? X

17:57—Missed call, Will.

17:58—Text from Will:

Sorry, just wanted to check. You do eat sea bass, don't you? I know there's one kind of fish you don't like but couldn't remember if it was sea bass or sea bream? Not too late to pop to the grocery store if you don't like it!

Shit, I forgot I was supposed to be going to Will's for dinner. The phone vibrates in my hand, and a tinkling tune fills the air. *Will.*

I'm tempted to swipe from right to left and pretend I'm working late, but he'll only worry and call back.

"Hello?" I press the phone to my ear.

"Jane!" He says my name jubilantly, his voice infused with warmth.

"Hi! Sorry I didn't get back to you about dinner, but I've only just finished my shift. One of the dogs developed explosive diarrhea when I was doing final checks, so I had to strip his bed and get it in the washing machine."

"Mmm, explosive diarrhea. I love it when you talk dirty to me."

He laughs. I want to laugh too, but I can't.

"So, are you still on for tonight, then?" The smallest note of tension enters his voice. Ours is still a fledgling relationship in many ways. We're still on best behavior, still testing the waters, still figuring each other out. "Because I've got a bet with Chloe, you know."

Chloe's his daughter. She's nine. Will's not officially divorced from her mom yet, but they've been separated for eighteen months and, according to him, living separate lives a lot longer than that.

"What kind of bet?"

"She thinks you'll be dead by morning."

"You can't be that bad a cook!"

"The first time we took her to bonfire night, she sniffed the air and said, 'Smells like Daddy's cooking.'"

This time I do laugh, and the tension evaporates.

"That was a few years ago," he adds. "I have improved since."

"I'll be around in half an hour," I say. "I just need to lock up here and pop home for a shower first."

"Do you have to?" Will asks. "I was looking forward to a whiff of eau de diarrhea."

"You're grim."

"And yet you still like me, so what does that say about you?"

〜

21

My grin disappears the second I leave the staff room. I lock the doors to reception first, then walk through the building so I'm outside the dog compound. The sound of frenzied barking greets me as soon as I step out into the dusk. I enter the building and double check that all the doors to the kennels are shut, the bedding and toys are clean, and there's water in the water bowls. I completed my checks before I finished my shift, but I have to reassure myself everything's still in order before I leave for the night. As I round the building and approach the runs, the barking increases, and cages rattle as Luca, Jasper, Milly, and Tyson throw themselves at the fences. Only Jack stands motionless and silent, staring at me through his one good eye.

"You'll be okay, boy." I speak softly, my eyes averted so we're not making direct eye contact. "You'll be okay."

His tail wags from side to side, but it's a hesitant movement. He wants to trust me, but he's not sure whether he should. Unlike Luca, Jasper, and Milly, Jack's details won't be entered on our website to advertise him as available for adoption once his seven-day observation is over. Instead, like Tyson, we'll look after him until his neglect case comes to court, whenever that might be. He could be here for months, but I'm not planning on going anywhere. Or rather, I wasn't until the letter arrived earlier.

I check the other dog compound, then cross the yard to check on the cattery. Two of the cats press their paws against the glass and mew plaintively, but the others ignore me.

I pass quickly through the small animals facility, checking doors are locked and windows are secured. It's quieter in here, and my reflection, pale and ghostly, follows me from window to window as I hurry down the corridor.

"Hello! Hello!"

The sound makes me jump as Freddy the parrot makes his way along the cage toward me.

He tilts his head to one side, his beady eyes fixed on me. "Hello! Hello!"

He used to belong to a retired army major named Alan, who taught him to swear at visitors, particularly unsuspecting Jehovah's Witnesses and window salesmen. When Alan died, none of his relatives wanted anything to do with Freddy, so he ended up here. He's an expensive breed of bird, and I don't imagine he'll be here long, but we tend to rush any visitors of a sensitive disposition past him as quickly as we can.

"Bye, Freddy," I call as I head toward the main doors. "See you tomorrow."

"Bitch!" he calls after me. "Bye-bye, bitch!"

~

Will has been talking for the last ten minutes, but I haven't the slightest clue what he's on about. He started by telling me about something funny that happened at school this morning, some ten-year-old who confused tentacles with testicles in his lesson about octopuses, but the conversation has moved on since then, and I can tell by the look on his face that smiling and nodding isn't enough of a response.

The letter is burning a hole in my pocket. It has to be from a journalist—that's the *logical* explanation. But why not sign it? Why not include a business card? Unless they're deliberately trying to spook me into talking to them... It's been five years since I returned to the UK, and four years since a journalist last tried to get me to sell my story, so why now? Unless that's it—it's the five-year anniversary of our trip to Nepal, and they want to dig it all up again.

"You lied, didn't you?" Will asks, and I look up.

"Sorry?"

"About the sea bass? It's not the sea bream you don't like; it's the bass. That's why you haven't touched it."

We both stare at the untouched fish on my plate, the dill and butter sauce congealed around it like a thick, yellow oil slick. "I'm sorry. I've just got a lot on my mind."

"Spill." He runs a hand through his dark hair, then rests his chin on his hand, his eyes fixed on mine. "You know you can tell me anything."

Can I, though? We've known each other for three months, been sleeping together for half that time, and yet I feel we barely know each other, not really. I know that his name is William Arthur Smart, he's thirty-two, separated with a nine-year-old daughter named Chloe. He's a primary school teacher, he likes folk music, his favorite films are the *Star Wars* trilogy, and he can't stand the taste of coriander. Oh, and he's got a sister named Rachel. What does he know about me? I'm Jane Hughes. I'm thirty, childless, and work at Green Fields Animal Shelter. I like classical music, my favorite film is *Little Miss Sunshine*, and I don't like the texture of sea bream. I have two brothers and a sister—Henry, George, and Isabella. It's all true. Almost.

"What's the worst lie you've ever told?" I ask.

He frowns momentarily, then smiles. "I told my teacher my dad was Harrison Ford when I was ten. I said he might let me bring the *Millennium Falcon* in to school if I promised not to scratch it."

His answer is so typically Will that I can't help but smile. He's a good person. Nothing he's said or done in the last three months has given me reason to think otherwise, but I don't trust my instincts. You can spend years of your life with someone and still not know them. So how can I trust someone I barely know?

"Hello?" He waves a hand in front of my face. "Anyone there?"

"Sorry?"

"I just asked why you asked that. About the lie."

"No reason, just curious."

He stares at me for several seconds, then sighs softly and reaches for my plate. "I'll get dessert. And if you don't eat my

24

world-famous raspberry cheesecake, I'm taking you to a doctor to get your taste buds checked."

"Will," I say as he disappears into the kitchen.

"Yes?" He pokes his head out the door, my plate still in his hand.

"Thank you."

He looks confused. "But you didn't like it."

"I wasn't talking about the fish."

"What for, then?"

I want to thank him for not pushing me to talk about my past and for just accepting me at face value, but the words tie themselves in knots on my tongue.

"For this." I wave a hand toward the bottle of wine and the flickering candles on the table. "It's just what I needed."

He pauses, as though trying to work out if I'm being sarcastic or not, then grins broadly. "If flattering me is your subtle ruse to try to get out of tasting my cheesecake, I'm not falling for it. You know that, don't you?"

5

S o did you sleep with the bouncer?"

Daisy smirks from behind her mug of tea. "Someone had to distract him from throwing Al out."

Leanne looks up from her cell phone. "That's a yes, then."

It's been a week since we manhandled Al out of the nightclub, and the three of us are gathered in Leanne's tiny studio flat in Plaistow, East London, to talk about how best to help her. Daisy and Leanne are sitting cross-legged on her single bed, the cro-cheted bed cover pooling on the threadbare beige carpet, while I'm perched on the only chair in the room, a hard-backed pine affair by the window. There's a basic kitchen on the other side of the room—sink, microwave, fridge, and a two-ring portable electric burner—and a clothes rail along the wall opposite the bed, and a small chest of drawers with a fourteen-inch flat-screen TV on the top. Leanne's tried to cheer up the room with a print of a sunny poppy-filled field, a small porcelain Buddha, a plaque that says "Only Truth Will Set You Free" on the windowsill, and a spider plant next to the stove, but it's still undeniably bleak. In the two years that she's lived here, it's only the second time she's invited me around. Correction: Daisy invited me around. Leanne texted her to suggest they get together to talk about how best to help Al; Daisy suggested I come too.

"Right." Leanne sits up a little straighter and presses her glasses into her nose. She's been unusually chirpy ever since we turned up, which is slightly weird considering she told Daisy on the phone that Al was sacked from her job three days ago and she was worried she might be a suicide risk. "I've been thinking about how best to help Al, and I've come up with an idea."

Daisy puts her mug down on the chest of drawers. "Go on."

"There are three main issues here." Leanne pauses, relishing the fact that she's got a rapt audience, then holds up her index finger. "One: Al is physically stalking Simone and Gem. She sat outside Gem's house all night last night—literally on the front doorstep—waiting for Gem to come out. Simone called the police."

"Shit."

Leanne raises her eyebrows. "I know. Apparently they just had a 'friendly word' and told her to move on, but if she does it again... Anyway." She raises a second finger. "Two: Al is stalking Simone on the Internet. Now that she's lost her job, she's spending every bloody second on her laptop. I was there yesterday, and when she went to the bathroom, I took a quick look at the screen. She was on some kind of forum about hacking Hotmail accounts. And three," she adds before I can interrupt again, "well, it kind of ties in with one and two. She's spending too much time on her own. We need to keep an eye on her, but none of us can do that twenty-four-seven, unless"—she pauses dramatically—"we take her on vacation."

"Yes!" Daisy's silver bracelets rattle as she punches the air. "Let's go to Ibiza. I love it there. I know a guy who used to work for Manumission who could get us free tickets."

"Did you shag him?"

She gives me the middle finger.

"That's a yes, then," I say, and she laughs.

"So? Ibiza, then? Ian will give me the time off, and I've got a month until my next runner job. Whoop, whoop! Ibiza, here we come." The bed squeaks in protest as Daisy bounces up and down.

"How long for?" I ask. "I've got three weeks' vacation left, but I was hoping to save one of those weeks for Christmas."

"Quit. Honestly, Emma. It'll be the best decision you ever make. Go to Ibiza, and get another job when you come back. You can afford it. You've got three months' emergency money saved up. You said as much last week."

"Actually…" Leanne tentatively raises a hand, but Daisy ignores her.

"Go on, Emma, it's for Al. She'd love a couple of weeks in Ibiza. She went last year, didn't she?"

"Didn't she go with Simone?"

"How's that a problem? She won't be there this time. Will she?"

"I don't know, but she'll have lots of memories of going there with Simone, and—"

"Emma!" Leanne snaps. "Can I get a word in, please?"

"Why are you having a go at me? I wasn't the only one talking."

"As I was saying"—she peers over her specs at Daisy—"I think we should go on vacation, but we should go to a place where (a) she's a long way from Simone, (b) she doesn't have access to the Internet, and (c) she can get her head together."

"Like where?"

"Nepal," Leanne says.

"Where?"

"Nepal! It's in Asia, near Tibet."

Daisy wrinkles her nose. "Why would we want to go there?"

"There's an amazing retreat in the mountains called Ekanta Yatra. My yoga teacher told me about it. Look!" She flashes her cell phone at Daisy, then taps the screen. "Amazing fresh, home-cooked food, yoga, a river you can swim in, a waterfall, massages, facials. We could spend a day in Kathmandu, then do two weeks at the retreat, then we could fly to a place called Chitwan and go on a jungle safari. It would be the adventure of a lifetime."

Leanne's face is aglow. I've never seen her look so energized; she normally looks so wan and tired. She's desperately thin, and Daisy and I have speculated several times about whether or not she might have an eating disorder.

"Could I see that?" I reach out a hand for her cell phone.

She presses it into my palm without saying a word.

I scroll through the website. It would seem Ekanta Yatra's run by a group of Westerners who met when they were traveling through Asia and decided to start a "retreat from the world" nestled in the Annapurna mountain range, an area popular with hikers. It's beautiful, and the idea of spending a couple of weeks being pampered, reading novels, and swimming in a crystal clear river appeals, but...

"There's no Wi-Fi," I say.

"Is that a problem?"

"Well, yeah. I've started looking for new jobs, and I won't be able to check my email."

Leanne slips off the bed and takes five steps across the room to the kettle. She picks it up and refills it from the tap. "You don't have to come, Emma. No one's forcing you."

It's not that Leanne and I actively dislike each other; we are *friends*, but only when we're with Daisy or Al. We don't go for drinks together or have text message marathons. We'll laugh at each other's jokes and buy each other birthday presents, but we've never developed any kind of closeness or warmth. I don't know why that is. Maybe it's because I didn't like the way she looked me up and down the first time we met. Maybe it's because I forgot to get her a drink when I went to the bar to get a round. Or maybe it's because, sometimes, when you meet someone, you get a vibe that they just don't like you, and that vibe never quite disappears.

"I'll bloody force her," Daisy says, jumping off the bed and onto my lap. "You'll come, won't you, Emma?" She cups her hands around my face and nods it up and down. "See, look, she's saying yes. She says she'll come."

"It sounds expensive."

"No more expensive than a couple of weeks in Ibiza," Leanne says as she pours boiling water into three mugs.

"Al's lost her job," I say. "How's she going to afford to go?"

"I'll pay for her," Daisy says. "Or, rather, Dad will." She jumps off me and back onto the bed, but I catch her smile slip. I don't think she's ever forgiven her dad for sending her away to prep school when she needed him most. She was only six years old, and her little sister had died tragically a year earlier. Shortly after her baby sister's death, unable to cope with the grief, her mom killed herself. Daisy's dad, a stockbroker, justified the decision to send her to boarding school by saying it would give her life some stability, plus a mother figure in the shape of a house mistress, but to Daisy, it was like being abandoned all over again. It's why she's so ruthless when it comes to ending friendships and relationships. It's better to leave than be left, no matter how painful the separation might be.

"Well? Are you up for it or not?" Leanne turns to face us, a steaming mug in each hand. She's smiling again, but it doesn't quite reach her eyes. She squeezes past me to reach the chest of drawers. Tea slops onto the pine top as she sets the mugs down. "I thought we could go next month."

"Next month?" I catch Daisy's eye, but she shrugs. She's got Ian, her boss, wrapped around her little finger. He lets her work in the King's Arms whenever she's in between runner jobs, so he won't bat an eyelid if she suddenly announces she's off on vacation for three weeks. And Leanne's an aromatherapy massage therapist who rents a room in a beauty salon, so she can take off whatever time she likes. Geoff won't make escaping to Nepal for three weeks so easy for me.

"You are entitled to time off," Daisy says as though she's just read my mind. "Or you could just quit."

"Daisy…"

"Fine, fine." She holds out her hands as though in surrender. "But if you don't come, I'll never talk to you again."

"Is that a promise?"

"Ha-ha."

"Is that a yes, then?" Leanne twists her hands in front of her. "Are we going to Nepal?"

"Only if we can convince Al."

Daisy grins. "Leave that to me."

6

I have no idea why Al and Leanne are laughing. It's our first night in Nepal, the bar's packed, and since Leanne beat me to the last seat at our table, I'm half squatting, half leaning against the low wall that separates the seating area from the rock band. I say rock band, but the music the four Nepalese musicians are playing is like no rock I've ever heard. The drummer and the bassist are out of time, and the guitarist sounds like he's playing a completely different song. Daisy nods at me from across the table, then sticks out her tongue and holds her hands in the air, folding her fingers into devil's horns like a blond, perfectly made-up Gene Simmons.

"Yeah!" she shouts, then whips her hair back and forth as she head-bangs to a guitar solo that would make Jimmy Page weep. I reach for my beer as the table wobbles precariously.

"Whoa!" Daisy says, rubbing the back of her neck and looking toward the band for a reaction. The guitarist gives her the thumbs-up and shouts something unintelligible.

Leanne squeals with laughter as though it's the funniest thing she's ever seen, while Al, to my left, drains her bottle and reaches for her cell phone. There's no Wi-Fi in the bar, but that hasn't stopped her checking for texts every couple of minutes.

"Shots!" Daisy shouts, jumping to her feet. "Then drinking games. Fuzzy Duck or I Have Never?"

"Fuzzy Duck!" Leanne says, pushing back her chair to stand up.

Daisy dismisses her with a wave of the hand. "I'll get these. You can get the next lot."

Silence descends on our table as the band stops for a break, and Daisy weaves her way through the bar, her denim shorts riding low on her hips, the strap of her red bra escaping from beneath her black tank top and resting on her shoulder. Every man she passes glances up at her. She's the only woman I know who sashays as she walks.

Leanne nudges Al. "Have you seen that couple making out over by the window? She's got her hands down his shorts. It's gross."

"Yeah," Al says without looking up from her cell phone.

It's like she can sense that everything we've done tonight—the head-banging, the jokes, the observations, the drinks—has been for show, to try to cheer her up and distract her from thinking about Simone. It hasn't worked. Al's normally right up there with Daisy, telling stories and bantering, but she's crawled into her shell since we first discussed coming to Nepal a month ago, and no amount of cajoling or teasing will tempt her back out.

"I'm going to the bathroom." She stands up, shoves her phone into the pocket of her cargo pants, and shuffles away.

Leanne and I watch her go.

"Looking forward to Pokhara tomorrow?" Leanne asks.

"I can't wait. I need a massage like you wouldn't believe. How long's the bus journey again?"

"About six hours."

"Wow."

"I noticed a little corner shop just down from our guesthouse. We should grab some water and snacks and things after breakfast."

"Good idea."

We lapse into silence as I gaze around the bar. We're on the first floor of a building on the main stretch of Thamel, the tourist district of Kathmandu, and the sound of car horns drifts through the open windows. The walls are painted a deep red and decorated with fairy lights and paintings of temples and mountain ranges.

"Guys!" Daisy bounces back into view with a tray bearing eight shot glasses in her hands, just as Al rejoins us at the table. "There's a wall over by the bar that loads of people have signed. We need to write something. Come on!"

~

"I don't know what to write." Daisy bites down on the piece of chalk in her hand, then cringes as a squeaking sound fills the air.

"I do." The tip of Al's tongue pokes out of the corner of her mouth as she drags the chalk over the wall. The whole expanse has been painted with blackboard paint, and it's filled with sketches, messages, dates, and obscenities.

"'Fuck you, Simone!'" Leanne rolls her eyes as she reads aloud what Al has written. "Seriously, Al, you can't leave that up there."

"Why not?" Al folds her arms over her chest and stares admiringly at her handiwork.

"Because it's really negative. This vacation is supposed to be about new starts."

"Okay then." Al pulls her sleeve over her hand and rubs at the wall. "There you go."

"'Fuck'?" Leanne asks, and everyone laughs. "That's it?"

"That's the best you're getting out of me. Your turn, Emma." She hands me the chalk.

"Oh God." I look at Daisy, who's still deliberating what to write, a pale chalky patch now smeared on her bottom lip. "I don't know what to write either."

"Give it to me, then." Leanne snatches the chalk from my hand, and before I can object, she steps toward the wall and starts scribbling. When she steps back, there's a self-satisfied grin on her face.

"What the hell?" Al squints at what she's written. It's longer than the things other people have written, and to fit it all in, she's had to twist the sentence over and around other scribbles like a snake.

"It's a Maya Angelou quote," Leanne says. "'The ache for home lives in all of us, the safe place where we can go as we are and not be questioned.'"

I have to fight not to roll my eyes. Trust Leanne to be pseudo-deep when everyone else has drawn dicks and balls and written things like "I love beer" on the wall.

"Okay, I've got it." I twist the chalk from her fingers and read aloud as I write. "Emma, Daisy, Al, Leanne—the adventure of a lifetime."

Daisy steps forward and nudges me out of the way. She rubs out "the adventure of a lifetime" and replaces it with "best friends forever."

"There." She stands back and pulls the three of us into an awkward hug. "Perfect."

Al rummages around in her backpack, pulls out two cans of lager, and chucks one at me. We left the bar half an hour ago, and we're back at the guesthouse, ostensibly to sleep, but Al seems to have other ideas.

I catch the can of beer. "What's this for?"

She settles back on her bed and kicks off her sneakers. "Not being a dick."

"What do you mean?"

"Tonight. It was like the Daisy and Leanne Show. Well, the Daisy Show, with a one-woman audience."

"They were trying to cheer you up." I pull the tab on my beer and take a swig. We drew lots to decide who'd share with whom in the guesthouse. Leanne wanted to share with Al and for Daisy and me to share, but Daisy thought it would be fun to "mix things up a bit," especially as we'll have to share rooms at the retreat and in the jungle too.

"I know, and I would have laughed if it wasn't so sad."

"Al!"

She smirks at me over the lip of her can. "Come on, Emma, admit it. I could see you cringing."

"Well." I shrug. "Maybe a bit. I felt like I should have held up a neon sign pointing to our table that said, 'We Are Having FUN!'"

"Best friends forever!" Al bursts out laughing, and the tension I've felt all evening finally dissipates.

There's a knock at the door, and we both freeze.

"Come in," Al shouts.

The door swings open, and Daisy's blond head peers around the doorway.

"Are you two bitches having fun without me?" She points at our beers with mock horror. "And you're drinking the duty free!"

Al reaches into her backpack and chucks a beer at Daisy. "Join in. Let's be friends forever!" She cackles with laughter, and the sound fills the room.

7

PRESENT DAY

J ane? Have you got a minute?"

I'm elbow deep in dried dog food when Sheila calls my name. She's standing in the doorway of the supplies room with a woman I've never seen before. Unlike Sheila, who's nearly six feet tall and all bosom and bum, the woman standing next to her is tiny. She's barely five feet tall, and her Green Fields standard-issue navy polo shirt hangs flat from her shoulders, skimming her nonexistent chest. Her gray pants nearly cover the toes of her black sneakers.

"Of course." I stand up, tip the scoop into one of the twenty metal bowls on the table to my right, then wipe my hands on my pants and cross the room.

"Jane, this is Angharad, one of the new volunteers. Angharad, this is Jane; she runs the dog section."

"Hi!" I smile at the newcomer. From a distance, she looked about nineteen, but up close, I can see she's nearer my age. She tucks a strand of her neat bob behind an ear as she smiles up at me.

"Hi." She holds out a hand, and I shake it.

"Angharad's between jobs at the moment," Sheila says, "so

she thought she'd do a bit of volunteering while she's looking for something permanent. She particularly requested the dog section—a big dog lover, apparently."

"Great." I smile at Angharad.

"Okay, so, I'll leave you to it, then." Sheila nods, then turns to leave.

⌐

"You said you came to work by bike. Do you live nearby?" Angharad asks as we speed past Freddy and head toward the wild boar pen up near the top field.

"In a cottage down the road. I can see Green Fields from my backyard."

"Wow, that is close. Have you worked here long?"

"Three years, give or take."

I'm giving her the official guided tour of the shelter. She'll already have been shown around when she attended the volunteer evening, but I'd rather chat as we walk than stand opposite each other in the silence of the supplies room.

"Where did you train?"

"Bicton, near Exeter. I did a general degree in animal science management and welfare when I was twenty-five."

"You were a mature student?"

I can tell by the expression on her face that she's waiting for me to go into more detail, to explain what I did before my degree and why I waited until I was twenty-five to study animal welfare, but I ignore her unspoken questions. Instead, I point at the pigs. They greet us with a series of increasingly noisy grunts and squeals as we approach them.

"Bill and Ben. I shouldn't imagine you'll have anything to do with them if you're going to spend most of your time in the dog compound, but watch out for them if anyone asks you to help out.

They're half wild boar," I explain. "We're not sure what they're crossed with, and they're a damned sight more dangerous than they look. Clever too."

Angharad gestures toward the multiple locks, clips, and chains on their pen. "That's a lot of locks."

"They've escaped several times since they arrived, but I think we've outfoxed them. They're vicious buggers too. Turn your back on them for a second, and they'll bite you. That's why we always lock them in their shed if we're cleaning their run and vice versa. They locked me in once."

She laughs, and I'm astonished by the way it transforms her. Gone is the studious look of concentration that's been etched on her face since we were introduced. Her laugh's a snorty chuckle, so infectious I find myself laughing too.

"You're kidding," she says as the laughter dies away.

"I'm not. I was cleaning their shed on my own, the door was closed, and one of them flipped the stable catch over with his nose, locking me in. I had to reach over with a broom and flip it back to get out."

"You don't think they did it on purpose?"

"Who knows? I don't know much about boars and pigs. At least with dogs you can predict how they're likely to react, most of the time, anyway."

"If only it was that easy with people." She gives me a sideways glance. I don't meet her gaze.

"Quite." I gesture for her to follow me back down the track. "They're harder to figure out than the pigs."

~

"So?" Sheila asks as I reach into the fridge for my lunch box. "How's she getting on?"

"Angharad?" I sit down on one of the hard plastic chairs that line the staff room wall and pop open a Tupperware lid. The scent of warm cheese-and-tomato sandwiches drifts unappealingly upward. I should have taken Will up on his offer of a slice of cheesecake for my packed lunch. "She's okay. She was pretty quiet when she started, but now she's warmed up, there's no shutting her up. She's full of questions. Gets on with her work, though. She didn't complain when she had to clean up Jasper's vomit or spend an hour in the laundry room washing blankets and bedding."

"You think she'll be back tomorrow?"

"I think so. She did seem keen to get to work."

I take a bite of my sandwich as Sheila taps away at the computer in a corner of the room, but then subtly spit it into a tissue. The bread is soggy from the damp tomato. Not that I have much of an appetite, anyway. Other than a couple of bites of cheesecake, I've barely eaten since yesterday morning.

"She was very keen to work with you, you know."

"Sorry?"

"Angharad," Sheila says. "When she came to the volunteer night, she specifically requested that she work with you."

"Really?"

"Yeah. She asked who worked in the dog compound, and when I listed everyone's names, she said, 'I'd like to work with Jane, if I could.'"

I look up sharply. "Why would she say that?"

Sheila stops typing and glances at me over her shoulder. "Who knows? Maybe she saw your name in the local paper when we had the fundraising? Maybe you helped one of her friends adopt a dog? Your guess is as good as mine."

The computer bleeps, and Sheila twists back to look at it, then swears under her breath.

"Why do people do that?"

"Do what?" I wrap the cellophane around my sandwich and put it back in the box.

40

"Enter spam into the contact form on our website. What's the point? It's not like I'm going to click on their stupid impotence pill links or whatever. I mean, look, this one's just ridiculous; it doesn't even make sense. 'Daisy's not dead.' What does that even mean? Is that an animal? Wasn't there a ferret named Daisy?"

The Tupperware box clatters to the floor as I stand up. I cross the room as though in a dream and peer over Sheila's shoulder at the computer. The email software is open.

"See?" She points at the screen. "There it is. 'Daisy's not dead.' That's all it says. Weird, isn't it?"

"Jane? Where are you going? What's wrong?" Her voice follows me as I run from the room and head for the bathroom, one hand clutched to my throat, the other pressed to my spasming stomach. "Jane?"

8

FIVE YEARS EARLIER

Y ou should have seen him!" Daisy gets up from her chair
and mimes running alongside a car, her coat caught
in a closed door. "His stubby little legs pounding the
pavement, his fat face bright red, and Emma hanging out of the
window screaming, 'Stop the car! Stop!'"

She finishes her story with a flourish, and there's a beat—a
split-second pause as Al and Leanne glance over at me—and then
the silence is destroyed by an explosion of laughter.

Daisy continues to scream "Stop, stop!" at the top of her voice
while she jumps up and down, her wedge sandals thumping the
patio, a near-empty bottle of red wine in one hand, a full glass
slopping around in the other.

I take a sip of my own wine and stare into the fire pit as it pops
and crackles, watching sparks leap into the air. It's our second
night in Pokhara, and we're sitting on the patio in our swimsuits.
Damp towels lie at our feet like sleeping dogs, the sky is a black
blanket speckled with holes, and the night is alive with the
sound of motorbikes, car horns, and cicadas. This was supposed
to be a treat—a couple of nights' luxury in a hilltop Pokhara

hotel—before we hike up the Annapurna range to Ekanta Yatra tomorrow. I don't know if it's the humidity, the really shitty email Geoff sent me the day before the vacation questioning my ability to do my job, or the fact that Daisy's spent three days getting laughs at my expense, but I'm finding it hard to join in with the frivolity. Back home, I could retreat to my flat in North London when things got a bit overwhelming, but the four of us haven't spent a second apart since we got here.

"Oh, come on, Emma!" Daisy shouts. "Cheer up!"

"I'm not miserable."

"Have you told your face that?"

She laughs and glances at Al as if to say "Right?" but Al doesn't respond. If anything, her smile slips, just the tiniest bit. This is the drunkest any of us have seen Daisy in a while.

"I'm fine, Daisy," I say. "I've just heard that story before, that's all."

"Ooh." She raises her eyebrows and widens her eyes. "Sorry if I'm boring you, Miss Emma Woolfe. Are my storytelling skills lacking? I do apologize."

"Well, *I* think you're funny," Leanne says. She's sitting cross-legged on her chair, her bony knees poking over the arms, a thin gray cardigan wrapped around her shoulders.

"Thank you, darling." Daisy takes a little bow, then totters over to me. "What's up with you, party pooper?"

"Nothing. Forget it." I reach for my wineglass and stand up. "I'm going for a walk around the grounds. I'll see you guys in a bit."

I slip away quickly, Daisy's mocking voice following me out into the darkness of the yard. She's doing her "northern voice," a cross between Yorkshire and Geordie. I'm not even a northerner—I'm from Leicester—but "everyone who lives north of Watford is a northerner," according to Daisy. Daisy and Al both claim to be from London, but Al's actually from

East Croydon, while Daisy's from Elmbridge in Surrey, "the Beverly Hills of Britain," apparently, not that Daisy spends much time there. She went straight from Cheltenham Ladies College to university in Newcastle. Apparently, she was being groomed to go to Oxford or Cambridge, but she was more interested in shagging boys on the grounds after dark than studying for her exams, and she only scraped three Cs. And then after university, we all moved to London.

"Daisy, you're hilarious!" Leanne laughs at Daisy's impression of me like it's the funniest thing she's ever heard. It's been seven years since she first did it at university, and apparently the joke still hasn't worn thin.

I make my way slowly around the swimming pool, checking the wet tiles for snakes, lizards, and frogs, then follow the winding steps down into the gardens. It's darker here, away from the glare of the hotel lights and the glow of the fire, but the moon is full and bright, and I head for the crest of the hill and perch on the edge of a wooden bench there. We've only been in Nepal for a couple of days, and I still feel as though I've been transported onto another planet. Forty-eight hours ago, we were in Kathmandu, with its roaring, beeping, haphazard traffic, men on bicycles piled up with treacherous, wobbling loads, and monkeys jumping from building to building, their young clinging to their chests. Now, in Pokhara, the Annapurna range looms like a dark dragon in the distance, while the lake below, black against the glittering lights of the city, glistens in the moonlight. London couldn't feel further away than it does right now.

I take a sip of wine, then place the glass on the ground. It wobbles precariously but doesn't tip over. I'm drunker than I thought. The sound of someone shouting along to Madonna's "Holiday" drifts across the night air toward me. There's a pause, a loud splash from the swimming pool, and then the singing continues. It's Al. The laughter is all part of the act that she's okay, just like the ceremonial burning of Simone's photo in the fire pit earlier and the solemn promise to "never, ever, get involved with a baby dyke again." Two thousand miles away and a bottle of red wine in her hand, and she's over the love of her life. If only it were that easy.

Leanne joins in the singing, her thin reedy tones picking out the words "holiday" and "celebrate," then falling silent for the rest of the song because she doesn't know the words. Al laughs and Leanne laughs, Al dances and Leanne dances, Al sings and Leanne sings. Leanne does exactly the same with Daisy—it's her MO. She reminds me of one of those birds who jump from one rhino's back to another, hitching a ride, pecking for food, and enjoying the protection of the bigger animal.

Movement from the bushes to my right makes me glance around. The leaves at the base rustle ever so slightly as a gecko creeps out. Its padded fingers grip the ground, and its bulbous eyes swivel from side to side. I stare at it, transfixed. I've only ever seen a gecko in the zoo before. It's strangely beautiful and almost otherworldly with its black, unblinking eyes.

"Here you are!" Daisy comes crashing down the steps toward me, a fresh bottle of wine in one hand, a glass in the other, and a blanket thrown over her arm.

"Don't hate me, Ems!" She throws herself onto the bench beside me and wraps her right arm around my neck, pulling me into her. Red wine sloshes out of the bottle and drips down the front of my swimsuit. "I was only having a laugh."

"I know." I peel the bottle from her fingers and place it on the ground, then untangle myself from her arm, but she continues to push the blanket into my face in a clumsy attempt to mop up the wine. "But I wish you'd stop doing it at my expense."

"Stop being so sensitive. It's just a bit of fun."

"Yeah, because I loved being the punch line of my family's jokes as a kid." I can hear the whiny, self-pitying tone in my voice, but I can't stop myself. Daisy's an aggressive drunk; I'm a maudlin one.

"Oh, for God's sake." She lets out an exaggerated sigh. "Sometimes I think Leanne's right."

"What about?"

"You."

I inch away from her. "Go on."

"No." She peers at me. She took her contacts out earlier because they were gritty at the end of the day, and she's too vain to wear glasses. "You'll get pissed off."

"Tell me."

"No." A smile plays on her lips as she shakes her head. She's so drunk this conversation has become a game. She knows it's dangerous, but she can't stop herself from playing it.

"Just tell me, Daisy."

"Okay, okay. Fine. She thinks you can be a bit of a party pooper sometimes. You say stuff that lowers the mood. Your parents are doctors, they're still together, your brothers and sister are successful, and you've got a job that pays okay, even if your boss is an asshole. Compared to what Leanne's been through, what the rest of us have been through, you haven't really got that much to moan about. That's all."

"And you agree with Leanne, do you?"

"Sometimes."

I stare at her in bewilderment. Seven years Daisy and I have been best friends, and this is the first time she's said anything about me being a drama queen. Leanne's been trying to drive a wedge between us for years, ever since we met at university. "The three amigos," that's how Leanne referred to herself, Daisy, and Al when they stayed up in Newcastle for the first Christmas holidays because none of them wanted to go back to their families. I wanted to stay up with them too, but Mom pulled a guilt trip on me. She told me Granny wasn't very well, and how would I feel if I missed her last Christmas because I chose to get drunk with my friends instead (Granny's still alive and well). Leanne went out of her way to exclude me when I came back in the New Year. She invited Al and Daisy to the movies, to club nights, and to dinner parties at their halls of residence, all the while telling Daisy that she'd invited me but I'd made excuses about studying and said no. I know Leanne and Daisy have been spending more time together in London than usual because they both work flexible hours, Daisy in the pub and Leanne in the salon, and consequently they'd been "babysitting" Al in the run-up to the vacation, but I never once thought they'd spend their time badmouthing me.

"Thanks, Daisy." I stand up. "I try to talk to you about you teasing me, and you use it as an excuse to have a dig at me."

"Stop being so bloody sensitive." She stands up too. "And anyway, that story wasn't about you. It was about that loser you picked up. That's who I was making fun of. It was funny."

"It wasn't funny. Elliot could have been run over."

"Elliot, was it? And there was me thinking he was some random guy who was just after a shag. He was rude, and he deserved to be kicked out of the taxi. I did you a favor, Emma."

"No, you didn't. You kicked him out because he called you a drunken bitch. Daisy, you threatened to find out where he worked and hunt him down if he shagged me and didn't call afterward."

"And?"

Her eyes glitter. There's no reasoning with her, not when she's like this. The evening can only go one of two ways now—she'll either have a raging argument, or she'll pass out. And if I keep quiet, hopefully it'll be the latter.

No such luck. Daisy's on a roll now and won't shut up.

"Because he tried to kiss me, you know, Emma—lovely Elliot, who you're so keen on defending. He was all over me while you were in the bathroom at Love Lies. That's the real reason I kicked him out of the taxi—not because he called me a drunken bitch, but because he was a shit and didn't deserve you."

I'm just about to respond when—"Surprise!"—Al leaps from the top step and lands next to Daisy. Still soaking from the pool, she wraps Daisy in a wet bear hug and clamps a hand to her mouth. Daisy puts up a halfhearted fight to free herself, but she and Al both know it's in jest. Al looks across at me and smiles. "No arguing, you two. We're on vacation, remember? Oh! Look at that gecko."

"What gecko?" Leanne makes her way gingerly down the steps. She pulls the gray cardigan tighter around her shoulders, but it doesn't stop her shivering. "What are you two doing? We could hear you shouting from the pool."

"Here." Al crouches down on the ground and reaches out a hand to the creature. The gecko speeds away and zips under the bench.

"Leave it." Daisy tugs at the black strap of Al's swimsuit. "Let's get some more wine and go back in the pool."

"I've never seen one of those before." Al peers intently under the bench.

"Al!" Daisy yanks her swimsuit again, but this time she's swatted away.

"Not now, Dais."

The playful expression on Daisy's face vanishes, and she twists away, wrapping her arms around herself as she turns her back to us and looks out toward the lake.

"I'm going to get my camera. Come with me and grab a blanket." Al stands up and gestures at Leanne, who's still standing on the bottom step, staring at us through the darkness. "You look cold."

"Yeah." Leanne hesitates. She can sense tension between us, and she's torn between going after Al and staying to find out what's happened.

"Come on," Al urges, grabbing Leanne by the elbow and angling her up the stairs. "We'll grab some more wine too. I think the hotel manager's still awake."

Daisy doesn't acknowledge Al's and Leanne's departures as they stumble up the steps and crash through the undergrowth. Instead, she continues to stare out at the lake. I head for the steps too. Staying and arguing isn't going to solve anything. We're drunk, we're tired, and we need to sleep.

"Is this how it's going to be?"

"Sorry?" I turn back.

"This. Is this how it's going to be? You and Al making excuses not to spend time with me?"

It's at times like this that I wonder how much more I can take. Daisy pushes and pushes and pushes, almost as though she's deliberately stretching the boundaries of our friendship to see how much I'll put up with. If I stay, she'll berate me for being a pushover, for not standing up for myself; if I go, I prove her theory that everyone will eventually abandon her. It's a catch-22 situation.

"Don't look at me like you don't know what I'm talking about, Emma. First you wander off when we're all having fun around the fire, then Al shrugs me off when I ask her to go in the pool with me. And then there was our first night in Kathmandu when you and Al pretended to be jetlagged instead of carrying on drinking with me."

"We *were* jetlagged."

"You were laughing and drinking beer in your room. Why couldn't you have done that in a bar with me?"

"Daisy, it was one can each, hardly a party. Come on." I take a step toward her and put a hand on her shoulder. "You need to go to bed."

"No." She shrugs off my attempt to drape the blanket over her, swiping it away, knocking it to the ground. "I don't want to go to sleep. I want another drink, and I want to go back in the pool. Where's my wine?"

She glances toward the bench. The bottle of wine is on the ground where I left it. The gecko has moved back out from under the bench and is a couple of inches from the wine bottle.

"I don't think you need any more wine, Daisy."

"Don't tell me what I need."

She pushes me out of the way and totters toward the bench. The gecko scuttles toward the wine bottle. Daisy slows her pace, inching forward on the toes of her cork wedges as though she's taking care not to startle the creature. I keep expecting the gecko to zoom off as she approaches, but it doesn't move. It grips the ground by the wine bottle with its suction-like feet, the only movement the back and forth motion of its eyes.

Daisy stops walking. She bends at the waist and reaches her right hand toward the wine bottle. Her left leg twitches, she steps forward, and she stamps the gecko into the ground with the sole of her wedged sandal. At the same time, she grasps the neck of the wine bottle and whips it into the air. She glances around at me, her expression victorious. "Got it!"

I stare at her in disbelief. She just stamped on the gecko. Deliberately. The pause, the leg twitch, the step. She didn't need to do any of that to get the wine bottle. She was close enough just to grab it.

"What are you staring at me like that for?" She raises the bottle to her lips and takes a swig.

"You just stamped on the gecko."

"Did I?" She hops on one leg and grabs her left ankle with her right hand. She hikes it up for a closer look, squinting into the gloom, then promptly loses her balance and has to grab the bench to stay upright. "Fuck."

"Didn't you see it? It was right next to the bottle."

"Was it? I can't see a thing in this light. Come on." She loops her arm through mine. "Let's go see what the other two are up to."

9

You okay?" Al touches the back of my hand. "You didn't come to breakfast."

"I couldn't find my pills."

We're sitting on the backseat of the rusty, ramshackle bus that will take us to the base of the mountain so we can trek up to the retreat. It's a lot more rickety than the bus that took us from Kathmandu to Pokhara, but according to Leanne, rather than a six-hour slog, this journey will only take half an hour. I made it on the bus first and took a seat by the window, folding up my waterproof jacket to cover the springs poking through the ripped leather seat. Al, Leanne, and a sunglasses-wearing Daisy filed on several minutes later. Al immediately tucked herself in next to me.

"Not your malaria pills?"

"No, the antianxiety ones. I looked everywhere. I'm sure I packed them."

"They'll be in a side pocket or something. Don't worry. I'll help you look once we get to Skanky Yaka, or whatever it's called."

"Cheers, Al."

We lapse into hungover silence. We didn't carry on drinking for long last night. When we returned to the patio, Leanne had already gone to bed, and with no sign of the hotel manager, we only had Daisy's half bottle of wine to drink between the three of us. By the time I dragged myself into the room I was sharing with Leanne, she was snoring softly.

I glance across the bus. Leanne's laughing uproariously at something Daisy's just said. She looks remarkably fresh-faced in her *My Little Pony* T-shirt and skinny jeans, while Daisy looks like she dragged herself out of bed and crawled into her clothes. She notices me staring and presses a hand to the side of her head.

"You as hungover as me?" she asks.

I nod. "I feel like hell."

Satisfied with the response, she sits back in her seat and whispers something to Leanne, who glances at me and laughs.

I close my eyes to try to conjure up the memory of Daisy stamping on the gecko, but the images in my mind are blurred by my hangover and lack of sleep. If she couldn't focus on me without her contact lenses in, and I was sitting across from her on the bench, how could she even have seen it? I'm misremembering what happened. I have to be. There's no way she deliberately stamped on a living creature, not after the accusations her mom leveled at her when her sister died.

Al snorts with laughter beside me, and I open my eyes.

"I don't suppose you got a photo of that gecko, did you?" she asks. "I just remembered I was supposed to get my camera, but I was so obsessed with finding more booze, I completely forgot about it."

"No." I shake my head. "No, I didn't."

"No worries." She shrugs. "I'm sure we'll see loads more."

～

Thankfully, we arrive at the Maoist station within minutes. Their desk is on a platform at the end of the rickety bridge that connects the café at the base of the mountain with the start of the trail. None of us are shocked to see them there—you're warned about the "tourist tax" in all good guidebooks—but the guns they clutch to their sides take us all by surprise. Shankar, our trek guide, nods for us to approach. I try to read his expression. While many Nepalese people support the Maoists, others are fearful of them. But Shankar's eyes give away nothing of his thoughts.

Daisy approaches the desk first, her shoulders back, chin high. She runs a hand through her hair and smiles at the man behind the desk as she hands him her passport, trek visa, and 150 rupees, but he doesn't acknowledge her. His expression doesn't change as he flips through the passport and then slides the money to the man at his left, who slips the notes into a money belt around his waist. Daisy reaches for her passport, then jumps as the man slaps his hand on top of it.

"I tell you when to take," says the man behind the desk. He stares at her for an unbearably long time, then lowers his eyes to her visa on the desk in front of him. He flips the passport open again and compares the name on the visa with the name on the passport, then looks back up at Daisy.

"Why you here?"

"Um…" She clears her throat. "Just to trek up to the summit."

Leanne has told us what to say. She seems to think the Maoists will charge us extra if they think we're going to be staying in a Western establishment rather than one of the Nepalese-owned hostels.

"You sure about that?" He continues to stare at her.

"Of course. I'm dying to see the view from the top. It's supposed to be amazing."

He pushes Daisy's possessions across the desk toward her, then dismisses her with a wave of his hand. He doesn't speak to Al, Leanne, or me, and our documents are processed wordlessly.

When we've been checked, the two armed men standing on either side of the gate take a step back to let us enter the trail.

Daisy grabs my arm the second we're all through. "Wow." She pushes her sunglasses onto the top of her head. She has bags under her eyes, and dozens of red blood vessels streak the white around her eyeballs. "That was mental."

She releases me and links her arm through Shankar's before striding off up the path. If she notices him flinching at the unwanted physical contact, she doesn't let on.

~

The muscles in my thighs burn from weaving my way from left to right and back again as I climb the three thousand steps up the Annapurna mountain. I was expecting actual steps—I think we all were—but these aren't evenly sized concrete blocks; they're slabs of rock dug into the side of the mountain, so uneven and wonky you have to look where you're placing your feet. They're the rustic, higgledy-piggledy winding steps of a fairy tale. Or a nightmare. With the exception of Al, we all go to a gym back home in London, but running 5K in thirty-three minutes on a treadmill prepares you for this in the same way that jumping in puddles prepares you to swim the English Channel.

It's 2:00 p.m., and Shankar is leading the way, leaping from stone to stone, as enthusiastic and energized as he was when we started our trek five hours ago. Daisy and Leanne follow in his steps, both breathing heavily, both swearing whenever they look up and see how many more steps there are to go until we reach the end of the trail. Green mountains striped with brown paddy fields and capped with snowy peaks wrap around us, hiding us from the rest of the world. I have never been anywhere so breathtakingly beautiful or so backbreakingly harsh. We passed donkeys earlier, roped together, stumbling up the steps with huge saddlebags strapped to their backs, their knees buckling, their hooves slipping under the weight of their heavy loads. One of the donkeys was carrying a fridge, strapped on top of its saddlebag like it was the most normal thing in the world. Watching the poor animals climb and stumble, heads down, eyes sad, was more than I could bear. I wanted to set them free and tell their handler that he was cruel for forcing them to live such a miserable life, but I bit my tongue.

Al trails behind me, her face puce, her enormous backpack waving from side to side with each step she takes, the belt undone around her waist, her hands on her hips. Every dozen or so steps, she stops, takes a puff of her asthma inhaler, and continues on again. If I were Al, I'd ask to slow down or take more breaks, but she's ox-like in her determination to get to the retreat before nightfall and hasn't complained once. I hear the puff-puff of her inhaler and stop walking. That's twice in the last five minutes.

"You okay?"

She shrugs off her backpack, then bends forward and grips her knees with her hands. She sucks at the mountain air like a fish on a hook.

I put a hand on her shoulder. "Stand upright if you can. Leaning over like that squashes your lungs." My brother Henry had asthma as a child, so her attack doesn't faze me. Though the fact that we're 3,500 yards above sea level and at least five and a half hours away from the nearest hospital does.

Al straightens up, puts her hands on her hips, and cranes her chin toward the sky as she continues to gulp in air. Her cheeks are still a violent shade of red, but it's not them I'm looking at. It's her lips. They're pink, not blue. That's a good sign.

"Nice deep breaths," I say. "Slowly. Don't panic. In…and out…in…and out… Relax your shoulders. You're tensing them because you're scared. Relax your shoulders, and exhale for as long as you can, then a nice deep breath in again."

I can hear Daisy's voice in my head as I speak, saying the exact same words to me a couple of months ago when I was in the grip of a panic attack. We were in a crowded theater, people filling every seat, and it was hot, really hot. We were watching a thriller Daisy wanted to see, and each time the main character jumped, I jumped. Each time she saw shadows where there weren't any, I saw them too. As her world grew smaller and more claustrophobic, so did mine, and I became convinced that there wasn't enough air in the theater for everyone to breathe, and I had to get out.

"Everything okay, miss?"

Our guide nimbly picks his way back down the mountain toward us, his tiny rucksack strapped to his back. Shankar's weather-beaten face is as lined as befits a man in his late forties, but he moves like a man twenty years younger.

"She breathe okay?" he asks as he reaches us.

"No. She's not. I think the altitude might be affecting her asthma. Maybe we should go back down."

"No!" Leanne says so loudly I jump. I hadn't realized she and Daisy had joined us too.

"I'm sorry?"

"We...we should carry on," she says, the base of her neck coloring. "It can't be much farther to the retreat, and they might have a doctor or a nurse there."

"But if the altitude is making her asthma worse, the best thing for her to do is go down again," Daisy says.

I nod in agreement. Thousands of people do this trek every year, but occasionally, people die. None of us wants to be part of that statistic.

"I still think we should continue to the retreat," Leanne says. She glances from Al to the steps, as though she's desperately hoping Ekanta Yatra will magically appear before us. "We've come this far. It would be such a shame to give up now. You can make it a little bit farther, can't you, Al? We can take it slowly, take lots of breaks. And like I said, I'm sure there will be someone there who can help."

Daisy and I exchange a look. Normally, Leanne would be the first to put her best friend's health before everything and charge down the mountain to get help. And then there's the fact that she's disagreeing with Daisy. That *never* happens.

"Yeah, yeah, we heard you," I say, "but conjecture isn't going to magically conjure up a nebulizer, is it? Are there doctors and nurses up there or not?"

Leanne shrugs. "I don't know. Probably. There are a lot of people there from different professions, and—"

"We're going back down." Daisy holds up her hands. "We're not gambling with Al's health. Come on." She gives Leanne a small shove. "Let's go."

"No!" Leanne twists sharply to one side, and for one heart-stopping second, I think she's going to hit Daisy. "You can go back down if you want, but I'm—"

"Could everyone please stop talking about me as if I'm dead or something!" Al steps out from beside me and holds up her hands. "I am here, you know. Seriously, I appreciate the concern, guys, but no one is going to miss out on the vacation of a lifetime just because I'm a twenty-a-day lard ass with crap lungs and a heavy load." She pats the roll of flesh that overhangs the waistband of her black combat shorts.

Daisy shakes her head firmly. "Nice speech, but no one loves a dead hero."

"Fuck off, Dais!" Al laughs, then looks at Shankar. "How much farther do we have to go? Like, how many more hours?"

He shrugs. "Thirty minutes, maybe forty?"

"All right, then." Al reaches down for her backpack, but Shankar grabs it first. There's a standoff as they each hold a strap and lock eyes, urging the other to back down. Normally, there's no way Al would ever let a man do something she's capable of doing herself.

"Miss. I carry. You breathe." There's a quiet tenacity to the way Shankar speaks, and although Al shakes her head, I can see her resolve waver. Her high color has paled, but she's still breathing shallowly.

"I'll take yours," she says, reaching for the smaller rucksack on the guide's back. "We can swap, but only until I've got my breath back. Five minutes, ten minutes tops."

Forty-five minutes later, Shankar shrugs off Al's backpack, flipping it onto the ground as though it's a pillow, and points to the building down a small track to our left. "We are here."

Rising out of the white blanket of cloud that surrounds us are three separate houses linked by fenced walkways, their three-tiered roofs silhouetted against the landscape like Chinese temples. The window frames are painted in shades of red, ocher, and turquoise, and stone steps lead up to an enormous wooden door on the front of the main house. A high wall runs around the perimeter of the grounds, a large wooden gate closing the retreat off from the world. Prayer flags flutter in the wind, and the sound of laughter drifts across the breeze.

"Wow." I unbuckle my own backpack, twist my body sideways so the pack drops to the ground, lean back, and groan with pleasure and relief as I press my shoulder blades together.

Daisy skips toward Leanne, grips her arm, and presses her cheek against the top of her shoulder. "Oh my God, it's even more gorgeous than it looked on the website."

Leanne grins at the compliment, drops her backpack, and wraps an arm around Daisy. "Told you! And you all thought I was going to bring you to some kind of shack."

"Actually," says Al, climbing the last few steps, "I thought we'd be sitting in a paddy field, meditating for twelve hours a day before being force-fed mung-bean sandwiches."

"The paddy fields are back down the mountain," Leanne says, pointing. "Off you go!"

"There's the river!" Daisy lets go of Leanne and points excitedly into the distance. I strain to see through the trees, then spot something blue and shimmery. "Is that the waterfall I can hear?"

"Probably." Leanne reaches for her backpack and hauls it back onto her shoulders. "Come on, they're expecting us."

Daisy squeals and hurries after her as she makes her way down the track. I wait for Al to catch up. She slips Shankar's rucksack off her shoulders and hands it to him. He slips it on effortlessly.

"Thank you." She holds out her right hand. "I couldn't have made it up here without your help."

Shankar shakes her hand while simultaneously touching his left hand against his right forearm as a sign of respect. "No problem, miss."

"For you." Al reaches into her pocket and pulls out a hundred rupee note. "Please." She presses it into his hand.

He accepts the money with a smile and tucks it into the little leather wallet attached to his belt, then turns to go back down the mountain.

"You'll come in?" I ask. "The least we can do is offer you a sandwich and a cup of chai. I'm sure the owners won't mind."

The smile slips from his face. "No, thank you."

"Please, you can't walk all the way back down again without a break. It wouldn't be right."

His gaze flicks to the left, to the retreat at the end of the track. "No." An emotion I can't read flickers across his face, and then it's gone.

"But..." The words fall away as Shankar turns on his heel and, without another word, starts back down the mountain.

"Emma, Al, come on!" the girls shout from below us.

A tall man with shoulder–length black hair, wearing cut-off camouflage pants and a gray, long–sleeved T-shirt, is standing beside them, holding the gate open.

"Hi," the man shouts, raising a hand in greeting. "I'm Isaac."

10

Sheila sent me home, no questions asked. She heard me throwing up in the ladies' bathroom and immediately diagnosed me as suffering from an upset tummy. She didn't even give me the opportunity to object.

"I saw you nibbling the corner of that sandwich, and I knew something was wrong. It's not like you not to have an appetite. Get yourself home, Jane. We don't want to risk you passing it on to everyone else. We're short-staffed as it is."

I think she would have driven me home herself if I hadn't pointed out that I had my bicycle with me. No point driving me home when I only live a five-minute cycle away and it's all downhill.

That was two hours ago. I've spent the last thirty minutes sitting in front of my laptop. I thought it would be harder to find Al. I thought that, after five years, she'd be impossible to track down, but unlike me, she hasn't changed her name. She's even got a Facebook profile. Alexandra Gideon. There were only three listed, and two of them live in the States. Her cover image is of the Brighton seafront, and the profile picture's a rainbow, and that's it—that's all the information I've got to go on, but I know it's her. She always said she wanted to leave London and move to Brighton.

It's been four years since we last spoke. We kept in touch for the first few months after we got back from Nepal, talking on the phone every day, trying to make sense of what had happened, but then Al sold her story to the press, and everything changed. I couldn't understand why she'd done it. I called her, over and over again, begging her to explain why she'd gone back on what we'd agreed, but she ignored my calls. I don't know if it was the money or the attention or what, but it was the worst kind of betrayal, especially after everything we'd been through.

I hold down the Delete button, and the cursor zips from right to left, swallowing the message I've been trying to compose for the last half an hour. I start again:

Al, it's me.

No. I created this Facebook account as Jane Hughes, and she won't know who that is.

Al, it's Emma. I know you probably don't want to talk to me, but I need your help.

I delete the last sentence.

Al, it's Emma. I think Daisy's still alive. Please contact me. Here's my cell phone number...

I touch the button beneath the swipe pad, ready to click Send, but then change my mind again. Does she already know? Whoever typed the message onto the Green Fields website could already have contacted Al. If I found her in minutes, they could have too.

I reach for my cell phone and click on Will's name. The call goes straight to voice mail. His tone is professional and impersonal, but the sound of his voice is comforting.

"Hi, Will, it's Jane. Could you give me a call when you finish school? I need to talk to you; it's important."

I place the phone on the desk next to the laptop. I stare at the screen, drumming my right index finger on the button under the swipe pad.

Delete or Send? Delete or Send? My heart tells me to trust Al. My head says not to.

I click Send.

~

The second Will sets eyes on me, he gathers me into a tight hug.

"Sorry, darling. I thought I'd mentioned that it was parents' evening tonight." He pulls away, his hands on my shoulders. "You okay? You sounded worried on the phone."

"Yeah, I..." I hand him a bottle of red wine. "I've had a bit of a weird day and..." The sound of two people talking drifts toward us as a couple of dog walkers stroll past the end of Will's yard, their high-visibility jackets glowing in the light from the house. "Can we talk inside?"

"'Course, yeah." He reaches an arm around my shoulders and ushers me into the house.

It's warm and bright in the hallway. Dozens of black-and-white photos of Will with Chloe and various friends and relatives smile down at me from one wall. On the other is a faux Banksy print of a large *Star Wars* AT-AT walker saying "I'm your father" to a smaller AT-AT walker (I only know what they're called because Will told me).

"I need to explain why I was being so obtuse last night," I say as I head toward the living room. "The reason I was asking about lying was because—"

"Hi, Jane!" Chloe waves at me from the sofa where she's sitting cross-legged with a loom band maker in one hand and a crochet hook in the other. She doesn't shift her gaze from the Disney movie blaring out song tunes from the television in the corner of the room.

"Hello!" I glance questioningly at Will. He normally only has his daughter for weekends during term time.

"Ah, yes, Chloe. The other reason it took me a while to get back to you. Sara rang during my last meeting. She sliced her thumb on a food processor blade and needed me to take Chloe so she could go to the emergency room." He glances at the clock above the fireplace. It's after nine. "We agreed it would be best if Chloe stayed here for the night. God knows how long it will take her to be seen."

Sara is Will's soon-to-be ex-wife. They're separated but amicably so. According to Will, their relationship gradually became more like brother and sister in the years after Chloe was born, but it wasn't until Sara admitted that she'd developed a bit of a crush on a colleague and Will felt feelings of relief rather than jealousy that they confronted the issue. Sara went on to have a relationship with her colleague, but it fizzled out almost as quickly as it began.

"Here." He thrusts my bottle of red wine at me. "Why don't you go into the kitchen and get this opened while I take Chloe upstairs? We can have a proper chat once she's in bed."

"Okay."

"I can make a bracelet for you, if you want, Jane!" Chloe says, waving the loom board at me. She has the same generous wide smile as her father. "What are you favorite colors? Or I could make you a rainbow one, if you like."

"A rainbow bracelet would be wonderful."

"I could make collars for the animals you look after too. Or you could sell them in the shelter to raise money for—"

"Bed!" Will says with a smile on his face. "You've seen Jane now. No more excuses. Let's get you upstairs."

Chloe's face falls. "But..."

"We can talk about your ideas this weekend, Chloe." I glance at Will, who nods. "In fact, we could discuss them at Green Fields. I'll give you the VIP guided tour."

"No way!" Chloe throws her loom bands to one side and runs at me. She wraps her arms around my hips and buries her head in my stomach.

I rest a hand on the top of her fine, mousy hair.

"You're very lucky, you know," Will says. "They don't let just anyone wander around Green Fields."

"I'm afraid you won't be able to meet the dogs," I add. "They get upset when too many strangers visit."

"That's okay." Chloe gazes up at me. "I only really want to see the cats and the ferrets and the mice. And the swearing parrot."

"The what?" Will pretends to look aghast, and Chloe giggles. "I'll pretend I didn't hear that. Come on, teeth time."

"Night, Jane." Chloe gives me another squeeze, then skips past her father and climbs the stairs two at a time.

Will and I exchange smiles, then he presses a hand to my cheek. "Thank you. You've made her very happy."

I shrug. "It's nothing."

"Still..." His gaze lingers, the emotion behind his eyes weighty and intense. We had a discussion on our third date about how neither of us wanted to get into anything "heavy," and we're still not officially "together," even though Will insisted I meet Chloe three weekends ago. We "bumped into" each other while they were feeding the ducks at the pond in the center of the village, and he introduced me as "my friend Jane." She accepted the introduction unquestioningly, but her eyes grew wide and round when I told her what I do for a living. She's been badgering her dad to spend time with me ever since.

My chest tightens with anxiety. I shouldn't have told Chloe about visiting the shelter this weekend, not when I'm about to tell Will that I've been lying to him since the moment we met. I got carried away by her excitement; I forgot that none of this is real.

"I should open the wine." I touch his hand briefly, then break eye contact with him and step away. "Give Chloe a good-night kiss for me."

He turns and heads for the stairs. Like his daughter, he takes them two at a time, then disappears into the bathroom off the landing.

~

It's cooler in the kitchen than the rest of the house. Will may have joked about burning the dinner, but his cooking prowess is demonstrated by the well-stacked spice rack to the right of the stove and the shelf full of cookbooks, the pages rippled and stained. The wine rack to the left of the stove is well stocked with a variety of red, white, and rosé bottles and two magnums of champagne, and there's a plentiful supply of chocolates in the cupboard above the mug tree too—presents from grateful parents, no doubt.

I dig around in the cutlery drawer until I find the bottle opener, then yank the cork out of the bottle of red wine. I don't wait for it to breathe. Instead, I half fill the largest wineglass I can find in the mismatched selection in the cupboard and down half of it. Then I refill the glass and pour another one for Will.

As footsteps reverberate on the ceiling over my head, I wander down the hallway and back into the living room. I turn off the television, tidy the spilled loom bands into their correct color compartments, then, with nothing else to do, I sit on the sofa and reach for Will's iPad.

I swipe from left to right to unlock the screen. Will only bought his iPad a few weeks ago, and he still hasn't gotten around to setting a password. I sent Al the message at seven o'clock. Has she read it? If she's as addicted to Facebook as half the girls at work, she'll have read it the second her phone bleeped with a new message notification. She may even have replied.

The sound of Will's laugh and Chloe's high-pitched giggle floats down the stairs as I log in to Facebook.

The messages icon at the top of the screen is still blue. No message from Al. She hasn't even read it yet. I'm just about to log out when I notice there's another tab open in the browser. Will's been reading a tabloid newspaper online—one he's ranted about several times. I click on it.

The headline alone fills a third of the page.

Humiliated, Abandoned, and Betrayed.
British Woman Escapes Deadly Cult That
Robbed Her of Two of Her Friends and
Nearly Stole Her Own Life

Alexandra (Al) Gideon, 25, from London talks exclusively to Gilly McKensie about the dream vacation that turned into a vacation from hell when she and her three friends—Daisy Hamilton, 26, Leanne Cooper, 25, and Emma Woolfe, 25—journeyed to Nepal. Now Al puts the record straight about what really happened and the mystery behind Daisy's and Leanne's disappearances...

I stop reading. I already know what it says. It's the article Al sold, the reason we haven't spoken for four years.

But why has Will been reading it? There's no way he could connect me with that story. Unless...

I reach into my back pocket, but the note's not there. It's still in my work pants, lying in a crumpled heap on my bathroom floor after I took them off to have a shower after work. Did the same person who sent me the note contact Will to tell him I'm not who he thinks I am? That might explain the real reason he didn't reply to my voice mail for a couple of hours—he wanted to check me out on the Internet first.

A floorboard creaks above my head.

Unless he was the one who sent the note?

I reach for one of the school exercise books on the coffee table and flick through it. On one of the pages, there's an image of a plant, drawn in pencil, with the various parts labeled in school kids' untidy handwriting—stem, stamen, petal, etc. Underneath, written in blue ink, are the words:

A great piece of work—well done.

The handwriting is small and neat.

The floorboard creaks again, louder this time, and panicking, I reach for my messenger bag, slip the book into it, then walk into the hall.

"Sorry, Will," I shout up the stairs. "I've got to go. There's been an emergency at work."

"Hang on, Jane," he shouts back. "I won't be a—"

The door clicks shut behind me before he can finish his sentence.

11

FIVE YEARS EARLIER

Help yourself to a beanbag, and make yourselves comfortable," Isaac says as he ushers us into a cool, dark room. His voice is deep and resonant with a soft Scottish burr. He rubs a hand over his stubbly jaw. "Just dump your backpacks wherever. I'll grab you some chai. You must be exhausted after your trek."

"You're not kidding." Daisy flashes him a smile as he slips back out of the room. She groans as she wriggles out of her backpack. It slips to the floor with a thump. Al, Leanne, and I do the same and then grab a beanbag each from the pile in the corner of the room and collapse onto them.

"This is the meditation room," Leanne says reverently. "It says on the website that they meditate three times a day. The first session is at five a.m."

Al laughs. "Well, I won't be spending much time here, then."

I gaze around, taking it all in. The floor is a dark polished wood, the walls roughly plastered and painted a vibrant turquoise and adorned with prayer flags and fairy lights. There's a bookshelf at one end of the room and a wooden altar at the other, with a large gold skull taking pride of place in the center, a metal gong to its right, and several church candles arranged on golden plates to the left. Plumes of gray smoke swirl in the air from the dozens of incense holders arranged in front of the gold skull and in plant pots and wooden holders around the room, and the air is thick with the rich, heady scent of jasmine.

"Here we go," Isaac says a few minutes later, ducking his head as he passes through the doorway and wanders back into the room, carrying a tray of steaming metal cups.

He takes the tray to Leanne first, crouching down to offer her a mug. She sits up straight and beams at him, then bites down on her bottom lip as though trying to suppress her smile. Al twists around and gives me an incredulous look. In the seven years we've known Leanne, she's never reacted to a man like this. Her normal modus operandi when a man approaches her is wariness, swiftly followed by sarcasm and put-downs disguised as jokes. She's only been out with two guys in the whole time I've known her; she went out with the leader of the Socialist Society at university for six months before they split up, for unknown reasons, and then she dated some Dutch guy she met at yoga after we all moved to London, but they finished after three months when he moved back to the Netherlands. Al thinks he broke her heart, but Leanne never talked to any of us about how she felt, not even Al. Unlike the rest of us, who always analyze our failed relationships to death, Leanne refuses to talk about her private life. Scratch the surface, and you get more surface.

Isaac straightens up and takes the tray to Daisy, who flicks back her hair and pushes back her shoulders so her cleavage is on full display as he squats down. She makes no attempt to hide her attraction to him—why should she? If Daisy's interested in a man, she makes it blatantly clear, and with her long, blond hair, narrow waist, and perky boobs, nine times out of ten, she gets him. Unlike the rest of us, she's never been dumped and never had her heart broken. She'll pursue a man until she gets him, but she never lets her defenses down, never lets herself fall for anyone. She'll dump a guy or move on if there's any danger of that happening. You don't have to be a psychologist to work out that it's got something to do with her mom committing suicide when she was five, and then her dad abandoning her at boarding school when she was six.

Al gives Isaac a cursory nod as he presents her with a cup of tea. He says something I can't hear, and she laughs and gives him a high five. My stomach twists as he straightens up once more and makes his way toward me. I don't know why, but attractive men make me feel insecure and self-conscious. My mouth dries up, and I struggle to make conversation.

"Hi, Emma." Isaac squats down in front of me. His eyes are the warmest brown, framed with dark eyelashes and eyebrows. They smile at me as he hands me the last cup of chai. "You okay?"

"Yeah." I press my lips together. "I'm fine."

"Cool." His gaze slips from my face to my legs. "Did you fall over on your way up the mountain?"

"Yeah, how did—"

"Your pants are ripped." He gently runs a finger over the tear in my dusty cotton pants. I flinch, even though the skin on my knee is no longer tender. "Sorry, didn't mean to hurt you." He pulls his hand away sharply. "If it still hurts, Sally in the kitchen has a first aid kit."

"It's fine, honestly."

"Okay." He smiles warmly and stands up. Then he crosses the room, picks up a beanbag, and plonks it in front of us. "So." He opens his hands wide. "Welcome to Ekanta Yatra. I know you've all had a look at the website, so I'll keep this brief, because I know you'll all be desperate to have a shower or a sleep or whatever.

"I founded Ekanta Yatra three years ago, along with Isis, Cera, and Johan—you'll meet them soon. We were all traveling separately and became friends when we found ourselves staying in the same guesthouse in Pokhara. We were all looking for somewhere that would be a retreat from the world, and we pooled what little money we had and bought this place. It was basically a shack when we bought it."

"It looks lovely now," Leanne says, and Isaac smiles at her.

"Cheers, we've worked hard. Johan's the big hulking Swede you'll see shuffling about. He's in charge of the vegetable patch and the animals—anything outside, basically. Isis is a short, gray-haired woman. She's got a background in massage and holistic therapies, so she's your go-to woman for your facials and aromatherapy sessions. Cera's the tall, elegant woman you'll see drifting about. She keeps the place running efficiently and makes sure everything is clean and tidy and that the kitchen's got all the supplies it needs. And I'm Isaac. I run the meditation sessions and the seminars and, um...I make a mean cup of chai too."

Everyone laughs.

"That's about it, basically. Everything else you need to know is in your welcome packs on your beds." He reaches into his back pocket and pulls out a small green tin. He pries off the lid and offers us the contents—half a dozen hand-rolled cigarettes. "Anyone want one?"

Leanne's smile slips. "But we're in a pagoda. I thought smoking... Well, I thought you couldn't."

"We meditate in here," Isaac says, a rollie dangling from his lower lip, "and we do yoga outside on the patio, and all these sort of things, but this isn't a religious retreat. We're a community of people making a life for ourselves outside of mainstream society."

He pauses to blow a stream of smoke up toward the ceiling. "When you look in your welcome pack, you'll see that we've got set times for meals and meditations and seminars, but what you guys choose to do is up to you. You can get as involved as you like, or not get involved at all. Ekanta Yatra is a place where you can escape from all the stresses and strains of everyday life and just *be*. There's a lot the outside world could learn from the way we live here."

"I'm always up for learning new things." Daisy slips off her beanbag and crawls toward Isaac, slinking through the gap between Al and Leanne like a cat. She takes a cigarette from Isaac's tin and looks up at him expectantly, the cigarette dangling from her lips.

"I think you could all learn a lot." He lights her cigarette, but his eyes are on me.

"Hi, girls," says a voice behind us, and Isaac glances away.

A tall, willowy woman with pale lips and dreadlocks the color of dark sand twisted on top of her head is standing in the doorway. She makes her way toward us, drifting through the room barefoot, her sari-like skirt sweeping the wood as she walks, her beaded necklace reaching down to her bare navel. Her smile is beatific, her eyes soft and compassionate. There's a serenity about her that's mesmerizing.

"Hello," she says, her benign gaze flitting over each of our faces as she stops next to Isaac. She reaches out a hand and ruffles his hair, then glances at Daisy. Her smile widens. "I'm Cera. I look after the house, so if there's a problem with the solar showers, or you need a snack between mealtimes, or anything else, just let me know."

"Hi!" I raise a hand in greeting. Al and Leanne do the same.

"I'll show you where you'll all be sleeping in a few moments," Cera continues, "and then I'll give you the guided tour, but first, if you could all give me your passports, please."

"They think we're going to skip off into the night without paying," Al says. She catches my eye and grins. Six years ago, the four of us hitchhiked up to Edinburgh from Newcastle and stayed in a B and B run by the snootiest woman on earth. The bathroom was gross, the sheets were stained, and the bedroom curtains smelled of rotten eggs, but she refused to give us a different room when we requested one. The woman just sniffed, said something about *bloody students*, and stalked off. We went out drinking until 4:00 a.m., returned to get our bags, and left without paying. It was Daisy's idea, of course, but the rest of us didn't need much persuading. It wasn't as though we'd actually slept there, was it?

"You'll have to get past me first," Isaac says and winks at Al. Then he stretches his arms above his head and stands up. "I'll leave you to it, then, Cera," he says before strolling across the room, his cigarette still dangling from his fingertips. He raises a hand as he reaches the doorway. "See you later, girls!"

"Bye, Isaac!" Daisy calls from beside his abandoned beanbag. If she were a dog, she'd be bristling.

The next couple of weeks are certainly going to be interesting; Daisy doesn't take kindly to rejection.

~

"Wow." Daisy peers around the door to the shower block, then glances back at us. "The website wasn't lying when it said the living accommodation is basic. There's a kitchen sink in here. Literally."

"Let me see." She steps out of the way so I can take a look too. She's right. There are two shower stalls, each with a rustic-looking door; two toilets with equally basic doors; and right at the end of the room, there's a kitchen sink with a colorful mosaic-framed circular mirror hanging above it.

"Are they sit-down toilets or holes in the floor?" Al shouts out.

I step into the shower block and push at one of the toilet doors. "Proper toilets."

"Well, that's something." Daisy rolls her eyes and walks back into the girls' dormitory. She stands beside the mattress she's been allocated in the corner of the room and nudges it with the toe of her flip-flop. "At least we had proper beds at boarding school. God knows what's going to crawl over me in the middle of the night."

"Don't be like that." Leanne, sitting cross-legged on the mattress beside her, slaps her guidebook shut.

"Yeah, come on, Dais." Al looks up from the cigarette she's rolling. "It's not like we didn't expect to rough it. We're in Nepal, not the Hilton."

"Roughing it is fine. Sharing a room with you guys is fine. But this?" She gestures at the rough, cherry-red wooden walls and the row of mattresses on each side of the room. "It's like a sheep shed, piling all the women into one room together. God knows who we're sharing with."

"Daisy…" I move to put an arm around her, then change my mind. The best way to deal with her when she's in this kind of mood is to ignore it. She's barely said a word since Isaac left us in the meditation room—not when Cera showed us the rustic dining room, the basic kitchen, the yoga patio, the orchard, the vegetable patch, the goat enclosure, the chicken pen, or the massage huts— and she was the only one of us not to squeal with excitement when we were led down to the river and the waterfall. The only time the vaguest flicker of interest registered on her face was when we returned to the house and Cera gestured to the walkway to the right and said it led to the boys' dormitories. It vanished when we were led to the left. It's astonishing, really. We travel halfway around the world to one of the most breathtakingly beautiful mountain ranges in Asia, and she's in a huff because Isaac didn't flirt back with her. I'd laugh if she wasn't my best friend.

"I bet the other women snore," Daisy says. "And smell."

"Well, you'll be in good company, then," Al says. "I couldn't sleep for all your farting and snoring last night."

"Sod off, Al," Daisy says, but the edges of her lips twitch into a smile. She yanks her sleeping bag from its sheath, lies down on top of the mattress, and starts rummaging around in her backpack. "Who fancies a shot of lemon voddy? I think we've earned it."

Everyone holds up a hand.

"Have you seen this?" Leanne waves the welcome pack in the air. "There are three yoga sessions a day, right after meditation. I'm thinking I'll do two a day—one in the morning, one in the evening."

"Why the hell would you want to do that?" Al licks the rolling paper, rolls the cigarette over itself, and sticks it behind her ear. "Unless you want to add *supremely bendy* to your ad."

"What ad?"

"The one you put in phone booths in London."

"Oh, ha-ha. Seriously, are any of you up for meditation or yoga?" Leanne persists.

"Nope." Al shakes her head. "I intend to sit on my ass and do precisely nothing for two weeks."

"Daisy?"

Daisy pours vodka into the bottle lid and knocks it back. She winces, then looks at Leanne. "Did you say something?"

"I asked if you want to try a bit of meditation or yoga."

"Maybe." She shrugs her shoulders. "Do many men do yoga? Does Isaac?" She glances at me. It's only a split-second look, but it's enough to confirm my suspicions about her bad mood.

She squeals as a balled pair of socks hits her square between the eyes.

"You are SO boring!" Al chucks another pair of socks at her, this time clipping Daisy's left ear. "Men, men, men, men, men. Give me a shot of that vodka, then let's go down to the river. Anyone up for skinny-dipping?"

12

"Remind me again why we're doing this," Al says as she stirs a pot of dal so vigorously that hot, gloopy lentils threaten to overflow the rim of the saucepan.

"Because someone"—Daisy fake glares at Leanne—"thought it would be nice to help out with the community. At five o'clock in the bloody morning."

Everyone laughs, including Leanne, and I swipe at my eyes with my forearm. They're smarting so much I can barely see for tears. Al and I have been chopping onions for the curry, and the mountain of vegetables in the sack on the floor doesn't seem to be shrinking.

Three days have passed since we first arrived at Ekanta Yatra, and we've spent the majority of our time outside, reading or sleeping in the many brightly colored woven hammocks that hang from the plum and walnut trees in the orchard, doing yoga on the patio to the rear of the main house, and daring each other to stand in the waterfall for as long as possible, laughing and screaming as the icy-cold water thunders onto our heads and freezes our bodies. It's come as a shock to actually do some "work" again.

"This can't all be for breakfast?" Al looks imploringly at Rajesh, the chef, who's sitting on a squat wooden stool, peeling potatoes.

His knees are spread wide, potato peelings sprinkling the top of his enormous stomach like sprinkles on a cupcake.

"Yep. Takes a lot of food to fill thirty people."

I put down my knife and wipe my face with the hem of my T-shirt. With no air conditioning, a window that's so rotten it only opens a fraction of an inch, and curry-scented steam filling the room, it's sauna-hot in here. Raj was already in the kitchen when Shona, one of the community members, shepherded us in. After Raj told us what he wanted us to do, he squatted down on the stool and started on the potatoes. This is the first time he's spoken since, and the sound of his voice makes me relax just the tiniest bit. There's something very disconcerting about chatting away with someone sitting silently beside you, observing everything but not saying a word. There's a lot of that here—community members drifting around, carrying bundles of God knows what from room to room, cleaning, meditating in random places, pausing in doorways. They rarely speak to us, but they're always watching, always listening. I can't shake the feeling that they're waiting for us to do something, but what, I have no idea.

"And you do this every day?" I ask. "Work in the kitchen?"

"Of course. It's my job."

"You wouldn't rather be out in the garden, tending to vegetables, getting fresh air?"

Raj drops a peeled potato into the bucket at his feet and looks up at me, the knife dangling loosely from his hand. "I just told you, Emma. It's my job."

A bead of sweat appears in his hairline. It rolls down his forehead and disappears into the thick, bushy arch of one eyebrow. His nostrils flare, pulsing as though to a silent beat, as he continues to stare at me.

"Can we get some water?" Daisy asks, just when I can't bear the weight of Raj's gaze a second longer. "I'm gasping."

"There's water in the tap." He gestures toward the sink. As he glances away, I feel unshackled.

"Eww." Daisy wrinkles her nose. "You haven't got any bottled stuff, have you?"

"Nope." Raj shakes his head. "We're running low on supplies. Ruth and Gabe, two members of the community, have gone to Pokhara to stock up. They should be back soon." The tiniest of smiles lifts a corner of his mouth then vanishes. "Apparently."

~

Standing outside one of the huts, I stifle a yawn. We were just preparing to crawl into our sleeping bags and pass out after kitchen duty finally ended when Cera drifted into the girls' dorm and told us that the huts had been prepared for our complimentary massages. None of us were going to turn that down, no matter how tired we were, so Al, Daisy, and I dragged ourselves outside and down to the huts. Leanne stayed behind to attend a talk Isaac was giving on detoxing your mind. I think Al's exact words to describe that decision were "fucking mental."

I yank open the wooden door to the hut and step inside. Not that there's far to step. The hut can't be much more than seven feet long and four feet wide. Everything is white—the floor, the ceiling, the walls, the pile of blankets fashioned into a narrow bed in the center of the room. Even the candle—the solitary source of light, burning on a table in one corner of the room—is white. The only things that aren't white are the two circular metal rings screwed into the far corners of the hut. It seems I'm about to have a massage in what used to be a goat shed.

A man stands opposite me, his legs spread wide, his arms crossed over his broad chest, shadow obscuring half of his face.

"Come in, and close the door behind you. Take a seat." He gestures at the pile of blankets.

I do as I'm asked, but I don't pull the door fully closed. The air is thick with the scent of jasmine incense. It fills my throat, the smoky fragrance so cloying I can taste it. I eye the man warily as he takes a seat himself, sitting cross-legged opposite me.

"Hi! I'm Kane." He holds out a meaty hand for me to shake. He's only an inch or two taller than me, and probably a couple of years younger, but with his shaved head and weighty frame, his presence dominates the hut.

"Emma."

He smiles broadly as I shake his hand. It transforms his face. His heavy brow lifts, deep dimples appear on either side of his wide mouth, and any worries I may have had about sharing such a small space with a complete stranger dissipate.

"Have you ever had reflexology before, Emma?" he asks.

When I shake my head, he explains to me how all the parts of the body are connected to the feet and how, if I have a blockage in any particular area, he'll be able to sense it.

"I've helped a lot of people," he continues. "They've come to me with back pain, skin conditions, depression, IBS, the lot, and with a course of treatments, I've helped them. Really helped them." He slides a book across the floor to me. "These are testimonials from the people I've treated. Have a look."

I flick through page after page, words like "improved," "transformed," "magical," and "healed" jumping out at me. I'm just about to tell him about my panic attacks when he holds up a hand.

"Don't tell me what's wrong with you. I'll know as soon as I touch your feet. Lie down for me, Emma, and slip off your flipflops. I'll begin by cleansing your feet."

I close my eyes and try to relax as Kane rubs my feet with what feels like cold, wet towels and then slathers them with oil. I feel terrified and excited at the same time. Terrified that Kane may be able to sense why I have my panic attacks and excited that he may be able to do something to relieve them. Now *this* is what I imagined when Leanne first mooted the idea of a retreat in Nepal—holistic treatments, massages, and relaxation—not early starts, peeling potatoes, and strange, staring men.

"You're a kind person." I jump at the sound of Kane's voice and open my eyes. He's still down at the other end of the hut, on his knees, pushing his thumbs into the balls of my feet. "You care about others, but you feel taken for granted sometimes."

I try to reply, but he shakes his head.

"I don't want you to talk. You carry a lot of pain around with you, but you don't talk to anyone about it," he continues as he presses his fingers into the pads of my toes. "You feel like you deserve to hurt, but you're wrong. You must forgive yourself for what you did, Emma."

I want to tell him that he's full of shit, that he's got the wrong person, but I couldn't speak even if I wanted to. I'm floored by what he's just told me. I don't know how he's picked up so much about me, but it's all I can do to keep breathing.

"Okay." He waggles first my left foot, then my right foot, from side to side. "Now let's see what's physically wrong with you. Tell me if anything I do hurts. If it does, don't worry. That just means there's congestion that needs to be cleared.

"How about this?" A single tear winds its way down the side of my face as he presses into the ball of my right foot, but the pressure has nothing to do with the reason I'm crying.

I shake my head to indicate no.

"This?"

He slides his fingers to the side of my foot, but there's no pain, so I shake my head again.

"How about here?"

I feel him jab at my ankle. "No."

"Here?"

"No."

Kane inhales noisily through his nose, and my first thought is that I'm doing something wrong. I'm not responding as I should. Why doesn't anything hurt?

"Here?"

I yelp as he prods a tender spot under my ankle. I spoke too soon.

"Family history of diabetes?"

I nod my head, astonished.

"And here?" I twitch as he rolls my calf under his hand. "Problems with your lungs?"

I nod again. He must have picked up on the fact that I feel like I can't breathe when I have a panic attack.

"And here?" His fingers dig into the soft, fleshy instep of my right foot. "Digestive problems," he says, his tone jubilant, and I wince as he presses the same spot again. "Diarrhea. Food passes right through you."

"Ummm…not really."

"Are you sure? Because I can definitely feel some tenderness here."

"Well, sometimes, I guess."

"And difficulty sleeping? You suffer from insomnia."

I shrug. I don't want to say no. He was doing so well.

"I can sort it." He continues to knead the sore spot with his fingers. "If we do a couple of sessions a week, you'll be good in no time. Now, if you'd like to strip down to your underwear, we can get started with your massage. There's a towel to your right. If you lie on your front and pull that over you, I'll turn my back. Shout when you're ready."

He turns and stands with his back to me, his hands thrust deep into the pockets of his shorts. Do I really want his hands all over me? Having a massage from a woman in a beauty salon or spa is one thing, but letting some random man massage you? Kane clears his throat. If I wanted to, I could gather up my clothes and slip out of the shed. I could be back in the house before he even knew I'd left. I glance back at the door, at the thin shaft of sunlight illuminating my blanket bed, and I yank off my T-shirt and shorts and flip over onto my stomach. I pull the towel over me so it covers my underwear.

"Ready?" Kane asks.

"I'm ready," I say.

The massage stops, and the cool breeze from the half-open door tickles the top of my scalp. I am lying on my front on the blankets on the floor, my limbs are dead weights, and my thoughts are jumbled, dancing on the edge of my subconscious as I fight sleep. I part my lips to ask Kane if I should leave now, but I'm so tired, I can't open my eyes.

"Shh," Kane soothes as he adjusts his position, straddled across my lower back, and he places his hands on my shoulders again. He presses the base of his palms into my flesh and circles them around slowly, sliding his hands over my oiled skin, then presses his thumbs into my tight muscles. They click as he rubs out months of tension, and I groan with relief.

I mentally will him to work on my neck, sore and stiff after four nights sleeping on a thin mattress, but his hands remain on my back—slipping and sliding over my skin, skimming my shoulders. His touch is lighter now, his fingertips barely grazing my body, and a shiver runs through me. It feels sensual, like I am being caressed rather than kneaded, but I don't fight it. Instead, I wait for him to continue to pound my knotty muscles.

Kane's hands slip down to the base of my spine, and his fingers wrap around my hips, then slide over my waist, and I gasp as he strokes the sides of my breasts as his hands travel back to my shoulders. Suddenly, I am hyperaware, my body prickling, anticipating where his fingers will go next.

"Shh." His hands move to my shoulders, and as his thumbs rub at the tight knots above my shoulder bones, I force myself to relax again. It was an accident. He didn't mean to do that. I'm being oversensitive.

His hands slide back down my sides. They pause as they reach the curve of my breasts, and his fingers brush my nipples as he reaches under my body.

"Kane!" I flip over onto my side, one hand covering my breasts, but Kane isn't the man massaging me.

"You okay, Emma?" Isaac sits back on his heels and smiles down at me.

"No." I reach for my clothes. "No, I'm not. Where's Kane?"

"Kane was needed elsewhere. You looked so relaxed, I didn't think you'd mind if I took over."

Mind? Of course I mind. I haven't had many massages, but even I know professional masseurs don't just change over without informing the client, never mind the inappropriate touching. I should have requested a woman to massage me; I should have trusted my instincts.

"I have to go." The smile doesn't leave Isaac's face as I wriggle out from beneath him and shuffle backward toward the door, my clothes pressed to my chest. "I...I have to go."

～

Someone grabs me the second I slam the hut door shut behind me.

"Hear that?" Al clutches my arm and points down the river, toward the third hut in the row.

I'm scared that Isaac will burst out of the hut at any moment so, still pressing my clothes against me, I grab Al's hand and pull her away, toward the orchard, before she can say another word. She looks confused but willingly follows me as I run, the barren soil scratching the soles of my bare feet. When we reach our favorite hammock, I turn my back to her and pull on my bra, T-shirt, and shorts, my eyes never leaving the closed door of hut number one.

"Daisy's having sex," Al says, pointing toward the third hut as I turn back toward her. "With Johan, that long-haired Swede—listen."

All I can hear is cicadas chirping, birds singing, and my heart pounding in my ears, but as I stare across the orchard, another sound reaches me. A man grunting loudly and a woman shrieking and moaning in pleasure. I've heard the sound before. I heard it when Daisy and Al drunkenly slept together in my flat seven years ago (a one-off event none of us ever talk about). I heard it after I passed out on the sofa after a night of heavy drinking a few weeks ago and discovered Daisy on the living room floor with the man I'd brought back.

"Al," I say, "there's something I need to tell you about my massage. Kane was doing it, but then…"

She turns to look at me; her eyes are wet with tears. "What is it? What's wrong, Al?"

She passes a hand over her face and shakes her head, but the tears keep falling.

"Al." I clutch her arm. "What is it?"

"Did…" She clears her throat and takes a deep breath. "Did Kane tell you anything weird? Did he say anything to you about someone you'd lost?"

"Lost? What do you mean?"

"Isis knew about Tommy, Emma. She said his name." She pulls away, runs her hands through her hair, takes a few steps toward the house, then turns back. "She was doing Reiki on me, her hands cupped over my face, and I had my eyes closed, and I could smell something warm and minty on the palms of her hands, and then she said his name—'Tommy'—just like that. 'You lost your brother Tommy.'"

Al's brother Tommy died in a motorbike accident when he

was eighteen and she was fifteen. It happened the day after she came out to her parents, after she'd been suspended from school for punching a girl who was spreading a rumor that Al was a dirty dyke who checked out seventh-grade girls in the changing rooms. Her dad had flatly refused to discuss the matter, while her mom reacted with tears and recriminations, blaming Al's lesbianism on everything from the ibuprofen she'd taken when pregnant with Al to the fact that they'd let Al play with her brother's toys. Al couldn't deal with it, so she packed a bag and caught the bus into town. Tommy found the note she'd left on the kitchen table when he got back from work and went after her. He was hit by a car that was pulling out at a T junction. Eyewitnesses said Tommy was driving over the speed limit, and the driver didn't see him until too late.

"Seriously, Emma. She knew everything about him. She knew about the motorbike. She knew how old we were. She knew his last words and about Mom and Dad arguing about whether he'd want to donate his organs. She knew everything."

"Have you told anyone here about him? Maybe she overheard you talking to Leanne or Daisy."

"No. I haven't mentioned Tommy once. Not once. And no one knows what his last words were apart from me, Mom and Dad, and you guys."

"Someone must have told her."

"Who? I've never told anyone apart from you, Daisy, and Leanne. Isis said that if you let go of all your worldly attachments, it opens up a channel within you that the spirit world can reach, and…and… Fuck!" She clutches her hands to the sides of her head as though she's trying to shake the thoughts out. "She said Tommy was in the room with us. She kept saying his last words to me, over and over and over. I can't stay here, Emma. This isn't what I came here for. It's not what I wanted. It's fucked up. It's too fucked up."

I catch Al as she falls into me and hold her quivering shoulders as she sobs into the crook of my neck. The door to the hut next to mine opens, and Isis steps, blinking, into the sunshine. She catches my eye and smiles. I don't smile back.

13

'm still staring at the note. It's not Will's handwriting. The letter *a* is formed differently throughout the note, with a loop at the top, more like the *a* on a keyboard rather than an enclosed *o* with a tail.

I thump the van's steering wheel with the flat of my hand in frustration. *Of course* it's not Will's handwriting. What possible motive would he have for trying to scare me like that? Everyone who knows him—including his head teacher and the board of governors—thinks he's a good man. He's either fooled us all and he's a high-functioning sociopath, or he's as trustworthy and caring as he appears.

I was being ridiculous even considering he was responsible for the letter. Ridiculous and paranoid. I was lying to myself when I said that your past doesn't shape your future. Or maybe it was wishful thinking. Your memories are the one thing you can't run from, the one thing you can't change.

I slide my cell phone out of my pocket and tap the keyboard with my thumb. I need to apologize to Will for running off when he put Chloe to bed last night. I overreacted when I saw he'd been reading Al's article about Ekanta Yatra on his iPad. Whatever his reasons for reading it, surely he can't have had any kind of malicious intent. We need to talk. *I* need to talk. I compose a careful text.

Sorry about last night, Will. The alarm went off at work, and I was worried someone had broken in to take their dog.

I delete the last sentence. I have to stop lying.

Sorry about last night, Will. I need to talk to you. Could we meet for drinks at the George tonight? 8pm okay? x

I press Send, then scroll through my contacts, pausing when I reach "Mom Cell." It's been three months since we've spoken. She insisted, as she has done ever since I returned from Nepal, that I move home and "give up the charity nonsense and get a proper job." Oh, and see a psychologist. I've told her over and over again that I'm fine, that I'm doing what I've always wanted to do, and I'm happier than I've ever been, but she won't listen. According to her, I need to go home to deal with my "unresolved trauma." I don't know where she got that phrase from; she probably read it in the papers.

I don't know why I expected her to be different when I got back from Nepal. Maybe because I'd changed, I expected she would have too.

I tuck my phone back in my pocket and open the van door. Sheila texted me this morning to ask if I'd mind doing a pickup, as the pet owner only lives a few miles away from my cottage. Usually, the Green Fields inspectors do the pickups, but on this occasion, it's just a couple of rabbits from a retired woman who can't get to the shelter to drop them off herself. It's simple enough for me to handle.

Joan Wilkinson greets me at the door with a rabbit under each arm and tears in her eyes. She's so thin I can see the ridge of her collarbones through her flowery housecoat. Her cheeks and eyes are sunken, her mouth lined with wrinkles, and her sparse gray hair is clipped back on either side of her head with a pink, sparkly Hello Kitty hair clip. She has to be at least seventy.

"You from Green Fields?" she asks, squinting at the name badge on my polo shirt, then peering past me to look at the van.

"Yes, I'm Jane. I heard you need our help. Rabbits getting a little bit out of control, are they?"

Joan hugs the rabbits closer. One of them, a gray one, objects by pounding her stomach with its left leg. "I can cope, you know. I didn't want to call you, but my neighbor made me. She said they've been getting into her garden and it's only a matter of time until her dog goes after one."

"These two look well." I gesture at the rabbits she's holding to reassure her. "Lovely coats, bright eyes, nice and alert. Could I come in for a little chat?"

She eyes me suspiciously, then eases the front door open a little wider with her elbow. "You're out of luck if you want tea, because my milk's gone off, but you can have water, if you like."

"No problem," I reassure her with a smile. "I had a cup of tea before I left home."

The stench of ammonia hits me the second I step through the front door into the hallway. It's like stepping into a rabbit cage that hasn't been cleaned for years.

From hip level upward, the living room looks normal: on

the mantelpiece stand porcelain figurines of ballerinas alongside framed, faded photographs of weddings, picnics, and children playing in a yard; a pile of *Reader's Digest* magazines is stacked haphazardly on the coffee table next to a green corduroy armchair; and a cream lace doily slip is spread across the back of the dusty-pink sofa. It's all just as I'd expect of an elderly lady's home. But the floor tells a completely different story. The beige carpet is spotted with dark patches of urine, speckled with sawdust, and pebbled with rabbit feces. There are rabbits everywhere, at least ten or twelve, hopping over torn newspapers, shredded toilet rolls, and rotting vegetables, nibbling at the anemic spider plant in the corner of the room, and peeking out from beneath the furniture. The air is ripe with the scent of sawdust, animal hair, and feces.

This isn't a straightforward "pensioner unable to care for a couple of rabbits" collection; it's a job for one of the inspectors. Officially, I should call Sheila and request an inspector visit, but I want to check that none of the animals are in any immediate danger.

I am careful to keep my expression neutral as I pick my way through the detritus and perch on the edge of the armchair. Joan hovers beside me, the two rabbits still wriggling in her arms. Her eyes are wide, her lips pursed.

"Have you kept rabbits for long, Mrs. Wilkinson?"

"All my life." She avoids eye contact, her gaze fixed on a point somewhere to the left of my face. "I was given a rabbit for my fifth birthday. I only got to keep him for a few months."

"What happened?"

"We went to India. My father was a missionary; my mother was a nurse."

"I see. That must have been upsetting."

"It was."

"And did you have pets in India?"

She shakes her head. "Mother said it would be unfair to the animals because we'd only have to move again."

"Right."

"I got these two after my Bob died." She glances at the faded wedding photograph framed on the mantelpiece. "He wouldn't let me keep rabbits. He said Spot would go after them."

"Spot's your dog?" There are no signs of a dog in the living room—no leads, bedding, or bowls.

"Yes."

"Where is he?"

"Ran away."

There's something about the way her eyes just flicked toward the door at the end of the living room that makes me nervous. "Did you report it?"

She shrugs. "I might have. I can't remember. It wasn't my fault he ran away. He didn't want to live here after Bob died."

"How long since your husband died, Mrs. Wilkinson?"

"Eighteen months." Her eyes mist with tears, and it's hard not to feel sorry for her. Cruelty cases may seem cut and dried when they're reported in the media, but they're not always about evil men and women abusing animals. So many of the cases involve lonely, desperate people with mental health issues. They take on an animal, thinking it will be good company, but find they can't cope. If you're struggling to look after yourself, how can you look after an animal too?

"I'm so sorry for your loss. That must have been very upsetting. Do you have children or relatives who look in on you?"

She shakes her head again. "My parents are dead, and my brother lives up in Leeds. It was only ever me and Bob. We couldn't have children."

"I'm sorry."

"Don't be." She looks back at the point just to the left of my head. "We were happy enough."

I gesture toward the door at the other end of the living room. "Do you mind if I have a look around?"

"Why?" The wistful look in her eyes vanishes.

"Just to get an idea of how many rabbits you've got."

"Sixteen."

"Okay. I'd still like to take a look around, if I may, just to see them for myself. Is that okay?" I take a step toward the door, but she grabs me by the wrist. Her grip is surprisingly powerful for a woman of her age and build. The two rabbits she was holding escape and hop toward the curtains.

"You can go in the kitchen, but don't go in the pantry."

"Why not?"

"There's a fly problem. I don't want you letting them out and upsetting the bunnies."

There are three more rabbits in the kitchen, one in a wire cage, the other two in the cupboard under the sink. The door is long gone, the hinges ginger with rust. The sink and surfaces are stacked with crusty pots, pans, and dishes, crumpled newspapers, bills, plastic bags, and assorted junk. There are two doors at the end of the kitchen, both closed. The glass-fronted one leads outside. The doorknob on the other door, the one I assume to be the pantry, is hanging off.

I head toward it, picking my way over split trash bags and rotting food, a single lightbulb, hanging from the ceiling on exposed wires, humming ominously over my head. It isn't just the inspector I need Sheila to call. Social services will have to get involved too.

"You've seen everything you need to see," Joan says from behind me. "And I'd like you to leave. I've changed my mind about you taking my rabbits."

I was expecting this. I've been careful to try to hide my reaction from her, but she's not stupid. She knows I'm not going to take a couple of rabbits away and then leave her to it. I could just go. I could explain what's going to happen next, then return to my van and call the shelter, but I can't leave without looking in the pantry. If there's an animal in there, and if it dies because I didn't act, I'd never forgive myself.

"I'd like to look in the pantry, please, Joan."

"No." She shakes her head violently. "No."

"Please. I want to help you."

"I don't need your help."

"I think you do."

I reach for the door handle, and two things happen at once. As I step into the pantry, a swarm of flies hits me in the face like a buzzing black cloud, and the door slams shut behind me. I cover my face with my hands as the flies buzz around me, landing on my arms, my hands, my hair, my neck. The air is thick with the stench of death. I gag repeatedly into the crook of my elbow. With no window, it's pitch-black apart from the pale pool of light at the bottom of the door. It takes a while for my eyes to adjust to the gloom, but then I see it, lying at my feet and swarming with maggots: the decomposing body of a dog.

I reach for the doorknob, but it's gone, lying at my feet next to the remains of the dog. It must have fallen off when the door slammed shut. I barge the door with my shoulder, then kick it as hard as I can. It holds fast.

"Mrs. Wilkinson?" I pound on the door with one fist, my face still buried in the crook of my elbow. There are flies in my ears, in my hair, creeping down the front of my polo shirt.

"Mrs. Wilkinson!" I bang again. "Joan, you need to pick up the doorknob on your side and feed the pole part back into the hole so I can reattach the knob on my side. Joan? Are you there?"

I stop banging and listen, but I can't hear a thing above the drone of the flies.

Panic rises in my chest, and I take a run at the door, smashing into it with the full weight of my body.

I'm about to shout Joan's name again when my back pocket starts to vibrate.

"Sheila!" I press the phone to my ear. "I'm at twenty-seven Allinson Road. I'm trapped. She's locked me in! She's going to hurt me, Sheila. Please, please, get me out!"

14

FIVE YEARS EARLIER

You guys *have* to come to Isaac's talk." Daisy leans against the wall, one hand on her hip. "Johan might be there, and I don't want to look like a loner."

Al grins. "And what? We sit there like gooseberries while you try to make Isaac jealous by flirting with Johan? Bloody hell, Daisy, I can read you like a book."

"*I'm* going to Isaac's talk."

"Of course you are." Daisy rolls her eyes at Leanne, who is wearing a purple sarong and a gray tank top with a multicolored beaded necklace that hangs past her waist. She looks like a shorter, bonier version of Cera. "And"—she turns her attention back to Al and me—"so are you two."

The four of us are having a standoff in the shower block at the back of the girls' dormitory. It's 6:55 a.m., and Isaac's talk starts in five minutes. Other than Leanne, who's been to each and every one of his talks since we arrived, the rest of us have successfully managed to avoid them. With titles like "Freeing Your Toxic Mind," "Achieving Contentment by Breaking Unhealthy Attachments," and "Harnessing Health through Positive Thought," they don't exactly appeal.

"You can badger me all you want, Daisy," Al says, resolute, "but I'm not going. I don't want to run into Isis."

Daisy sighs. "Oh, for God's sake, Al. You're not still going on about that, are you? Isis is about as psychic as my backpack."

"She knew things about Tommy that only you guys know."

"Then she must have overheard someone talking about him. Leanne, are you sure haven't mentioned him?"

Leanne, who's been picking at the knot in her sarong with her spindly fingers for the last couple of minutes, looks up. "I haven't, Daisy, I swear. I wouldn't do that to Al. It's too personal."

"Emma?"

"God, no."

"Then maybe you were talking in your sleep or something? Seriously, Al, if Isis freaks you out that much, just tell her to sod off if she tries to talk to you. You don't have to listen to her voodoo claptrap if you don't want to. You managed to avoid her last night, didn't you?"

"Only because I went to bed early and pretended to be asleep when she came in. She was staring at me the whole way through dinner. She would have come over if I hadn't left the room."

"And what's your excuse for not coming to the talk, Emma? I thought you were Isaac's biggest fan?"

She asks the question lightly, but there's a hint of irritation in her voice. I deliberately haven't told anyone what happened with Isaac during my massage yesterday. Al was too upset after her experience, Leanne hasn't stopped going on about how inspiring and amazing Isaac is, and if I tell Daisy, she'll have a go at him and that'll be it—vacation over. For now, I'm going to pretend it never happened and avoid being alone with him.

"I'll go if everyone goes." I look at Al. "Or stay behind with you, if that's what you want..."

Leanne gives me a dirty look, then lays a hand on Al's wrist. "Al, please come. I've hardly seen you since we got here." She nestles her head against Al's shoulder and looks up at her with dark, pleading eyes. "I miss you. I'll have a word with Isis if she comes over to talk to you. We get on really well. She'll listen to me."

Al looks at Leanne for the longest time, then exhales noisily through her nose. "Okay. But if she so much as looks at me, I'm out of there."

～

The meditation room is largely empty. It's just me, Al, Leanne, Daisy, the two Swedish girls who arrived yesterday, and a man I vaguely recognize from breakfast. He's older than the rest of us by at least twenty years. I think he's named Frank. He entered the room ten minutes ago and headed straight for the bookshelf at the back. He's been sitting in the corner, flicking through a book about Maoist culture for the last ten minutes. Every now and then, he glances up and smiles or nods at me. The first time he did it, I smiled back. Now it's just gotten weird, and I'm studiously avoiding eye contact.

Al hasn't spoken since she entered the room. She's sitting with her back against the turquoise, roughly plastered wall, her knees pulled up to her chest, her eyes on the door. Leanne is sitting beside her, on the other side of Daisy, listening to the full no-holds-barred details of her sex marathon with Johan yesterday. Daisy is attempting to whisper, but she's so excitable, everyone in the room can hear every word. The Swedish girls keep nudging each other and laughing.

The door opens, and Johan and Isis appear in the doorway. They're an unlikely double act. He's late twenties, tall, six foot four at least, and slim with broad shoulders, while Isis is short and petite and quite a bit older, with gray cropped hair, purple hessian pants, and a gray tank top. As they stroll into the room, Daisy and

Al snap apart. Their reactions to the new arrivals couldn't be more different. Al slumps into herself, head down, and rubs at the back of her neck with her hand, while Daisy sits up straight and pushes back her shoulders. She tips her head to one side and smiles coyly at Johan, but he walks straight past her and crouches beside Frank. They have a conversation, after which Frank nods and reaches into his back pocket and hands over a passport. Johan pockets it, then straightens up. He nods at Isis as she sits down to the right of the altar, in front of the gong, and strolls straight back out of the room.

"Asshole," Daisy says as the door closes behind Johan.

No one says anything else, and we sit in uncomfortable silence for several minutes before the door clicks open again and Isaac appears in the doorway. My cheeks grow warm, and I look down at my hands, knotted in my lap, before he can make eye contact with me. The next time I look up, he's lounging on a beanbag in front of the altar, facing the group.

"I'm so glad to see so many of you here, especially when I know some of you weren't sure about coming to this session."

I glance at Al, but she's looking at the floor.

"Yesterday, we talked about detoxing the mind." He reaches into his shirt pocket for his tobacco tin and proceeds to roll a cigarette, nimbly handling the thin papers with his long fingers. "This session continues that theme, only today we won't be talking about attachment, anger, or ignorance. Today, we'll be talking about clearing emotional damage."

I shift on my beanbag. Al isn't the only one who feels uncomfortable sharing her secrets with strangers.

"I was physically abused as a child. My stepdad beat the shit out of me on a regular basis," Isaac says. "He hated that my mom had had a kid with another man, so first he got her pregnant, then he turned her against me. She put me into foster care when I was eight years old."

He stops speaking, and the sentence hangs in the air, demanding a response, but no one says anything. I look at the floor and trace a knot in the dark wood with my finger.

"It fucked me up for a long time," Isaac continues, "a really long time, and without really knowing it, I fucked up other people too, because of what had happened to me."

He sparks his lighter, and the scent of burning tobacco fills the air. "As I grew up, I became your quintessential bastard. I adored the chase, but the second a woman started caring about me or putting pressure on me to emotionally commit, I was off. Sometimes they refused to let me go, and then I'd have to get cruel." He pauses and looks at Isis, who nods thoughtfully. "I didn't want anyone to care for me. I didn't need looking after or saving or loving. Fuck that shit."

Isaac cranes back his neck and blows a long stream of smoke up toward the ceiling. He rocks back ever so slightly, then looks at us. "I thought I was protecting myself by not letting anyone get close. I thought I was stopping myself from getting hurt, but I was actually making things worse. I was screwing myself up." He shrugs. "And then I met this lot"—he looks at Isis again—"while I was traveling, and I figured some stuff out. I went to India, I studied with yogis, and I learned to let go."

I'm suddenly aware that what he's saying is having an effect on Daisy. Her eyes are trained on his face, but her hands are fidgeting in her lap, her fingers pulling and twisting at the tassels on her skirt. I know she's thinking about her mom and sister. Isaac wasn't the only one who had a shit childhood.

"How?" she asks. Her voice sounds unnaturally high and strained. "How did you let go?"

Isaac smiles. "You want an easy solution, don't you, Daisy? You want me to say 'chant this meditation,' 'get this massage,' 'visit this temple,' and all your shit will go away."

"No." Daisy makes a face; she looks awkward, embarrassed. "I don't want you to do anything apart from answer my question."

"Touché!" He laughs, and the atmosphere in the room lifts. "Okay, I'll tell you what did it. I opened up and started talking. About everything, to anyone who'd listen, every dirty little detail. Every filthy, fucked-up secret I'd kept to myself for twenty-four years. I thought that by keeping it to myself, by blocking it out and pretending it hadn't happened, I was stronger than the abuse my stepfather had inflicted on me. But I wasn't. I was its slave. I was carrying it around with me everywhere like a monkey on my back, and it affected everything I did, everything I said, and everyone I met. So I put my shit out there—I put it all out there—and when I did, it didn't have the strength to hurt me anymore."

"So, what, now you don't treat women like shit?" The vulnerability has disappeared from Daisy's voice, and her normal confident, scathing tone has returned.

Isaac looks at her steadily, his eyelids narrowed against the stream of cigarette smoke escaping his lips. "I don't treat anyone like shit now."

Daisy doesn't look away, and they continue to stare at each other for one thump of my heart, two, three, four. The room is silent, and everyone is still, but there's a frisson in the air, an invisible cord connecting Isaac and Daisy.

"How about you, Daisy?" Isaac's whispered question breaks the strained silence, and everyone shifts position. "What baggage are you carrying that's weighing you down?"

Daisy's cheeks pale, and a fine sweat beads across her top lip.

"I…" The word escapes from her lips, then she closes them again. She glances around the room as though she's just woken up and realized where she is. She catches Al's eye and smiles. Al is up on her haunches, her upper body twisted toward the door as though she's seconds from running out of the room. "I think someone else should go first." Daisy looks at me and laughs. "Emma?"

I shake my head. Any secrets I have are staying hidden.

The rest of the group stays silent. The two Swedish girls are sitting so closely together they look like they're conjoined at the arm. Frank is staring out of the window, his eyes unblinking.

"I'll go first," Leanne offers. She's sitting cross-legged now, her sarong puddling on the floor around her.

"Thank you, Leanne." Isaac nods at her, and she lights up like a beacon.

"The last time I saw my mom," Leanne says, not taking her eyes off Isaac, "she told me that God must hate her. When I asked her what she meant, she said, 'Well, the abortion didn't work, and I got saddled with you, didn't I?'"

One of the blond Swedish girls gasps, and I close my eyes. The room sways, and I feel sick. I can't listen to Leanne talk about abortions, not after what happened to me.

Something twitches on my knee, and I fight to stay calm. It's just Daisy's hand. I focus on it, on the warmth of my skin under her palm, and imagine the sound of her voice.

You are on a beautiful beach in the Caribbean, lying on a towel on the warm sand. Dig your fingers and toes into the sand, Emma. Feel how warm they are. Feel the sun on your face.

Daisy was the only one who could talk me down from my panic attacks at university, the only one I trusted to see me in that kind of state. She'd stroke my arm and talk to me, conjuring up my ideal vacation, making me live it in my mind. She didn't make me close my eyes, and she didn't make me focus on my breathing, but by taking my mind somewhere else, she'd break the cycle of hyperventilating, rapid heartbeat, and "I'm going to die" thoughts, and my anxiety would gradually dissipate.

"My mom was drunk when she said that about the abortion," Leanne continues, and I open my eyes again. "She's always drunk. My dad was killed in a car accident when I was fifteen, and Mom's been drinking ever since. She said he was the love of her life, but that didn't stop her from bringing men back from the pub. I lost count of how many there were."

She stops speaking and stares at the floor. She is utterly still, lost in thought. Isaac rises soundlessly from the floor, crosses the room, and sits directly in front of Leanne, cross-legged. For a couple of seconds, he says nothing. Daisy and I share a glance.

"Look at me, Leanne," he says, so quietly I barely catch the words.

Leanne slowly raises her head. Isaac leans forward and looks deep into her eyes, the expression on his face so tender, so concerned, that she immediately tears up.

"Did one of your mom's boyfriends hurt you, Leanne?" he whispers.

She shakes her head.

"Who crept into your room when your mom was passed out on the sofa, Leanne?"

She drops her chin, but Isaac catches it, lightning fast, and tips her face back up toward his. "Who hurt you?"

She attempts to shake her head, but Isaac tightens his grip on her jaw.

"Who?" he asks, his voice louder, his tone more urgent. "Who hurt you, and what did they do?" He pushes the strap of her gray tank top down over one shoulder, revealing her pale-skinned, bony frame. "Who made you hate yourself so much you stopped eating? Who made you feel that starving yourself was the only way you could feel in control?" His voice is so loud now that it's bouncing off the walls and filling the room. The scent of the incense sticks—dotted around the meditation room, wedged into church candles, plant pots, and wooden holders—is overpowering. The air is thick, jasmine scented, and heavy with emotion. The rough walls seem to be closing in, constricting the space, forcing the nine of us closer. I want to stand up, throw open a window, and let some air into the room, but I'm rooted to my beanbag.

"Who raped you, Leanne? Say his name. Say it out loud. Say it, and let go of the hold he has on you."

There's a gasp, and for a second, I think it escaped from my lips, but then I spot Al scrabbling to her feet. Isis rises too and grabs for her, but Al pushes her away.

"Fuck this shit!" she shouts as she runs toward the door. "It's sick. It's fucking sick."

Daisy's hand on my knee clenches, and I instinctively grab it. Her eyes are wide and startled, and for the first time in as long as I've known her, she looks freaked out.

"Stay here," I say. "Look after Leanne. I'm going after Al."

Daisy doesn't respond; she's still looking through the open doorway. Al is whirling around in the hallway, tearing photographs from the walls and ripping tablecloths from the tables. There is an explosion of shattering glass and porcelain as vases, ornaments, and candlesticks crash to the ground.

15

've wrapped a blanket around Al and forced an extra pair of socks onto her feet, but she still won't stop shaking. In desperation, I pull her into my arms, cocooning myself around her.

"Shh," I whisper, even though she hasn't said a word since she ran from the meditation room and into the girls' dorm. "Shh, Al, it's okay."

She presses her head into the nook between my neck and my shoulder and shivers violently. After a couple of seconds, she pushes herself away from me, her eyes flashing with anger.

"Did you see that? Did you see what that fucking asshole was doing to Leanne? He was making her... He was trying to get her to say..."

"I know."

"We need to get back in there." She throws off the blanket and rises to her feet. "He's fucking with her head."

"It's okay." I tug at her hand. "Daisy's with her."

"And? She won't do anything." She twists her wrist out of my grasp. "Isaac's playing you all for fools. It's embarrassing, the way the three of you hang off his every word."

"That's not true." I'm stung and incredulous.

"Isn't it?"

"No."

"Did *you* know one of Leanne's mom's boyfriends raped her?"

I shake my head.

"No, neither did I, and I'm supposed to be her best friend. Why would she tell that to him and not me? What is it with everyone keeping fucking secrets from me? As if it wasn't bad enough that Simone lied to my face and slept around behind my back, now I find out that my best friend can't bring herself to confide in me about one of the most awful things that can happen to you, but she'll spill everything to that fucking twat—who's a complete stranger. How is that supposed to make me feel?"

"No one's keeping secrets from you, Al. Well, yes, Simone did, but that's different. And you know what Leanne's like. She gets wrapped up in this hippie bullshit, and it was really intense in there. Isaac pretty much forced her to talk about her childhood."

Al glares at me, and for a second, I think she's going to hit me. Instead, she twists and lands a punch on the cherry-red wall behind us. There's a crack as her knuckles make contact with the wood, and she winces with pain as she sinks to her knees.

"Let me see that." I reach for her right hand, but she pulls away, her fingers cradled to her chest.

"You're not the only one who's wary of Isaac," I say.

"You're just saying that."

"Am I? Kane and Isaac swapped places during my massage without telling me, and Isaac felt me up."

Her jaw drops. "You're kidding?"

"I'm not."

"What did he do?"

"He touched my tit."

"He grabbed your tits? Fuck, Emma." She immediately pulls herself back to her feet. "That's sexual abuse."

"He didn't grab them. It was more like"—the base of my throat grows warm—"he tweaked one of my nipples as he was running his hands up my sides."

"Tweaked?" She makes the motion with her left hand. "Deliberately?"

"Well, no, it wasn't rough. It was… I don't know… It was probably an accident."

"You wouldn't have mentioned it if you really believed that."

"I…" I shake my head. "I don't know."

"Have you told Daisy?"

"No. I thought she'd go off the deep end at him."

"And so she should."

"Please, Al." I gesture for her to sit down on her mattress. The mood she's in, she'll storm into Isaac's study and swing for him. "Can we drop it? I don't want to spoil our vacation by making a fuss about something that might have been an accident. Seriously, if I were scared of Isaac, would I really have just sat in a room with him?"

"If you're sure?" She looks at me intently but sits down as requested.

"I'm sure. Can we just forget I said anything? And please don't tell Leanne or Daisy."

She looks thoughtful. "You know Daisy slept with Johan because she was pissed off with Isaac, don't you? And I think she's a bit pissed off with you too, for flirting with him at the welcome meeting."

"I didn't flirt with him."

"That's not what she thinks."

"Oh, for God's sake." I knew there was a reason Daisy's been a bit off with me. I pick up one of her discarded tank tops, fold it up, and place it next to her backpack. "If anyone should be pissed off, it should be me. She was trying to tell me the other night that Elliot, the guy I picked up before we left London, tried to kiss her while I was in the bathroom at the Love Lies nightclub—when actually it was the other way around. When I got back from the bathroom, he asked me to go to the bar with him and told me, and I quote, 'You want to watch out for your mate. She was all over me like a rash as soon as you left the room. It was embarrassing. I had to push her off.'"

"And you believed him?"

"Yeah." I pick up another T-shirt, fold it neatly, and place it on top of Daisy's tank top. "It's not like it's the first time it's happened. A few weeks before that, we met a couple of guys at Heavenly and went back to one of their houses. The guy she picked up went home after a couple of drinks, and I passed out on the sofa. When I woke up, she was rolling around on the floor with the guy I'd kissed."

"No!" Al looks aghast. "Did you say anything?"

"Not then, no. I pretended to go back to sleep, but I confronted her about it the next day in the taxi home, and she just laughed and said, 'You said in the club that you didn't like him that much.' She acted like she hadn't done anything wrong."

"It's like she's in competition with you."

"I know. It's weird and embarrassing, and I need to talk to her about it, but—" A shadow passes across the open doorway to the girls' dormitory.

"What?" Al follows my gaze.

"Someone was out there, listening."

Neither of us says anything for several minutes as we stare at the doorway. Nothing happens.

"Who do you think it was?" Al asks.

"No idea. Hopefully not Daisy. I can't deal with another argument."

"Another argument?"

"It's not important." I pick up a pile of Daisy's necklaces, lying discarded and tangled on top of her backpack, and start unpicking them. I forgot I didn't tell Al about the argument I had with Daisy before she stamped on the lizard. Al was having such a good night. It was the first time in weeks she hadn't mentioned Simone. "By the way, I don't suppose you know if Johan gave Daisy a psychic reading during her massage?"

"What? Where did that come from?"

"Kane said a couple of things to me before my massage that were a bit close to the bone, but he didn't pretend to be psychic."

"What do you mean 'pretend'?"

The curt tone to her voice makes me look up. "You don't believe it, do you? That Isis is actually psychic?" I know Daisy and Leanne both denied telling Isis about Tommy, but someone must have. "I think it's really cruel, giving you false hope that Tommy's watching over you, and—"

"Stop." She stands up awkwardly, cradling her hurt hand to her chest. All the color has drained from her face. "I'm not talking about this anymore."

"I'm sorry, Al." I reach for her. "I didn't mean... Please, sit back down. Let me look at your hand."

"No." She shakes me off, stepping past me. "Leave me alone."

"Al, wait!" I hurry after her as she sprints out of the dorm and across the wooden walkway to the main building, but the toe of my flip-flop catches on something, and I hit the ground with a thump. If Al heard me fall, she doesn't turn back.

"Shit." I sit up gingerly and peel back my pant leg. My knee is bleeding.

"You okay?" There's a hand at my elbow. I vaguely recognize the small, dark-haired woman at my side, a mop and bucket lying discarded beside her. Her name is Sally; she's one of the Ekanta Yatra community members.

"It looks worse than it is." My flip-flop, the leather thong ripped from the base, lies a couple feet from my foot. "My sandal must have broken."

Sally wipes her hands on her pale blue apron, crouches down, and takes hold of my calf between both her palms, gently tugging it toward her. "Shout if it hurts."

She twists my leg clockwise, then counterclockwise, rolls my ankle around, and then asks me to bend and straighten my knee as she checks to see if I've broken any bones. Finally she nods.

"It's not broken, but it'll need a clean. Can you walk?" She stands up and offers me an arm, clutching the mop and bucket with her free hand. "There's a first aid kit in the kitchen. You can lean on me, if you like."

~

As Sally helps me along the walkway and through the hallway, we pass a man and a woman on their knees sweeping up the devastation Al created after she ran out of Isaac's session. Broken glass and shards of pottery clink together as they brush the mess into their pans. Neither of them looks up as we walk past and into the kitchen.

"Here." Sally pulls a rickety wooden chair out from under the heavy kitchen table, and I lower myself down onto it. A thin streak of blood winds its way down my calf to my foot.

She goes into the pantry and returns with a small plastic tub. She places it on the table, then roots through it for some cotton balls and a crusty-lidded bottle of antiseptic.

"It should stop stinging in a minute," she says as she dabs at the blood. "Do you need anything for the pain? I think we've got some aspirin, if you want it." She glances up at me from her kneeling position on the wooden kitchen floor. "Or I could find something stronger?"

"No, I'm fine, honestly. It doesn't really hurt."

I look away from her smiling, friendly face to the red plastic bucket and gray tatty mop propped up against the wall, and a question forms in my mind.

"Sally?"

"Yes."

"Where were you? When you heard me fall over? There wasn't anyone else in the dorm."

"I was in the shower block," she says as she reaches for another cotton ball and crosses the room to the sink. "I was cleaning."

She holds the cotton ball under the tap and turns on the faucet. If she was in the shower block, then she wasn't cleaning very vigorously, or we would have heard her. You can hear *everything* that goes on in there—every splish, every splash, every flush. Everything.

So if she wasn't cleaning, then she was listening. She heard me tell Al that Isaac felt me up during my massage. She heard me call Isis a fake psychic. She heard every word we said.

"Emma? Are you okay?" Sally glides across the room, the damp cotton ball outstretched. Black spots appear in front of my eyes, and a rush of nausea makes me slump forward over my knees.

"Emma?" She crouches in front of me. "Emma, are you okay? You look a little green. Would you like a glass of water?"

"I'm sorry," I say as she floats back to the sink and returns with a glass of water. She presses it into my hands, and I gulp at it. "I'm really sorry if you heard us talk—"

She's about to reply when Rajesh the chef bowls into the room, his white apron splattered with red, orange, and brown stains, and wraps Sally in a huge bear hug, sweeping her off her feet. "Ah, my beautiful Sally." She squeals in surprise, and his big, dark face lights up with delight as he gazes down at her. His expression morphs into horror when he notices me watching.

"What's *she* doing here?" He pushes Sally away from him.

"This is Emma." Her smile falters. "She's one of the new girls. She fell over on the walkway. I was dressing her knee."

"You should have warned me you had company. I need to talk to you." He glances back toward the hallway. "In private."

"Okay." Sally swallows noticeably. "What... Where?"

"In there." He points toward the pantry, then glances at me.

"I've made a new spice mix. It's experimental, and I need a second opinion."

I don't believe a word he's saying. What's going on?

"You'll be okay now, Emma. Just stick this on." Sally hands me a bandage, then follows Raj across the kitchen to the pantry. They both disappear inside and shut the door.

~

My knee aches as I rise to my feet, but it doesn't buckle, and I'm able to hobble my way out of the kitchen and into the hallway. It's empty, the man and woman and their dustpans and brushes long gone. The photographs Al swept onto the floor when she ran out of Isaac's talk have been replaced on the table, in their frames but minus their glass. The statue of the Hindu goddess Kali is still in its usual place, and the only tangible sign of her destruction is a small space between two wooden candlesticks where a white china skull previously sat.

The door to Isaac's study is ajar. The rumble of voices drifts toward me.

"Everything's under control," Isaac is saying. "No one's going anywhere."

"But what about Al?" It's a female voice this time, possibly Cera's. "She's really volatile."

"It's fine. Johan's going to deal with her."

"But what if Paula talks to her? You know she's been threatening to tell the new girls all about—"

"I told you, it's under control. She'll be fine after her detox."

"That's what you said about Ruth."

"Paula won't refuse. And besides…" Isaac lowers his voice to a whisper, and I can't make out a word.

I take a step closer to the door. I know who Paula is. Cera introduced us to her when she gave us the guided tour. She's the red-haired girl who looks after the goats. She was swearing like a trooper while trying to fix some broken fencing with an old ladder. She barely made eye contact when Cera introduced us. And that's the second time someone's mentioned this Ruth person in as many days. Raj said yesterday that she'd gone to Pokhara to get supplies with Gabe, whoever that is.

I take another step toward the study door. A heavy hand on my shoulder yanks me back.

16

H ere, drink this." Will hands me a cup of steaming tea, then sits beside me on the sofa. "I've added lots of sugar."

"Thank you."

It's been two hours since the police released me from Joan's kitchen. Sheila was with them. She took one look at me, then bundled me into her car and drove me home. She spent the first five minutes of the journey yelling at me for being so irresponsible, only softening when I burst into tears. She stayed with me until Will turned up, then she gave me a brusque hug and said, "You have to put your own safety before that of the animals, Jane. For those who love you, if for no one else."

That made me cry again.

Now, Will takes a sip of his tea, then sets his cup down on a coaster on the coffee table. "How are you feeling?"

"Still shaky."

"She didn't lock you in on purpose; you do know that, don't you?"

"Yeah." I glance away, embarrassed. I heard Sheila and Will talking in hushed voices at the front door before she left. She must have told him what I'd said on the phone about Joan deliberately locking me in so she could hurt me.

"Joan said the door often gets stuck. She was trying to help you."

"I know. The police said."

"It's a good thing Sheila called you when she did."

"Yeah. Thank God Angharad couldn't find the food rotation, or I'd have been stuck there for God knows how long."

Will reaches for his tea and takes another sip. "Do you think they'll prosecute her for animal cruelty?"

"I don't know. There will be an autopsy on the dog's body. If she was responsible for its death, the case will go to court. An inspector will seize all the rabbits. Mary at work's going to be busy."

"I imagine she will."

We lapse into silence, the only sound the chirping of birds in the trees outside. It's autumn, my favorite time of year. I love the nip in the air, warm sweaters, and the prospect of red wine and old films in front of a roaring fire.

"Jane." Will reaches a hand across the back of the sofa and touches me on the shoulder. "Is everything okay?"

"What do you mean?" I take another sip of my tea, but there's only a dribble of liquid left in the bottom.

"You've seemed…different…recently, and you sent that text earlier, saying we needed to talk."

"I know." I place my mug next to his on the table, close but not quite touching.

"Okay." He twists around so he's facing me, one knee pulled into his body, one foot on the floor. From the stoic look on his face, I know he's expecting a "It's not you, it's me" conversation.

"Last night," I say, "when you were putting Chloe to bed, I used your iPad."

"That's not illegal!" He laughs nervously.

I take a deep breath. "I saw the article you were reading, about Ekanta Yatra."

"You were talking about it in your sleep the other night after I cooked us both dinner. You were thrashing about in bed, and you kept muttering it—Ekanta Yatra, Ekanta Yatra—under your breath. It's a weird name, but that's why I recognized it, from the news, years ago. I should have just asked you about it the next morning, but"—he shifts uncomfortably—"you always get a bit defensive when I ask you personal questions. I shouldn't have Googled it, but I was curious. I thought it might help me understand you."

"Did it? Did it help you understand me?"

He looks at me steadily. "You were part of the cult, weren't you?"

"It wasn't a cult. That's what the media called it. It was a community. It was..." The words dry up. Talking about Ekanta Yatra and the trip to Nepal is like picking open a five-year-old scar. It's a wound so deep, I can only scratch at the surface.

"It's okay." He inches toward me and pulls me into his arms. "You don't have to talk about it."

"I do." I look up into his warm, trusting face. "Because I'm not who you think I am." I pause and take a breath. "Will, my name isn't Jane Hughes. It's Emma. Emma Woolfe."

"You're her." His grip on me loosens. "You're the girl in one of the photos. Your hair was redder back then, but I knew it was you. You're one of the four friends who went to Nepal. You're the other one who made it back."

"Yes." I shift out of his arms and gaze down at my hands, too scared to confront the hurt, confusion, and distrust that I know must be written on Will's face. The clock above the mantelpiece *tick-tick-ticks* into the silence.

"I'm sorry." I rub at a pale stain on my pant leg with my thumbnail. I'm still wearing my work clothes, and my calves are covered with rabbit hair. "I should have told you my real name."

"Why didn't you?"

"I haven't told anyone. Not Sheila, not Anne, not anyone at work. When I changed my name to Jane and moved here, it felt like I'd been given a fresh start. After Al's article came out, I couldn't go anywhere without people nudging each other and pointing at me, not in London and not in Leicester either: 'There's that girl, the one in the cult.'"

"You could have trusted me, Jane. I'd have understood why you made that decision."

"Would you?" I glance across at him. "Things were so casual between us at the beginning, and…" I shrug.

"And you didn't know where it was going?"

"No."

He shifts position on the sofa, as uncomfortable as I am now the focus of the conversation has moved to our relationship.

"Did you ever find out what happened to the other two— Daisy and…"

"Leanne."

"Yeah. The article said they just disappeared." He stares at me for the longest time, his eyes searching mine.

I say nothing, my mind whirling.

"Jane?" he asks, then pauses. "Emma?" He says the name tentatively, as though tasting how it feels in his mouth. "Do you know what happened to them?"

"No," I say. It's a half lie, but it's still a lie.

~

Despite being more open with Will during our conversation yesterday than I've ever been, I didn't tell him about the message on the computer saying that Daisy was still alive, or about the note—I slipped that deep into the middle of the filing tray on the china hutch in my kitchen. I also managed to slip the school exercise book I'd borrowed into his briefcase, stuffing it among the rest of his marking without him noticing. I shared some things with Will last night, but not all.

I told him my real name, but only the bare bones of my story. I told him why we'd chosen to go to Nepal. I told him how excited we all were when we first arrived at Ekanta Yatra. I told him how glorious our first couple of days there were, how we swam in the river, splashed one another in the waterfall, read books in hammocks, and drank beers around the fire. I told him how things started to change, how we changed, how dangerous the place became. I didn't go into detail about what happened with Isaac or Frank. I didn't tell him about Ruth or Gabe or Johan. I told him that I'd been scared, more scared than I'd ever been in my life, and he held me as I talked and stroked my hair away from my face. He kept saying that it was all over now and that it was okay to cry and let it all out, but my eyes stayed dry.

It's not all over, no matter how many times Will tells me it is.

I lay awake for hours last night, turning everything over in my mind as Will slumbered beside me. It was the fear that unsettled me the most—the way that fear had revved from zero to one hundred the second Joan's cupboard door slammed shut. One minute I was in the present, staring at the carcass of her dead dog, realizing the situation had just escalated to something prosecutable, and the next I was sucked back into the past, reliving the most terrifying moment of my life. Until then, I'd fooled myself into believing that I'd locked all that away, that I'd filed it in a box in my head marked "Do Not Open," but the note unlocked it all. And someone out there is determined it stays that way.

I must have slept at some point last night, because Will's cell phone alarm startled me awake just after six this morning. He got up and grabbed his T-shirt from the neat pile on the chair beside the bed. When we first started dating, he'd toss his clothes onto the floor with abandon, but my neat-freakery has changed all that.

"No." He held up a hand, one pant leg on, one pant leg off, as I threw back the duvet and moved to sit up. "You need to stay in bed. Sheila told you not to come in today, remember?"

"Will, I'm fine. I'd rather be at work than rattling around in here all day with nothing to do."

"You're not fine." He pulled up his pants, fastened them, then lowered himself onto the bed and put a hand on my leg. "You were sleep talking again last night. Actually, sleep whimpering would be more accurate. Do you want me to stay?" His brow creased with concern. "It's not too late for me to send some cover work in. I'm sure it would be fine."

"I'm not ill."

"I know you're not, but…" He squeezed my thigh firmly, but his indecision was written all over his face. His school is due to be inspected before half term, and there's a hell of a lot he needs to do in order to prepare for it.

I slid my hand over his. "Honestly, Will. I'm fine. If I really have to stay home, I've got an enormous pile of books I haven't had time to read, and there's always that sci-fi box set you lent me."

"*Battlestar Galactica.*" His face lit up. "You'll love it, Emma. I know you will."

"Hmmm." I wrinkled my nose, and he laughed.

"Honestly, you don't even have to be a sci-fi fan to enjoy it. The number of people I've recommended it to who've—"

"Become totally addicted to it. I know, I know." I gave him a playful shove. "You don't have to give me the hard sell. I'll give it a go."

"Okay." He leaned forward and kissed me on the nose. "Just take it easy today, okay?"

Ten minutes later, the front door clicked shut, his ancient Ford Fiesta spluttered to life, and he reversed down the drive, pulling out onto the main road. He raised a hand in good-bye as I stood at the window and watched him drive away.

That was three hours ago. Since then, I've cleaned the bath-room, vacuumed the living room, watered all the plants, and folded and put away the laundry. I attempted to watch *Battlestar*

Galactica but only managed one and a half episodes before I gave up and retreated to my bedroom with a book. It's a turgid affair. It's won all sorts of awards and plaudits, but the language is dense, the plot barely discernible, and the main character—

My phone vibrates on the bedside table, tapping against the base of my glass of water.

It's been two days since I sent Al a message on Facebook about Daisy still being alive. Maybe she's read it.

A wave of relief mixed with disappointment courses through me as I snatch up my phone. It's a text from Will.

> Hope you're doing okay. Think there must be a full moon tonight: tenth graders are HELL today. What do you think of BG? x

I smile, despite my disappointment.

> I'm sorry, I'm not a fan. I thought Gaius Baltar was really annoying. Sorry! X

There was a time when I would have pretended to love a TV show, a song, or a book just because everyone else did, but not anymore. My phone chirps almost immediately. Will must be in the bathroom; he never texts me during a lesson.

> You need to give him a chance. He grows on you. Kind of like I did ;)

I smile again and immediately begin tapping out a response:

> But you did—

I pause, thumb poised over the keypad as the sound of car tires crunching on gravel drifts through the open window. The engine dies, and I swing my legs over the side of the bed, stand up slowly, and pad toward the window. The curtains are open, so I stay close to the wall so I can't be seen from the driveway below. A black VW Polo I've never seen before is parked outside my cottage. There's no one inside.

I stand stock-still and wait for the doorbell to ring or knocks to hammer at my door. When nothing happens, I head for the bedroom, then freeze, my heart in my mouth as I hear the kitchen floor creak under the weight of footsteps.

"Hello?" I stand at the top of the stairs and listen. Voices drift toward me. "Hello, who's there?"

I glance at my phone, but it's just as I left it, in the middle of a message to Will.

"Hello?" I creep down the steps and sigh with relief as I catch sight of the TV at the far end of the living room. Gaius Baltar and Starbuck are arguing over a card game. I must have left the DVD on pause, and it restarted itself. I hurry down the last couple of steps, then freeze again.

There's someone in my kitchen, yanking open and slamming shut the drawers. I press 911 on my phone as the clatter and clank of forks, spoons, and knives being rifled through fills the air. I hold the phone close to my chest, my thumb hovering over the Call button, and creep around the bottom of the stairs.

"Angharad!"

She jumps at the sound of her name and swings around, a six-inch carving knife in her right hand. The color drains from her face, and she takes a step backward, her hand clutched to her chest.

"Jane! You scared me!"

I look from her to the front door, which stands several inches ajar, and shiver as a gust of icy wind blows into the cottage.

"What are you doing here?"

"I brought you a cake." The hand holding the knife trembles as she points toward a small Victoria sponge on my china hutch.

"Sheila told me you weren't well, so I nipped to the cake shop. Sheila said you like sponge."

"You didn't knock."

"I did, but you didn't answer. I could hear the TV through the mail slot and assumed you couldn't hear me, so I let myself in; the door was unlocked. Sorry." The color returns to her cheeks, and she flushes red. "I can tell by the look on your face that I shouldn't have, but I didn't want to leave the cake outside in case it rained." She sees me looking at the knife and places it on the counter next to the kettle. "I just put the kettle on. I was going to bring a cup of tea and a slice of cake up to you."

The door was unlocked? I did go outside earlier to bring in the laundry, but I could have sworn I kicked the door shut after I carried the basket inside. It must not have closed properly.

"Right." I glance back toward the TV, which is still blaring in the living room. Something about her story doesn't make sense. If I'd walked into someone's house with some cake and the TV was on and they weren't about, I'd assume they'd gone to the bathroom. Unless she knew I was up in my bedroom—but how on earth would she know that? I run a hand over my face as I walk back into the living room and turn off the TV. I'm tired after a bad night's sleep and disturbed by what happened yesterday. I left the front door open, and Angharad took it as a sign it was fine to come in. People around here leave their doors open all the time, I guess; it's that kind of community. She hasn't done anything wrong. She was just trying to be nice.

"Sorry I made you jump." I force a smile as I step into the kitchen. "I wasn't expecting company, and I'm still not really used to the whole 'leave your door open and friends let themselves in' thing. That's not something we did in Leicester."

"You're from Leicester?" Her face brightens, and I kick myself for not being more careful. "My ex-boyfriend was from Leicester. We used to go to Kick Up the '90s at Fan Club. Have you been?"

I shake my head. "It's been a while since I've been clubbing."

"Right. Well, it's not exactly rocking with them here, is it?"

"No."

It strikes me, as silence descends and we stand opposite each other in the kitchen, smiling tightly and nodding awkwardly, how, even though we're about the same age, I feel twenty years older than Angharad. She's bright and sharp and inquisitive, whereas I feel old and tired and jaded. Five years ago—that was the last time I went clubbing. I went to Love Lies with Daisy, and I met some guy. She kicked him out of the taxi on the way back to my house. What was his name? I look up as Angharad says my name.

"Sorry, I was miles away. What was that?"

"I was just talking about the clubs I used to go to while at university. Did you go? I know you said you went to university in Exeter, but I think you said something about university. Newcastle, was it?"

My memory of the past might be hazy, but I know for a fact I haven't told Angharad where I went to university or even that I went at all. I've been careful not to give away too much about my past since I moved here. Will's the only one who knows anything about my life as Emma. There's a part of me that's incredibly relieved that I don't have to filter what I say to him anymore, but I also feel vulnerable, as though I peeled off my protective layers and laid myself bare in front of him last night. As far as anyone else is concerned, though, I'm Jane Hughes, I left school at sixteen, then did a variety of shop and admin jobs before deciding to get a qualification in animal care and management when I was twenty-five. I've told Sheila the names of my brothers and sister, but that's it.

"No." I shake my head. "I think you must have me confused with someone else. I've never even been to Newcastle."

"Oh, right." A half smile plays on her lips as she raises her eyebrows. "Sorry, my mistake."

My gaze drifts from the kitchen table to the cake on the china hutch. My table is huge, a good eight-seater, and yet she chose to squeeze the sponge into the tiny space between the letter rack and the filing tray where I hid the note.

"Shall I cut you a piece?" Angharad follows my gaze and leaps into action, snatching up the knife. "I'm sure Sheila wouldn't mind if I'm a little bit late. She did say to give you her love."

"No." I press a hand to the side of my head. "No, thank you. Sorry, Angharad. I don't want to be rude, not after you've gone to so much trouble, but I've got a terrible headache. I think I might just go back to bed."

"Oh." Her smile fades. "Oh, okay then."

I shoot her a friendly smile. "I'll see you at work on Monday. I think we've got a new arrival booked in. I can show you how we do the registration process."

"Great." Her smile returns, but it doesn't reach her eyes. "Great, I'll see you then."

She looks at me for several seconds, as though deciding whether or not to add something else, then nods curtly and raises a hand in good-bye. "I'll see you on Monday, then, Jane."

She rounds the table and heads for the front door, pulling it closed behind her with a click.

I wait until the VW Polo purrs to life and crunches its way down the driveway, then I take a step toward the kettle and press my fingers against its shiny curved belly.

Cold.

I cross the kitchen to the china hutch, pick up the cake, and move it to the table, then turn back. The paperwork in the filing tray, previously squared up and piled neatly, is askew. I riffle through it, tossing aside gas bills, council tax forms, and articles I've snipped from the newspaper. The envelope—the one with "Jane Hughes" written in neat handwriting in blue ink on the front—is gone.

17

FIVE YEARS EARLIER

Within seconds, I'm surrounded. Isaac and Cera dart out from his study, and Sally and Rajesh hurry out of the kitchen. Daisy snatches her hand from my shoulder and stares at me in horror.

"What did you scream for?" She presses her hands to her chest. "Jesus fucking Christ, Emma, you nearly gave me a heart attack."

"What happened?" Isaac puts a hand on my shoulder, a look of concern on his face. He doesn't know I was listening to him and Cera talking about Al.

"Nothing. Daisy startled me when she touched me, that's all."

He glances down at my grazed knee. "What happened there?"

"She fell over." Sally skips to my side and links her arm through mine, but her eyes don't leave Isaac's face. Raj takes a step back toward the kitchen. "I was cleaning the girls' shower block when I heard a noise, and I found her on the walkway. One of her flip-flops broke, and she tripped."

Isaac stoops and peers at me. "And you're sure you're okay?"

I fan my hand in front of my face. It's hot in the hallway, and everyone's standing too close. They're all watching me, staring, waiting for me to speak. A bead of sweat dribbles down my back. I close my eyes momentarily, but when I open them again, the walls swell, opening out like a balloon then constricting again, squeezing everyone closer, closer, closer to me, until the pressure on my chest is so great I can't breathe.

"You're not going to faint, are you?" Sally sounds like she's talking underwater.

I want to tell her to stop hanging on to my arm and Isaac to get out of my face, but I can't speak. I can't move. I can't bear the sensation of Sally's fingers pressing against my skin or the scent of tobacco on Isaac's breath.

"Why don't we go for a walk?" Daisy asks, guiding me toward the front door, leading me into the fresh air. My knees buckle, but she holds me upright.

"Emma!" Sally calls out as we take the steps one at a time. "Do you need a stick? I could find you one if you need one."

~

I don't say a word as we round the building, cross the patio—normally crowded with bending, stretching yoga bodies, but now strangely deserted—and carefully pick our way down the slope toward the river. Instead, I focus in on Daisy's voice as she tells me to breathe. She says it over and over again.

"Breathe, Emma, just breathe."

She lowers me carefully onto a large, flat rock on the edge of the river, and I double over, my head in my hands. Everything still sounds as though I'm sitting at the bottom of a swimming pool, but my heart has stopped pounding, and the world has stopped pulsing. Fresh blood is dribbling from my knee and running down my calf. Sally's bandage is still in my hand.

"You okay?" Daisy peers at me as I suck on the cuff of my linen shirt and use it to wipe away the blood.

"No. No, I need my pills."

She stands up and looks toward the house. "Where are they?"

"I don't know. I haven't seen them since we were in Pokhara. I've looked everywhere."

"Shit." She sits down again, rests a hand against the base of my spine. My shirt is stuck to my back with sweat, but she doesn't remove her hand. "We'll find them. And you'll be okay. I'm here, Emma. You'll be fine."

I nod, but I'm not sure I will.

"What were you doing?" Daisy asks. "When I came in the front door, you were standing on your own in the hallway with the weirdest expression on your face. I thought you were supposed to be with Al."

I look up at her. "Why did you say it like that?"

"Like what?"

"Like you're annoyed that I've been spending time with Al."

"You have spent a lot of time with her since we got here."

"That's because Leanne's always skipping off to meditation or one of Isaac's seminars, and I didn't want Al to feel left out."

She looks at me for several seconds, then tips back her head and laughs. "Would you look at your face! I wasn't getting all *Single White Female* on you. I just thought it would be nice to spend a bit of time with my best friend, that's all. Anyone would think you're ignoring me!"

"I'm not."

"Are you sure about that?" Her bright blue eyes bore into me.

"Of course I am. Anyway, what happened after Al and I left Isaac's talk? Did he carry on giving Leanne the third degree?"

"No, he stopped, and Isis took her off somewhere. I tried to go with them, but Isaac wouldn't let me. He said that Leanne was like an open wound, that the infection from her past was seeping out and that I couldn't be with her or I'd contaminate her and she'd have to go through the process all over again."

I laugh. "You're kidding me."

"I swear I'm not. He seriously came up with that crap. It's a good thing he's so fit, or he couldn't get away with it. Anyway"—she dismisses the thought with a wave of her hand—"I went to look for them in the grounds but couldn't see them anywhere, so I went back to the house. And that's when I saw you standing in the hallway playing a game of musical statues all on your own."

"I was listening to Isaac and Cera talking in the study."

"What about?"

I squint into the distance. Isaac is leaning out of his study window, puffing on a cigarette. I would never admit it to Daisy, but there's something fascinating about him. On the surface, he seems really chilled and laid-back, but there's a lot more going on beneath the smiles and the pseudo-Buddhist bullshit. I'm not sure I buy what he said about getting over the abuse he suffered in his childhood by talking about it. I think the hurt's still there, but he's found a way to block it out. "Al. I think they were pissed off with her for smashing up the hallway."

Daisy follows my gaze. "You know he likes me?"

"Sorry?"

"Isaac. He fancies me. Leanne told me. He plays hard to get, apparently."

I suppress a smile. Daisy's propensity for self-delusion is astonishing, but her telling me that Isaac fancies her isn't to share her surprise or delight; it's to warn me off. This is her staking her claim. If it weren't so ridiculously childish, it would be irritating. "Right, okay. That's interesting."

"I know, I like a challenge, and according to Leanne, it really pissed him off that I shagged Johan." She smirks and runs a hand through her hair, preening even though Isaac is over a hundred yards away.

"Leanne told you that?"

"Yeah. I knew he liked me; I just couldn't figure out why he was being such an asshole about it. But now I know he had a fucked-up childhood, so that explains a lot. It looks like we've got more in common than I thought." Her lips twitch into a tight, self-satisfied smile, and she reaches for my hand. "Shall we go find Al?"

18

'm sorry, guys. I've made up my mind." Al puffs on her cigarette, throws it on the ground, and then lights another. It's the fourth one she's had since dinner.

The sky is a black blanket, it's spitting with rain, and we're sheltering under one of the mango trees in the orchard at the bottom of the lawn. The house shines like a beacon in the distance—the kitchen is bright with the light of electric lamps, while the study and meditation room glow with the warmer, dimmer light of dozens of candles. The fire pit on the patio crackles and sparks, illuminating Isaac and Johan. Their silhouettes are tipped together, as though deep in conversation. The yard is silent apart from the rushing of the river, the chirps of the cicadas, and Al sucking on her cigarette.

We didn't have to look far to find her. She was sitting in one of the massage huts with Johan, puffing on a joint. We heard her laughter as we walked along the bank of the river. It faded as she spotted us, and she barely said a word over dinner.

"But you can't leave." There's a whiny tone to Leanne's voice, whiny and desperate. She's wrapped in a Nepalese yak's wool blanket. Every time she waves her arms around to illustrate her point, the smell of damp dog drifts toward me. "We've only just gotten here."

"If this has anything to do with what I said earlier about Isis and what she said about your brother," I say, "I'm sorry. What I said was thoughtless and tactless. I didn't mean to upset you, I swear."

Al waves away my apology with a flick of her hand. The burning tip of her cigarette dances through the air. "Don't worry about it, Emma."

"Seriously, I feel really—"

"Let's not talk about it." She fixes me with a look. "Okay?"

"It's going to rain later," Daisy says, her gaze still fixed on the patio. "You heard what Johan said."

Al leans back against the mango tree and sparks her lighter, lighting another cigarette. The flame illuminates the deep graze on her knuckles. She punched the wall in the girls' dorm with a lot more force than I realized.

"Johan says a lot of things," Al says.

"I thought you liked him." Daisy sounds indignant.

"I do—he's a decent bloke—but that doesn't change anything. I'm still going."

Leanne shivers and pulls the blanket over her head. "Is this because you've got no reception on your phone? I know it's hard, because you can't check to see if Simone has texted you, but that's part of the reason we're here. You've got an unhealthy attachment to her. You need to acknowledge your past so you can free yourself from it. Isaac thinks—"

"I don't give two fucks what Isaac thinks."

Daisy and I exchange a look. Al's never snapped at Leanne like that before.

"Seriously." Al stands up straight so she's no longer resting against the tree trunk. "You need to listen to yourself, Leanne. Ever since we got here, it's been Isaac this, Isaac that. Toxic minds, unhealthy attachment, meditating on nothingness; you're even starting to sound like him."

"And is that such a bad thing?" The yak blanket slips from Leanne's head as she pulls herself up to her full five-foot height. Her beady eyes peer up at Al from under her glasses. "Isaac's happy, Isis is happy, Cera is happy, everyone here is happy—and we're not. Why do you think that is? Because they don't have any unhealthy attachments, and we do."

"I'd like to get unhealthily attached to Isaac," Daisy says, but no one laughs. She glances back toward the patio. I can't see Isaac's face, but I can tell from the angle of his body that he's gazing down past the gardens and into the orchard, watching us.

Al draws on her cigarette, then tips back her head and exhales. The gray smoke spirals into the darkness and then disappears. "So how did purging yourself of your past work for you, Leanne? Are you a happy little sunbeam now?"

Leanne bristles. "There's no need to be a bitch about it."

"Sorry!" Al holds up her hands. "I don't want to fall out with you, Leanne, honestly, but this place is doing my head in. I want to leave, I need to, and it's got nothing to do with Simone."

"Give it a couple of days," Daisy says. "There's going to be a big party once Gabe and Ruth get back from Pokhara. There'll be vodka, lots of it! Brought up here on a donkey—a donkey, for goodness' sake! Although how they can call themselves a business and run out of food and drink when they've got guests staying, I don't know."

Al shakes her head. "Sorry, mate, not interested. I'd rather be back down at the hotel in Pokhara with my feet in the pool."

"But *we* wouldn't be there."

"I'll cope. It won't be long until you lot join me." Al grinds her cigarette butt into the ground with the heel of her flip-flop. "I'd better go get packed if I want to leave tonight."

"Tonight?"

"I'm not spending another night sleeping in the same room as Isis. She creeps me out."

"Then sleep in the meditation room," Leanne says. "I'm sure they wouldn't mind if you dragged your mattress in there."

Al shakes her head. "Nah, it's cool. I've made up my mind."

"But it's spitting already, and Johan said the rain is going to get heavier! It's not safe trekking up or down the mountain in bad weather. And it'll take you hours."

"It's downhill, and unless Johan is channeling the Weather Channel straight into his brain, he's guessing about the weather."

I shake my head. "You're not going on your own. I'll come with you."

"She speaks!" Daisy feigns shock, and Leanne laughs.

"You don't have to," Al says.

"I want to. I can't bear feeling so on edge. I'd enjoy this vacation a whole lot more if I could get some more pills. I'm sure there'll be somewhere in Pokhara where I can buy some. Daisy bought Valium over the counter in Kathmandu." I glance at her, waiting for her to launch into her "You can't go, you're my wing woman" speech that I get every time I try to leave a London club early, but she merely raises her eyebrows and gives me a half smile.

"Please." Leanne grips Al's hand. "Don't go. Give it a few more days. I know I've been a bit crap at spending time with you, but we can fix that. We can go swimming more often, and Raj said he'd give us cooking lessons, if we want. I know how much you love his dal bhat."

Al shakes her head. "Nah, no offense. It's nothing to do with you, Leanne, honestly. I just need to clear my head, and it feels claustrophobic here. Look, we were only planning on spending another week or so here, anyway. I can meet you back in Pokhara, and then we'll get the bus to Chitwan and do our jungle trek."

Leanne lets go of Al's hand. "Um, about that…"

"What?"

"I haven't actually booked it."

"Why not?" Al glances from me to Daisy. "I thought the plan was Kathmandu, then Pokhara, two weeks here, then Chitwan. That's what we agreed before we came out here. Haven't you guys already paid for it?"

Daisy and I both nod as Leanne shifts from foot to foot and pulls the blanket more tightly around her. "I...I was going to book it, but then I thought I'd play it by ear just in case we... in case..." She glances up toward the patio. Isaac is alone now, the dim light of his cigarette tracing through the air. "Anyway, someone told me it was cheaper to book treks from here."

"So we're still going?"

"Well, as I say, I haven't actually booked it yet, but..."

"Don't you think we should? What if there's no availability for next week?" Al waves a hand dismissively. "Never mind. I'll organize it once I get back to Pokhara, if you can give me the cash."

"I haven't got it on me. I'd...I'd need to go to a bank."

"Right." Al shrugs. "Then I guess we'll have to wait until we're all back in Pokhara."

"The rain is getting heavier." I hold out a hand, palm up, and gaze up at the sky. Even in the darkness, there's no mistaking the menacing clouds looming overhead.

"Fuck." Al tucks her Marlboro Lights into her bra strap and sighs heavily, looking morosely out at the view. "Tomorrow it is, then. I can put up with Isis for one more night, I guess. Come on, let's get back inside before it pisses down."

She sets off toward the house at a surprisingly speedy pace, and I set off after her, only pausing to glance back when I reach the now-deserted patio. The heavy clouds above have finally broken open, but the fire pit is still alight, a single log glowing in its belly though Isaac is long gone.

"Daisy! Leanne!" I shield my eyes from the rain and shout

down to Leanne and Daisy, who are still standing beneath the mango trees, two dark, indistinct shapes in the gloom, their heads close together as though deep in conversation. "Come on, you'll get soaked!"

Neither of them acknowledges me.

19

J ane! Lovely to see you." Sheila envelops me in a bear hug, pressing my head to her sizeable bosom, then holds me at arm's length and looks me up and down. "How are you doing?"

"Great," I say, when the truth is I've never felt so tired.

After Angharad's visit yesterday, I had even less sleep than the night before. I got out of bed three times to search for the note. I looked through the filing tray and the letter rack. I got on my hands and knees and peered under the china hutch, nearly throwing my back out trying to pull it away from the wall so I could check behind it. I rummaged through the trash, my pockets, the living room, but there was no sign of it. It was definitely gone.

Will sent me a text at 5:00 p.m. saying they were putting in a late one at work to go over something inspection related before the weekend, and then he was taking his department off to the pub to say thank-you for all their hard work. He apologized profusely, explaining there was no way he could get out of it, but I was very welcome to join them. I turned him down. I've never met any of his work colleagues, and I find small talk with strangers exhausting, particularly when I have other things on my mind. Will isn't the sort of man to turn up drunk for sex after a night's heavy drinking, so I knew I'd be spending the night alone.

I did everything I could to avoid going to bed. I watched a crime drama on TV, then a documentary about life on benefits, and then, with nothing else that even vaguely appealed, I watched back-to-back episodes of *Battlestar Galactica* until I fell asleep on the sofa somewhere around 3:00 a.m. I woke with a start at 6:00 a.m., grateful to see the sun creeping over the horizon.

"You don't look great," Sheila says. "You need to eat some more of that cake Angharad brought you. She said you seemed a bit out of sorts. Are you sure you're okay?"

"Honestly, I'm fine." I wriggle out of my waterproof jacket and hang it up on the coat stand. There's no sign of the red, wool-blend winter coat it usually hangs beside. "Angharad not in?"

Sheila shakes her head. "She doesn't do Saturdays. You've got Barry working with you today."

Barry's one of the regular volunteers. He's sixty-three, almost completely bald, and as wiry as they come, but he's strong. You'd never know it from his soft, lilting Welsh accent, but he used to be a sergeant major in the army. The dogs know it, though: they never put a foot wrong when Barry's taking them for a walk. They respect and adore him in equal measure.

"You've got quite the fan there, you know," Sheila adds.

"What, Barry?"

"No." She laughs. "Angharad. Little Miss Twenty Questions she was yesterday at lunchtime. 'How long have you known Jane? Has she got a boyfriend? She's very secretive, isn't she? She never talks about her private life.' You know what, Jane? If I didn't know better, I'd say someone had a bit of a crush on you!"

"Sheila!"

"Not like that!" She laughs again, flashing the sizeable gap between her front teeth. "It just seems a bit hero-worshippy to me. I think maybe she's found her vocation here. I wouldn't be at all surprised if she starts inquiring about training and a full-time position. You know me; I'm a good judge of character. I employed you, after all!"

Tears prick at the back of my eyes, and I blink them back. I hate that I've lied to Sheila, hate that I'm not the person she thinks I am. It never occurred to me when she first interviewed me that we would build a relationship more akin to mother and daughter than employer and employee. Could I tell her? Could I sit her down at my kitchen table and, over a bottle of wine, tell her what I told Will? But I only told him part of the truth, and this is a different situation. I'm in a position of responsibility here. If I've lied about who I am and what I've done, how could she trust me with some of the serious cases we're dealing with? She'd have to let me go. I don't know what I'd do if that happened.

But it may already be too late. Someone searched through my things yesterday, and there were only two people in my house other than me. One was Will; the other was Angharad. And one of them took the letter.

~

My walkie-talkie crackles when I'm halfway up the top field with Jack. "You've got visitors in reception."

I wave at Barry, who's over on the other side of the field walking Bronx, a powerful Doberman with an excitable, inquisitive personality, and then point back down the field toward the gate to the shelter. "I'm going back."

He cups a hand behind his ear and shakes his head.

"Back!" I shout and gesture again. This time, he gives me a thumbs-up.

"Sorry, sweetheart." I crouch down and rub Jack behind the ear. He gazes up at me, his brown eyes warm and trusting, mouth open, dribbling saliva onto his chest. It's only been a few days since we brought him in, but the change is remarkable. He's not keen on Barry or any of the men who work here, but he seems to have warmed to me. He flinched the first few times I reached out to touch him, but now it's only sudden movements that scare him. He's not over his dog-fighting experience, not by a long shot, but his psychological scars are slowly healing along with his physical ones. I've been half expecting Jack's owners to pay us a repeat visit to demand him back, but there's been no sign of Gary Fullerton and his wife. I can't say I'm not relieved.

"Come on, then, boy." I straighten up, and we stroll side by side back down the field. "Let's go see these visitors."

Chloe throws herself at me the second I walk through the double glass doors to reception. Her small arms circle my hips as she presses her head into my belly.

"She was up at six this morning, according to Sara," Will says. "Too excited to sleep, apparently."

I reach out an arm to pull him into a group hug, but he sidesteps it and squeezes my hand instead. I mouth the word "Hungover?" but he shakes his head.

"I'm fine."

"It's my school fair this afternoon," Chloe says. "Will you come? I've made some loom bands to sell. Mrs. James said I can give half the proceeds to Green Fields. It would be so cool if you came. Please say you will."

"What time does it start?"

"Two p.m."

My shift finishes at lunchtime, so, in theory, I could make it. I glance at Will, who shrugs his shoulders, then turns away and plucks a cat toy from the merchandise display. He jiggles it up and down in his hand. The tiny bell inside makes a tinny, jangling sound.

"Will?"

"Yeah." He doesn't turn around. The annoying jangling sound continues.

He's either lying about being hungover or there's something else on his mind.

"I'd love to come to your school fair," I say to Chloe, "but I won't stay too long."

"Brilliant! Can we go see the kittens now?" Chloe gazes up at me, and I'm reminded of Jack with his big, trusting brown eyes. "Please!"

"Of course." I disentangle her and reach for her hand. She takes it, then reaches for Will's hand too. She swings our hands back and forth as we cross reception. To an outsider, we'd look like the perfect, happy little family. Happy, that is, apart from the strange sideways looks Will keeps giving me.

~

"They're so cute. Can I have one, Daddy? Please?" Chloe is sitting on the carpet with a tiny, tabby kitten desperately trying to clamber out of the circle she's made with her legs. We've completed the tour of the shelter and retreated to the "cat living room" where potential adopters can spend time with the cats in a more natural environment. We've furnished it with sofas, armchairs, beanbags, and a radio. "Daddy?"

Will, who's been looking at his phone since we sat down, looks up. "Sorry?"

"A kitten? Can we have one?"

He looks back down at his phone. "We'll see."

"Is that a yes?"

"We'll have to ask your mom."

"She'd say yes. I know she would. And if she said no, we could always keep it at your house, couldn't we? Couldn't we, Daddy? It could live at your house, and I could see it on weekends. I know you'd have to look after it during the week, but I'd be there more often during the holidays, and—"

"I said we'll see, Chloe."

She visibly jumps at his raised voice, then folds herself over the kitten, tears pricking at her eyes, scoops him off the floor, and presses him to her chest.

I lean in toward Will and say in a low voice, "Is everything okay?"

He looks at me for what feels like the first time since they arrived an hour ago. His eyes search mine. "Not really."

"Do you want to talk? Outside? Chloe will be okay in here with the kittens. We can keep an eye on her through the window."

He nods. "We're just popping out into the corridor for a bit, Chlo. You okay in here?"

She nods mutely.

"Chloe." He eases himself up from the sofa and crosses the room, then crouches beside his daughter and puts a hand on her shoulder. "I'm sorry I snapped at you just now. That wasn't fair. We'll talk some more about getting a kitten when we get home later, okay? It's not a decision we should rush into, no matter how cute these little fellas are."

"Okay, Daddy." Chloe doesn't unfurl, but she doesn't lean away when he pulls back her curtain of hair and kisses her on the cheek.

"We'll just be in the corridor." Will points toward the door.

~

"I'm sorry," he apologizes the second the door clicks shut behind us. "Sara's passive-aggressiveness used to drive me nuts, and you deserve more than that, Jane—Emma," he corrects himself quickly.

I cross my arms over my chest and brace myself for the "It's not me, it's you" speech I know is coming. He's too decent a man to have walked away when I first told him about who I really was, especially after what happened at Mrs. Wilkinson's house, but he's had a couple of days now to reflect. His daughter has taken a shine to me, and he's worried. Who wouldn't be?

"So the thing is"—he runs a hand through his hair and clears his throat—"I found myself in a bit of an awkward situation in the pub last night. We were talking about Graham's impending wedding to Claire, and then someone asked me if I was going to marry you." He waves away my sharp intake of breath. "Obviously, I told them that we're very early on in our relationship, but the question opened the floodgates, and suddenly everyone was quizzing me about you. Where are you from? What do you do? When did you move here? Where did you live before? Et cetera, et cetera. And I found myself..." He gazes through the window at Chloe, who's teasing the kittens with a small, gray catnip mouse. "I found myself repeating everything you'd told me. Not what you told me the other night, but what you'd told me before, and..." He looks back at me. "I felt like a liar. I felt like I was complicit in something I don't fully understand. And that made me feel uncomfortable, Jane. Really, bloody uncomfortable. I'm the head of biology, and I was telling barefaced lies to my staff, people who look up to me."

"But they're not lies. Other than my name, nothing I've told you was a lie. I just...I just left out some parts of my past."

"And I get that. I get that you wanted to leave all that behind and start a new life for yourself, but I couldn't help wondering if there's more."

"More?" My pocket vibrates as my phone bleeps, but I don't reach for it.

"You told me about Ekanta Yatra, but have you been hiding more than that?"

My phone bleeps again. "Like what?"

"Like a husband? Children?"

"No."

"A criminal past?"

There's a third bleep, and I grimace apologetically. *"No!"*

Will glances through the window toward Chloe. He's quiet for what feels like the longest time.

"I understand," I say when I can't bear the silence a moment longer. "You have to protect your daughter. I get that, Will, and if you want to break things off between us, I...I'll accept it."

"But I don't want to." He looks back at me with fear and confusion written all over his face, and my heart seems to squeeze in my chest. "I like you, Jane. Sorry, can I keep calling you that? You're not Emma to me, not yet."

"You can call me Jane. I'd rather you did, actually."

He smiles the smallest of smiles. "Good. To be honest, Jane, this is really hard for me to wrap my head around. It's not the sort of thing that you can have just sprung on you, and I need some time to process it. Can you do that? Can you give me a bit of time?"

"Of course. Shall I tell Chloe that I can't make it to her school fair this afternoon? I could make up some kind of excuse about work."

"No." Will shakes his head. "She'd be really upset. Let's go to the fair, then, you know..."

He leaves the sentence hanging, and I don't finish it for him.

"You should answer that," he says as my phone bleeps for the fourth time. "I'm just going to go let Chloe know that it's nearly two."

"Okay." I reach into my pocket, grateful for an excuse to turn my back so he won't spot the tears that are pricking at my eyes.

I swipe my fingers over the screen as Will opens the door to the cat living room and slips inside. The bleeps were alerts from the Facebook app telling me I've got four messages. But when I look at them, they're not from Al: they're from Daisy. Daisy, who is supposed to be dead.

20

Al stares at the river of water that's cascading down the stone steps. "Shitting hell. Where'd this come from?"

"Want to turn back?"

She shakes her head. "We've made it this far."

It's the morning after Al announced she wanted to leave, and we've been picking our way down the mountain for over an hour. Progress is slow. Johan wasn't kidding about the downpour. The ground on either side of the steps is a muddy swamp, and the trees are bent low and dripping rainwater. My waterproof jacket, which the camping shop salesman told me could withstand the heaviest of downpours, is stuck to my arms and clinging to my body. My shorts are hanging limply from my hips, and my socks, poking out the top of my hiking boots, are sodden.

It wasn't raining when we stepped out through the gates of Ekanta Yatra. We had all of ten minutes of clear skies before the heavens opened again. Daisy came to the gates to wave us off, but Leanne stayed indoors. Officially, she was helping Raj prepare the lunch, but we all knew she was sulking. Her attempt to talk Al into staying didn't end the moment we left the orchard; when she and Daisy finally returned from their private conversation among the mango trees, she continued to badger and cajole Al late into the night. Neither of us has had more than four hours sleep.

"Oh God."

Al stares at me. "What?"

"I just realized we left our passports behind. They're still in Isaac's study."

"Doesn't matter. Leanne and Daisy will grab them when they leave."

"You think?"

"Yeah, 'course. Leanne will remember. She's organized like that."

"Is she? She forgot to book the Chitwan trip. Don't you think it's weird that she remembered everything else—everything from mosquito spray to the coach to Pokhara to a guide to bring us up here—and yet she forgot that?"

"No." Al shakes her head. "She said she just wanted to play things by ear."

"But she's packed enough clothes to come on three vacations."

"What are you saying?" Al runs a hand over her face. Rain is dripping off her eyelashes.

"I don't think she wants to go back. You saw the way she reacted when we left. She might not have waved us off, but there were tears in her eyes when we left the kitchen."

"Don't be stupid."

"I'm not! Have you ever seen her as happy as she's been recently?"

"That's because she's on vacation."

"So am I, so are you, so's Daisy, and we haven't been skipping around, borrowing clothes from Cera and Isis and joining in with absolutely everything. You know Leanne; her default setting is sarcasm."

Al shrugs. "I think you're reading too much into it, Emma. Leanne's a hippie at heart, and Ekanta Yatra's a hippie paradise, and that's all there is to it." She reaches into her pocket and pulls out her inhaler. She puffs on it.

"You okay, Al?"

"I think it's the altitude. My asthma's been acting up since we got here."

"And it's got nothing to do with you smoking twenty cigarettes a day?"

She flicks me the finger. "Nah, the warmth of the smoke opens my tubes."

"Try telling that to your doctor."

"She was the one who told me to try it." She laughs good-naturedly. "C'mon, let's get going." She places one foot cautiously onto the first step. The dirt-brown water gushes around her boot and rolls down the hill, leaves and twigs twirling and whirling on the surface. It's hard to see where one step ends and the next begins.

"It's fine. Look." She takes another step onto the path and then, tentatively, another. "You just need to take it carefully and slowly, that's—argh!" Her foot slips from beneath her, and she falls backward, landing on her bum with a splash.

"You all right?" I take a pace toward her, testing my weight on the first step, and reach out a hand.

"Yeah." She twists around, plunging her hands into the water, and attempts to stand up. "Fuck. My ankle."

"Have you twisted it?"

"Yeah, I think so. Shit!"

"Don't move. I'll try to lift you." I inch forward, then crouch down. The water cascades over the top of my boots as I tuck my hands under Al's armpits and take the strain. "Ready?"

She nods.

"One...two...three..."

I take as much of her weight as I can, but she's a good fifty pounds heavier than me, and she plops back into the river.

"You're going to have to help me a bit," I say. "Can you put some more weight on your good foot?"

"Okay. Ready?"

"One…two…three…" She groans as she puts her good foot on the ground, and I yank her upward. There's a moment where we both wobble precariously, and my heel slips on the step, but we manage to stay upright. Neither of us says anything for several seconds as we stare down the mountain, and then Al sighs heavily.

"There's no way we can get down there. Not unless we both sit on our bums and make our way down toddler-style. We're going to have to go back and wait for the weather to improve. Shit!"

My heart sinks. The excuse I made to Leanne and Daisy about my antianxiety pills was only half the reason I want to leave. Despite the beautiful surroundings and the relaxed, easygoing way of life, cracks have started to appear in our friendship, and the quiet rumblings of discontent that were much easier to escape in London have begun to grow louder. When you're forced to live together twenty-four hours a day, there is no escape. You can't go home and ignore your cell phone for the rest of the weekend. Instead, the atmosphere follows you around, clouding the air, making it too dense to breathe.

"Leanne will be pleased we're back," Al says, but her voice is flat. She's even more disappointed than I am. She came to Nepal to try to escape the specter that was her relationship with Simone, but since her session with Isis, she's been forced to deal with other ghosts she'd rather forget.

"You can put your weight on me." I take her elbow, and slowly, we revolve so we're facing back up the hill.

~

It took us an hour to get part way down the mountain, but it takes us twice as long to get back up. By the time we reach the gates of Ekanta Yatra, we're both shivering, and Al is gasping for breath and wincing with every step. We knock at the gates for what feels like forever and are finally welcomed in by Johan, who takes one look at Al's ankle, then hoists her over his shoulder—backpack and all—as though she's featherlight and carries her into the house and through to the kitchen, where Sally, Leanne, and Paula are washing the breakfast dishes. Leanne takes one look at Al, and her face lights up but then crumples with worry as Johan eases her into a seat.

"Al, what happened?" Leanne shoves me out of the way in her desperation to get to her and crouches beside the chair. The skin beneath her eyes is puffy and swollen.

"I twisted my ankle. It's a mud bath out there." Al peels off her waterproof jacket and drops it to the floor, then looks back up at Leanne, her face creased with concern. "Are you okay? You look like you've been crying."

"I'm fine. I was just upset because I thought I'd never see you ag—" She presses a hand to her mouth as though she's just said something she shouldn't.

"God, you're a softie." Al reaches for a hug, and Leanne wraps her slender arms around her and clings to her, closing her red-rimmed eyes as she nestles her chin into Al's shoulder. She looks simultaneously delighted and relieved, like someone hugging a long-lost relative in an airport arrival lounge, not someone who said good-bye to a friend a few hours ago.

"Oh, no." Leanne pulls away from Al, her red-rimmed eyes wide and worried behind her glasses as she glances up at Johan. "If the weather's really bad, will Gabe and Ruth be able to get back from Pokhara okay?"

He crosses his arms over his broad chest, and his lips tighten ever so slightly. "Gabe's done the route so many times, he could do it blindfolded. He'll find an alternative route. Anyway"—he turns away—"I need to get out to the garden. If I don't put some straw on the veg, it'll rot."

"Thanks, Johan." Al smiles up at him but then winces as Sally eases off her boot and rolls down her sodden sock. "Hope you didn't put your back out."

"No problem." He strolls back out of the kitchen and heads for Isaac's study, his face still pinched and drawn.

Sally stands up and crosses to the sink. She picks up a tea towel from the draining board and runs it under the tap. "I'm afraid we don't have any ice, so a wet compress will have to do."

Al mouths her thanks, then smiles at Leanne, who is clutching her right hand, limpet-like.

"I'm so glad you're back," she breathes. "You have no idea how much I would have missed you."

"You'd have joined us in a week's time," I say. "It's not like you were never going to see her again. Unless..." The fog in my brain lifts. There's only one explanation for Leanne's over-the-top reaction to Al's return. "Unless you were planning on staying here and not coming back to the UK with us."

"Yeah, right, Emma," Al says. "Of course she wants to give up her cozy little studio flat with a fridge stocked with food to sleep on the floor and eat lentils for the rest of her life."

As Al laughs heartily, a flicker of irritation crosses Leanne's face. She doesn't say anything but instead eases off Al's other boot, then stands up. "I'll get you a nice cup of chai, Al. It'll warm you up."

"I'd love one too," I say slightly too loudly. "I'll drink it after I've had a shower. See you guys in a bit."

"See you!" Al raises a hand in good-bye as Leanne turns on her heel, crosses the kitchen, and takes one cup down from the shelf.

"I'll put some extra sugar in it for you, Al."

~

Daisy is standing in the hallway, leaning against the wall beside the table with her arms crossed. She's dressed in a floor-length maxi dress that's a size too big for her, with her hair piled up on her head and wrapped in an indigo scarf.

"Hi." I pull the kitchen door shut behind me. "We're back! Al slipped over and hurt her—"

"We need to talk. Let's go into the girls' dormitory."

Without waiting for a response, she leaves the hall and walks down the walkway and into the dorm. It's dark and gloomy, the sky black with rain clouds beyond the window.

"Sit down, please." She gestures toward my mattress, then sits down on Al's and arranges her dress over her crossed legs.

I ease my backpack off, letting it fall to the ground with a thump, then rotate each of my shoulders in turn. "What's this about? Why are you being so weird?"

Daisy smiles tightly. "I've been doing a bit of thinking."

"Dangerous stuff." I half sit, half fall onto my mattress and groan as I untie my boots and ease them off. My sodden socks cling to my feet. I yank them off too, then root around in my backpack for my towel, shower gel, shampoo, and conditioner.

"Don't." Daisy's smile vanishes. "Don't try to be funny."

"What's the matter with you? I thought you'd be pleased to see us."

"Not particularly."

"Oh, for God's sake, Daisy." I release the armful of toiletries I've gathered and give her my full attention. "What is it?"

"Enjoy talking about me behind my back, do you?"

"What?"

"Don't play the innocent, Emma; it doesn't suit you. Apparently, you and Al were having a good old bitching session about me."

"Who told you that?"

"It doesn't matter who told me. What matters is that you were overheard."

"Was it Leanne?" I think of the two of them, huddled together under the trees the night before.

"I told you, it doesn't matter."

"Fine, don't tell me who it was, then, but we weren't bitching about you."

"No? So you don't think I'm in *competition with you*." She throws back her head and laughs. "Seriously, Emma. You really believe that?"

"I didn't say that. Al did."

She rests her elbows on her knees and leans toward me. "But you said I was embarrassing and weird, didn't you?"

"I said it was embarrassing and weird when you go after men I'm interested in. Elliot, that guy you tried to push out of the taxi, told me you tried to kiss him when I was in the bathroom. And then there was that guy I met at Heavenly. I *saw* you on the floor with him at his house."

"My God, Emma." She looks up at the ceiling and smirks. "Elliot again! What is it with that guy? You seem determined to let him come between us."

"This isn't about him, Daisy. This is about you."

"No, Emma." She jabs me in the bicep with her index finger. "This is about *you* siding with some random bloke who couldn't give a shit about you over me. Your best friend for seven years."

I rub my arm. "I'm not siding with anyone. But I am sick and tired of everything being about men all the time. We can't go to the pub and have a drink without you eyeing someone up. We can't go for a meal without you spending the whole time analyzing the behavior of some guy you're interested in. And we can't go to a club just to have fun and dance; it's all about picking up men."

"That's not true."

"Isn't it? You picked up the bouncer when we went to get Al out of Malice."

"To stop him chucking her out!"

"We were leaving anyway! And now we're halfway around the

world, and you're obsessed with picking up Isaac." I gather up my towel and toiletries and stand up. "I can't be bothered having this conversation anymore. I'm going to have a shower."

"No." She grabs my wrist. "We're not finished yet."

I shake her off. "Yes, we are."

"I think we need to take a break," she shouts as I cross the room.

"What?" I turn to look at her.

"I had a little chat with Johan and Leanne after you and Al left, and they think we're unnaturally attached."

"What the hell are you talking about?"

"Our friendship. We've been living in each other's pockets for years, and a lot of resentment has built up over that time." She gestures toward the mattress I was sitting on. "The conversation we just had confirmed that."

The situation is so ridiculously melodramatic that I can't help but smile. "So you're breaking up with me?"

She shrugs. "I think we should spend less time together."

"Because of one argument?"

"No, because we're too attached to each other. Leanne was telling me what Isaac was talking about in the seminar she went to—about how our attachments to people and things make us stressed and anxious and jealous and bitter, and how, if we can let go of those attachments, it's easier to be happy."

"And you think you'd be happier if we weren't friends?"

She shrugs again, and for the first time in the conversation, she breaks eye contact with me and looks away. I don't know whether to cry or throw my shampoo bottle at her head.

"Guys!" Leanne speeds into the room and throws herself at Daisy. She laughs as they overbalance and fall onto the mattress, a tangled mass of clothing and limbs, and for a second, I relax, relieved that the horribly awkward conversation with Daisy has come to an end.

"Come on, Hopalong!" Leanne shouts as Al hobbles into the

room, her ankle heavily strapped. "It's still pouring outside, so I thought we could play cards. How about Hunt the Bitch?" She looks up at me and smiles widely. "Want to play, Emma?"

"Are you calling Emma a bitch?" Al asks as she gingerly lowers herself onto the mattress beside Leanne and winks at me.

"No." Daisy props herself up on her elbow and flicks Al on the nose. "Leanne got the name of the game wrong. It's Hunt the Cunt!"

Al and Leanne snort with amusement, and it's like our second night in Pokhara all over again, only this time, there's no playful tone to Daisy's teasing and no friendly sparkle in her eyes. She doesn't look at me once to check that I'm laughing along with the others. It's as though I no longer exist.

21

Normally, I'd find Daisy amusing as she tries and fails to smoothly transition between cobra and downward dog and ends up in a crumpled, red-faced heap on the patio, but I'm too fixated on Leanne to laugh. Her brow is knitted in concentration as her thin limbs twist and contort while she moves lithely between positions. Daisy and I have barely said a word to each other since our little "chat" yesterday morning, which has made things horribly awkward, particularly as we've been confined to the house for the last twenty-four hours because of the rain and Al's strapped ankle.

I didn't join in with Leanne's generous offer to play Hunt the Bitch, a bastardized version of Chase the Ace. Instead, I read my book while she, Al, and Daisy traded insults and threw cards at each other for the best part of half an hour. I drifted around the retreat for the rest of the day. With the rain falling heavily outside, some people spent their time gathered in the meditation room to chat and play musical instruments, while others slept or read in the dorms or hung out in the kitchen, helping prepare the meals. A few hardier types donned their waterproof jackets and went into the garden to tend to the animals and vegetables, but most people stayed inside. I sat with Al, Leanne, and Daisy in the meditation room for a while, but with Daisy ignoring me and Leanne acting like nothing was wrong, it was more than I could bear, and I took myself off to the kitchen to peel potatoes for Raj. He made idle chat with me, but the hollow feeling in my chest that I'd been carrying around all day didn't disappear. If anything, it grew stronger. I'd never felt more lonely, or more isolated, in my life.

The sense of relief when we woke up to a blue sky this morning was palpable. The ground was still wet, too wet to attempt another trip down the mountain, but the patio quickly dried, and Isis announced that yoga was on again.

"So now if you'll all lie down on your mats and assume the corpse position, I'll talk you through a little guided meditation," Isis says.

The group takes up their positions as one, all apart from Frank, who catches my eye. He doesn't smile or nod. He stares until I'm forced to look away. Leanne catches him looking and smirks. Despite her "Hey, guys!" faux friendliness and attempts to get us all to join in with countless games of Hunt the Bitch, the Post-it game, and charades, she couldn't be more delighted that a crack has appeared in Daisy's and my friendship. There's a natural pecking order in all friendship groups, and I'm fairly certain Leanne knows she's on the periphery. It's not enough that she's Al's best friend. She wants to be in with Daisy too. Two rhinos to feed off is better than one, especially if you've frightened the other bird away. The only person who's been genuinely friendly toward me is Al, and I haven't been able to get her on her own since our abortive trip back down to Pokhara yesterday morning.

I tiptoe past the group and sit down on one of the steps leading to the garden as Isis leads everyone through the meditation.

Al, who's spent the last half an hour in the kitchen having her ankle checked over by Sally, appears at the doorway to the house. She raises a hand when she spots me, then hops slowly toward me and gingerly lowers herself to the ground. "What's up? You look pissed off."

"Have you noticed that Daisy's stopped talking to me?"

"I noticed that things were a bit weird between you two yesterday, but I assumed it would blow over. What happened?" She digs around in the neckline of her T-shirt and pulls out the packet of Marlboros stashed under her bra strap. She lights one, then offers them to me. I only smoke when I'm drunk, but I take one anyway. The smoke catches in the back of my throat as I inhale. There's something strangely satisfying about the sensation.

I exhale heavily. "Someone told her about the conversation we had the other day. The one before we left, when I told you about her hitting on Elliot and that other guy."

"Jesus." She sighs. "Well, I didn't tell her."

"I know—someone must have overheard us."

"And she's pissed off?"

"She is with me. She wants us to have some 'space.'" I make quotation marks in the air with my fingers. "Apparently, she had a little chat with Leanne and Johan while we were trying to get down the mountain, and they told her that we're unnaturally attached, and she'd be happier if we stopped being friends."

"Seriously?" Al makes a face. "I know Leanne has bought into all this hippie bullshit, but Johan seemed sound when I had a smoke with him the other day. Maybe they were just saying that to placate her? You know what she's like when she's on one. Give it a couple more days, and she'll be fine."

"I just want to go home, Al. I've had enough. Yesterday was horrible. I felt like I couldn't breathe."

"I know what you mean. Listen, I'll have a word with Johan about the weather and when he thinks it might be safe for us to give the trek another go. Leanne thinks that's it now—that it's going to pour every night. You'd have thought she'd have known it's monsoon season here at this time of year, given the amount of time she spent on her laptop researching Nepal before we—"

She stops speaking as a wiry figure appears beside us. Frank crouches down and helps himself to one of Al's Marlboro Lights.

"All right, ladies," he says through the side of his mouth as he sparks it up. "Sorry to interrupt, but Isaac wants everyone in the meditation room for an emergency meeting. Apparently someone's died."

~

The meditation room is heaving. Warm bodies fill every space in the room, pressed together at the elbow and hip, necks craned toward the altar where Isaac is standing, arms spread wide, fingers gripping the wood, eyes closed. Daisy is sitting on the right of the room with her back against the wall, sandwiched between Johan and Raj. As we squeeze into the room on the tail of Isis and the yoga group, Leanne spots Daisy too. She raises her hand in greeting, then she's off, picking her way between the cross-legged bodies on the floor. Al follows her, then pauses halfway across the room and looks back at me. Her smile falters. She doesn't know whether to keep following Leanne or stay with me. More people file in, and the pathway between us is blocked. As Al continues across the room, I drop where I am. I make an apologetic face at Minka, one of the Swedish girls, and wrap my arms around my knees to make myself as small as I can.

The atmosphere is thick with expectation. No one is talking, and each time the floor squeaks or creaks as someone shifts position, everyone looks around.

A man I've never seen before sits at Isaac's feet. He's heavyset, with a shaved head, long, dark beard, AC/DC T-shirt, and cut-off combat pants. He can't be much older than twenty, twenty-two tops, but he surveys the room with the weary gaze of a man twice his age.

"Hi, guys." The sound of Isaac's voice startles me. "Thanks for gathering here so promptly. As you will have noticed, Gabe is back." He gestures to the man at his feet.

Several people shout hello and wave, but Isaac silences them with a shake of his head.

"But there's bad news about Ruth. Terrible news..." His voice cracks, and he closes his eyes. When he opens them again, tears spill onto his cheeks. He makes no attempt to wipe them away, and a low murmur fills the room. "A group of men in balaclavas tried to rob Gabe and Ruth on their way back up the mountain, and when Ruth objected, one of the men shoved her out of the way, and she fell and hit her head. The men took off with the donkey and the provisions, and Gabe tended to Ruth, but...there was nothing he could do. Ruth died before he could get her back to Ekanta Yatra."

There is a collective gasp followed by a crescendo of noise. Sally, sitting in the middle of the room beside Raj, clutches hold of him and buries her head in his chest. The only person in the room who doesn't react to the news is Gabe. He keeps his head down, his hands clasped in his lap.

Isaac holds up his hands, and the roar dims to a dull murmur. "We're going to hold a memorial celebration for her on Wednesday night. Anyone wishing to attend should meet on the banks of the river at ten p.m. If you'd like to help collect wood and build the pyre, you should meet us there this afternoon at three."

"You're going to cremate her?" I'm on my feet, and the words are out of my mouth before I can stop them. "Here?"

Isaac nods.

"Without telling her family that she's dead?"

"We are Ruth's family, Emma."

"You know what I mean. Her proper family. Her parents, sisters, brothers."

"We are her sisters and brothers," Isis calls out from the corner of the room.

"It's what she would have wanted," shouts someone else.

Voices ring out, one after another after another.

"She loved Ekanta Yatra."

"This place was her life."

"Ruth belongs here."

All eyes are on me, and suddenly I feel suffocated, as though the oxygen has been sucked from the room. I glance at Daisy for help, but she looks away. Al won't meet my gaze either. She's folded over herself, her face pressed into her knees, her hands gripping her calves. She can't deal with talk about death—not Tommy's, not anyone else's. She left the pub once when Daisy asked us what songs we'd want played at our funerals and then started drunkenly ranting about how it was up to us to make sure her asshole of a dad shouldn't be invited to her funeral.

"So that's it, then?" I ask. "You're just going to go ahead and cremate her without telling her family? Without telling the Nepalese police what happened? And you think that's okay?"

Isaac gives me a long, sorrowful look as though I'll never be able to understand.

"How do you suggest we do that, Emma? We don't have the Internet, phones, or mailboxes. Even if we risked these bastards attacking us again on another Pokhara run, then what? We don't have any contact details for Ruth's parents. I'm not even sure what her surname was."

An image of us glibly handing over our passports on our first day flashes into my mind. "What about her passport? If you give that to the British Embassy, they'll be able to track down her parents, even if she hasn't filled out their details in the back."

A dark-haired man sitting in front of me turns and hisses, "Sit down, you're embarrassing yourself," but Isaac dismisses him with a wave of his hand.

"Emma's new. She doesn't understand."

The man gives me one last scathing look before he shrugs and turns away.

"Ruth burned her passport after her detox," Isaac says. "Everyone does when they make the decision to abandon their old selves and become part of our community. It was her decision. I understand why you're having trouble processing all this, because it's not what you're used to. I'll happily talk it through with you later, if you'd like."

I want to ask Isaac what a detox is and what it involves, but I don't want anyone else to shout me down. They're all staring at me, willing me to sit down and shut up. The air is hazy with incense. I can taste it on my lips, my tongue, at the back of my throat. There's no air in the room, and it's hot. I glance behind me. Why is the door shut? Frank catches my eye and frowns.

"Would you like that?" Isaac asks. "A chat later?"

"Yes," I say without looking up. "Yes, fine."

I'd agree to anything if it meant everyone would stop staring at me.

"Great." Isaac claps his hands together and smiles, and the atmosphere in the room immediately lifts. "The other thing we need to talk about is security. We haven't had an issue with it before, but we don't know who these guys are or how dangerous they might be, so we need to take precautions. I suggest we start patrolling the grounds at night, just for a few weeks. Johan, you'll be patrolling with Emma. Isis, you'll be with Daisy. Cera, you'll be with Frank. Raj, you'll be with—"

I stop listening and sink to the floor. Frank reaches out a hand to steady me.

"It's a shame we didn't get paired." He leans so close that his lips graze my ear. His breath is hot and tangy with the scent of cumin and cardamom. "I'd really like the opportunity to talk to you alone sometime, Emma."

"I'm sorry." I force myself back onto my feet. "I think I'm going to be sick."

~

It's cold on the floor of the pantry. I've been sick twice, into an empty margarine tub I found in a pile of plastic in the corner, and the chill from the floorboards soothes my burning cheeks. The sound of footsteps and chatter drift under the door as everyone files out of the meditation room and heads outside.

A noise from the kitchen startles me, and I shuffle farther into the pantry and squeeze myself between sacks of rice and flour as the voices—one male, one female—draw closer.

"Are we safe? I don't want to get into trouble."

"It's okay, there's no one here."

"I'll shut the door."

A door clicks shut, then footsteps creak across the wooden floor of the kitchen. They grow louder as they approach the pantry, and I curl up, tucking my head into my knees. It's a pointless move; the second someone walks in, I'll be discovered. The door rattles on its hinges, as though someone is pressing themselves up against it, but it doesn't open, and a second later, I catch the wet, squelchy sound of two people kissing.

The kissing continues for several minutes, then suddenly stops.

"Gabe didn't bring any food back. Nothing, not even a bag of rice." I recognize Raj's voice. "What am I supposed to do with no new provisions? I can't conjure meals out of thin air, and we're nearly out of lentils. Even if I ration out what's left, we've only got one week, two tops, until we're all out."

A woman makes a sympathetic sound.

"Why Isaac sent Ruth with Gabe, I don't know," Raj

continues. "Gabe's been down the mountain with the donkey before, and the Maoists have never had a problem with him. He gives them a share of the supplies on his way back up, and they let him on his way."

"That's assuming it was the Maoists."

"Who else would have attacked them?"

"I don't know."

"Are you okay?"

"No, I'm not. Ruth was my best friend, Raj. I know we hadn't gotten on for a while, but that doesn't change the fact that I'm never going to get to talk to her again. I'll never be able to say sorry."

"For what? You told her to tone it down, Sal, but she wouldn't listen. You could hear her wherever she was in the complex, whining and complaining, making sure everyone heard. She was worse around the guests, speaking out of turn. You were right to distance yourself from her. Otherwise, it wouldn't just have been Ruth that Isaac called into his study…" Raj lowers his voice to a whisper.

"Hey, hey. It's okay. Don't cry." I imagine Raj pulling Sally into his arms and pressing her against his broad chest. "We're safe here, and I'll make do with the food. We've still got the veg patch, the fruit trees, and the chickens, and some of the goats are ridiculously fat. We'll be fine."

They fall silent again, and I tentatively unfold my legs. Pins and needles shoot from my foot to my hip as I stretch the leg out, but it's too numb to control, and my foot flies up and kicks the barrel opposite me. The catering-size tin of kidney beans on top of it sways precariously and topples. My fingertips graze the base, but it slips from my grasp and hits the floor with a clang. There's a pause followed by the whisper of Sally's anxious voice.

"Did you hear something?"

Rajesh laughs his low rumbling laugh. "Sorry, that was my stomach."

"Are you sure? I thought—"

"Let's go sit by the river for a bit. Dr. Raj's orders."

"But—"

"Come on, Sal."

If Sally continues to protest, I don't hear it as the sound of flip-flops on the wooden floorboards fades into the distance.

22

J ane, are you still in there?"

Chloe's plaintive whine drifts under the bathroom door.

"I'll be out in a second."

I'm crouched on an infant-size toilet at Ringwald Street Primary School with my cell phone in my hands. Seconds after I saw the Facebook notifications from Daisy's account, Chloe zoomed out of the cat living room and pressed the two kittens into my hands. After I'd safely secured them back in their enclosures, she grabbed my hand and half led, half pulled me to Will's car, insisting that I sit in the back with her. I tried to object, saying I'd brought my bike, but Will immediately offered to drop me back after the fair to pick it up.

"Jane, all the loom bands will be sold if you don't hurry up."

"Coming!"

My heart lurches into my mouth as the Facebook Messenger app opens.

Daisy.

The profile photo is tiny, but I can tell it's her. Small,

heart-shaped face framed by a mane of blond hair. Her head is tipped back, and she's laughing, a glass of champagne or Prosecco in her raised hand. There are four messages. I open the thread.

Help me, Emma!

It's so cold.

You never came back for me.

I don't want to die alone.

My hands shake, the stall starts to spin, and my stomach clenches violently.

"Jane!" Chloe shouts. "Jane, are you sick? Should I get Daddy?"

~

My hand is cold and clammy in Chloe's grip as she drags me through the narrow school corridors. They ring with the sound of laughter, chatter, and whining. Excitable children and harassed parents pass by me in a blur. My cheeks are burning, even though I splashed my face with cold water in the bathroom, and my tongue is sour with the taste of cold vomit.

"I can see Daddy!" We squeeze through the crowds at the entrance of the school, and I gulp at the fresh air.

"Daddy!" Chloe raises a hand and waves as she leads me through the playground. "Daddy, Jane's been sick. Oh, there's Mommy! Mommy!"

I try to pull away as a tall, slim woman wearing a knee-length red skirt, black boots, and black leather jacket turns at the sound of Chloe's voice, but it's too late. She raises a hand in greeting, then looks me up and down. I pull at the hem of my navy polo shirt beneath my waterproof jacket, suddenly aware that I'm still in my work clothes.

"Hello, darling!" Sara crouches down and opens her arms, then looks up at me as Chloe releases my hand and rushes to hug her. "You must be Jane. I've heard a lot about you."

Will, standing by her side, shifts his weight from one foot to the other.

"Jane was sick," Chloe says, extricating herself from her mother's embrace. "I heard her puking in the bathroom."

"Chloe, don't embarrass Jane." Sara shoots me an apologetic look. "Are you okay?"

"I'm fine. I…" I press a hand to my stomach. "It must be something I ate."

"You do look very pale." Will reaches into his pocket and pulls out his wallet. "Here." He hands Chloe a five-pound note. "Go get Jane a bottle of water."

"Okay." She takes the money and skips off across the playground, disappearing into a crowd of children surrounding the refreshment stand.

"Sorry." Sara holds out her right hand. "Will isn't very good at introductions, so I'll do it, shall I? I'm Sara."

I take her hand. She has a surprisingly strong grip. "Jane."

"Chloe's told me ever so much about you. She couldn't sleep last night; she was so excited about going to your shelter."

"Yes, Will said."

Sara glances at him and smiles tightly. "Of course. So…" She looks me up and down again. "Are you back off to work after this?"

"No, I've finished for the day."

"Do you often work Saturdays?"

"Occasionally. It depends on the rotation."

"Of course."

"Sara's an HR manager," Will says a little too loudly. "She works for BT."

I search my mind for something to say in response, but the best I can manage is "Great." All my attention is on the phone in my pocket, waiting for it to vibrate again. I'm simultaneously terrified and desperate at the prospect.

"It keeps me out of trouble," Sara says and laughs lightly. The second she stops, the silence is deafening.

"How is your thumb?" I ask, remembering her trip to the emergency room.

"On the mend." She takes her left hand out of her pocket, revealing a neat bandage.

"That's good," I reply, and then the awkward silence returns.

"I think Chloe's going to have to use her elbows to get through the line at the refreshment table," Will says, and as one, we all turn to look in that direction.

"I should get going," I say as Sara glances at her watch.

"Yes." She nods as if in agreement. "Me too, though I did promise Jo I'd visit her stall and buy a few raffle tickets first. Will, could you tell Chloe where I am when she gets back?" When he nods, she looks at me. "Lovely to meet you, Jane. I hope you feel better soon."

"Thank you."

The knot of anxiety in my stomach untwists ever so slightly as she strolls away, head held high, waving at other parents across the playground.

"Sorry," Will says the second she's out of earshot. "I didn't know she'd be here."

He's standing close enough that I could touch him if I reached out a hand, but the distance between us feels greater than that. It's as though we're both cloaked with invisible force fields; one step too close, and the other will be repelled. I'm struck with the sudden urge to tell him how much I enjoyed watching *Battlestar Galactica* the other night, after I forced myself to watch it, but it feels too intimate. It's the sort of conversation we'd have had before he decided we needed some space from each other.

"There she is!" His shoulders slump with relief as Chloe bursts through the crowd of children at the refreshment stall, a bottle of water raised victoriously above her head.

"Got it!" she shouts as she runs toward us and thrusts the plastic bottle into my hand. "Sorry it took me so long. I'd just gotten to the front when a lady in a blue hat started asking me questions about Jane." She uncurls her right hand and presents Will with a handful of coins. "Here's your change, Daddy."

"A lady asked you about me?" I press a hand to my chest.

"Yeah. She asked me if Daddy calls you Jane or Emma." She looks from me to Will and back again as though gauging our reactions. "And I told her that was a silly question, because everyone knows your name is Jane."

"Chloe." I fight to keep my voice steady as I slip my hand into my pocket and close it over my cell phone. "Did the lady ask you anything else?"

She shakes her head. "She tried to, but then Connor Murphy from third grade pushed in, and Jake Edwards said he'd punch him if he didn't go stand at the back, and then…"

Will and I exchange a look as she continues her story about the fight that never happened in her shrill, excitable voice. When he looks away, it's with a slight shake of his head.

"What did she look like, the lady?" I ask when Chloe finally draws breath.

"Just a normal lady." She shrugs. "In a blue hat."

23

FIVE YEARS EARLIER

T his has to be illegal."
   We are standing on the banks of the river, a rectangular wooden pyre looming out of the darkness beside us, the only light the soft glow of the flares that were dug into the soft mud this morning. Two days have passed since Isaac broke the news about Ruth's death. Somehow, I've managed to avoid the promised "chat" with him, although I've been nervously anticipating him approaching me at any time.

Al is beside me, her hand in mine. Leanne and Daisy are standing on the other side of her, crying silently. Every couple of seconds, they unclasp hands to wipe their cheeks with the back of their hands, but fresh tears take the place of the ones they've just rubbed away. There's something disingenuous about their over-the-top grief. They never knew Ruth, never even met her, but they're sobbing like they've lost a close relative.

"We need to go to the British Consulate," Al whispers back. We are flanked on either side by members of Ekanta Yatra, so we have to keep our voices low. "And the press. People need to know what's happening here."

"We need to get back to Pokhara first."

"We're stuck here for at least another month, according to Johan. I can't believe Leanne brought us here in monsoon season. What was she *thinking*?"

That this would happen, I think but don't say.

"Anyway." Al shrugs. "It doesn't look like Daisy and Leanne are bothered about leaving any time soon."

I glance at Daisy. She still hasn't spoken to me since our argument in the girls' dormitory. Instead, she's glued herself to Leanne's side, attending every meditation, every talk, and every yoga session. At mealtimes, she sits with Leanne or members of Ekanta Yatra, while I sit at a different table. Sometimes Al sits with me; sometimes she sits with Daisy. She's trying to be diplomatic, but it still hurts.

"It's sick." Al nods toward the pyre. "These people are living on a different planet."

She was shaking with anger when I found her in the orchard two days ago. I'd escaped unseen from the kitchen pantry, and Al was sitting under a walnut tree, the knuckles of her right hand red and raw. There was blood on the bark of the tree. Neither of us said anything for several minutes, then Al launched herself forward and smacked the hard ground with both fists.

"Her fucking family!"

I didn't need to ask who she was talking about.

"I want to punch Isaac." The muscles in the side of her jaw clenched tight. "I want to put my fist in his smug, self-satisfied face. All those fucking people, Emma, and you were the only one to speak up. What's wrong with everyone?"

She started to cry then, silently, sitting cross-legged on the ground with her hands covering her head. I sat down beside her, gently stroking her back until the sobs slowed and she straightened up and reached for her packet of cigarettes.

That was our last opportunity to talk in private. Isis and Cera joined us seconds later, saying they needed our help to clean out the chickens. They haven't left us alone since. Even now, when they're further down the line of mourners, I can still feel their eyes on us. It's almost as though they know what we're planning on doing.

"If we could have silence for the arrival of Ruth's body, please." Isaac's voice rings out loud and clear over the yard as he walks across the patio. He is flanked by Johan and Gabe, each carrying a flare in their right hand and an incense bowl, dangling from chains, in their left. The firelight illuminates their faces, casting dark shadows under their eyes, cheekbones, and chins. A cloud of smoke drifts after them. Six men step through the smoke. They're carrying a body draped in a shawl and raised high on their shoulders, the gray, waxy face of a woman partially revealed.

It can only be Ruth.

The line of mourners on the riverbank parts as they approach the pyre. Al presses herself against me. I can feel her trembling through the thin material of her waterproof jacket.

"I don't think I can do this."

"You can." Leanne looks across at her, her angular face peering out from beyond the swathes of material she's fashioned into a head scarf. "You're stronger than this."

"I'm not. I'm really fucking not."

She falls silent as the body is placed on the pyre, and Isaac reaches for the flare in Jacob's hand. He holds it toward the dry leaves and kindling at the base. As a single flickering flame licks at the dry wood, Al yanks her hand from mine and sprints off into the darkness, back toward the house.

"I'll go." Leanne puts a hand on my shoulder. The gesture disarms me. It's the first time she's touched me since we arrived here. Is she trying to reassure me or stop me from going after Al? She sprints off into the darkness before I can react, her scarf falling from her head and trailing behind her as she runs.

Daisy glances across at me from beneath her woolen hood. She's discarded her waterproof jacket in favor of a yak's wool blanket, like the Ekanta Yatra women wear. Her eyes are hooded and tired, her lips set in a thin, tight line.

"I don't know what Al's problem is," she says. "Ruth wasn't close to her family, and she obviously didn't have any other reason to return to the UK. Why else would she have burned her passport?"

"Dais—" Her name forms on my lips, but she turns and walks away, strolling down the line of mourners, before I can say it. She passes Frank, who sees me watching and raises a hand in a silent hello. I ignore him, too busy watching Cera enveloping Daisy in a warm hug.

The flames are dancing higher now, licking at the soft, frayed edges of Ruth's burial shawl. I can see the silhouette of her profile above it, the curve of her belly, the shape of her arms crossed on her chest. I can see all of that—I can see that there is a body on the mound of wood about fifteen feet from me—yet I still can't accept that it's real.

"It's hard to take in, isn't it?"

"It's surreal," I say as Johan stands beside me, blocking my view of Daisy and Cera.

Johan doesn't reply. His eyes are fixed on Ruth as the flames engulf her feet, her calves, her torso. The shawl catches fire quickly, and she's lost in a cloud of black acrid smoke.

"What's Isaac doing?" I ask, watching him walk counter-clockwise around the body three times before standing still.

"Saying good-bye. Hindus walk around a dead body three times—once for Brahma the creator, once for Vishnu the pre-server, and once for Shiva the destroyer: the trinity of Hindu gods. We do this to say good-bye to Ruth's body, her mind, and her spirit."

The fire crackles and pops, and several women in the line cover their noses and mouths with their scarves or arms.

I look at Johan. "Was Ruth a popular member of Ekanta Yatra?"

A muscle twitches in his cheek, and he swipes at his eyes as thick, gray smoke drifts toward us. It smells disgustingly of cooked meat.

"Popular?" The muscle twitches again, but his expression remains impassive. "Well, I liked her."

"Did Isaac?"

He doesn't reply. His eyes blink and water as the smoke swirls around us, but his gaze doesn't waver from Ruth's body.

"Did she come here alone?" I ask.

"No. She came with Sally."

Sally and Raj are talking farther down the row. They're angled toward each other so as to exclude anyone else from their conversation, but their bodies aren't touching. As they chat, the backs of their hands touch, and they intertwine their fingers. It's a small but intimate gesture. Sally senses me watching and slips her hand from Raj's. He looks at her in surprise and then sees what Sally sees—me watching them—and takes a step away from her.

"What is it?" Johan looks at me curiously, then toward Sally and Raj.

They nod hello. Johan nods back.

"Emma?" He looks back at me. "What did you see?"

"Nothing."

"Are you sure?"

"Yes."

"Good, because we're on patrol."

"What for?"

"Gaps or holes in the fence, any attempts at breaking in."

He gestures away from the river and toward the fence. There are flaming torches every few feet, but the majority of the perimeter is shrouded in darkness. "Isaac seems to think we're in danger from the people who attacked Gabe and Ruth."

He sets off without waiting for a reply, striding off toward the orchard. I remain where I am. Making polite conversation with him in full view of the others is one thing, but disappearing into the night alone with him is another. He was instrumental in turning Daisy against me, and I don't trust him, no matter how laid-back and friendly Al may think he is. Still, he might be able to answer some of the questions I don't want to ask Isaac. I wait a few minutes, then head slowly after him.

~

We walk in silence for five or ten minutes, striding around the perimeter of the retreat, only pausing so Johan can investigate small gaps in the fencing or unusual objects on the ground. So far, he's deposited a pink flip-flop, a trowel, and a small piece of wood into the canvas bag he's wearing across his body. When we reach the log pile, stacked waist-high with an ax propped up against the side, he pulls the piece of wood from his bag and chucks it on the top.

"Johan," I say as he puts his hands on the lock and chain that secures the front gate and gives it a hefty tug. It holds firm. "Can I ask you a question about the attachment thing?"

He shoulders the gate. It creaks under his weight but doesn't give way. "What about it?"

"You believe that you need to give up your attachments in order to find peace, right?"

"Correct."

We lapse into silence again as we turn back to walk through

the orchard. There's a mango tree just a few feet from the fence, on our side, its branches grazing the barbed wire, as though desperate for escape.

"So is it..." I pause to think how to phrase the question. "Is it frowned upon to be part of a couple, then? Here, I mean."

"Were you at the seminar where Isaac talked about attachment?"

"No, not that one."

"Right, well, you won't understand what we mean by the toxic mind, then. Basically, if we're to be truly happy, we need to free our minds of anger, ignorance, and attachment."

"So no falling in love? No"—Daisy's face flashes through my mind—"close friends?"

"You can love. Of course you can. We positively encourage you to love those around you, but we discourage the kind of love that claims another as a possession. When we love someone exclusively, we're welcoming all sorts of ugly emotions into our lives—jealousy, mistrust, suspicion, attachment, need, desperation, confusion, frustration."

"You say that, but what about trust, warmth, caring, intimacy—"

"We share all those emotions collectively, Emma." Johan stops walking and faces me. "But because we're not exclusively attached to individuals, there is no jealousy, no possessiveness, no anger. We can no more claim another person as our own than claim the air we breathe."

"But don't you miss it? Don't you miss having one person love you and you love them back?"

Johan's expression remains the same—emotionless, stalwart, in control—but something flickers in his eyes, a spark of regret or longing, and then it's gone.

"No," he says. "Why would I? I get to sleep with whomever I want, whenever I want, and no one gives me any shit. Isn't that every man's dream?"

He throws back his head and laughs, but the laughter seems forced, and the fine lines around his eyes don't crease when his eyelids shut.

He's lying.

24

There's no sign of Ruth's body on the bank of the river. All that remains of last night's cremation is a riverbank muddy with dozens of footprints and a black, ashy rectangle where the pyre used to be. The air is clear and still, and the sun is bouncing off the fast-flowing river. The tinkle of female laughter carries from the waterfall, where a small group of women play beneath the cascading water.

The fence looks smaller than it did last night, the barbed wire on the top less intimidating. Johan and I must have walked around the perimeter twelve or thirteen times before we heard the gong that signified the end of our shift. We chatted, but only superficially, small talk about the difference between Sweden and the UK and the dwindling food rations at Ekanta Yatra. When I asked about his family and friends back home, Johan began pointing out the various flora and fauna we were passing.

When our patrol was over, he walked me to the entrance of the girls' dormitory. Leanne and Al were curled up in a corner together, while Daisy slept alone a few feet away.

"Johan," I called as he headed back along the walkway.

He turned. "Yes?"

"Did you tell Daisy that she should break her attachment with me?"

"Why would I do that?"

"I don't know. I thought perhaps you'd told her to when she asked you for advice. I didn't dream for one second that she'd hear what I said to Al. I was just getting stuff off my chest. I didn't mean to hurt her. Could you talk to her for me? Could you explain?"

He sighed softly. "See what attachment is doing to you, Emma?" He turned and walked back into the main house.

～

"Hi, Emma, how are you?"

I start as Frank sidles up to me, his hands in his pockets, head down, his beardy chin pointing toward his narrow pigeon chest.

"You don't mind if I join you, do you?"

I want to say yes, I do mind, that I'm cherishing the time alone on the riverbank, watching the water swirl and drift, but instead I shake my head. Unlike the four of us, Frank arrived here alone, and he doesn't appear to have made many friends. His attempts to befriend me have been creepy at worst, desperate at best, but who am I to reject him just because he's got no social skills?

"Of course," I say. "How are you?"

"Freaked out."

"The cremation?" I nod toward the black, ashy reminder.

"That and…everything else."

"I know what you mean."

"Do you?"

"Yes, I do."

Frank's eyes are ever so slightly too close together, the pupils tiny dark pinpricks in the bright afternoon sunlight. "This is a thousand miles away from normal. It's sure not sitting behind a desk, staring at a computer screen."

"Is that what you did? Before you came here?"

"Yeah, I was a banker. In the City. I know, I know." He holds up two hands as though in surrender. "Don't tell anyone, or they'll feed me to the Maoists."

I laugh. "I'm sure that's not true, although you might want to keep it to yourself around Leanne. She's a paid-up member of the Socialist Workers Party; at least she was while we were at university."

"That's how you know each other? From university?"

"Yeah. We all met there. I met Daisy our first week on campus. I'd lost my roommate in the cram to leave a gig and was scanning the crowd for her when a posh blond-haired girl nudged me and said, 'I can't abide lines. If we crawl under the merchandise table, we can get out through the fire door.' The alarm went off, and they had to evacuate the entire Students' Union!"

"Sounds like something she'd do."

"You don't know the half of it!"

"You'll have to tell me sometime." He raises an eyebrow. "So how about the other two? Leanne and Al?"

"Leanne was in Daisy's sociology course, and Al was her best friend from the dorm. Leanne introduced Al to Daisy, and they... they got on really well." I pause. I don't mention the number of times Al ran her hand through her hair when she was introduced to Daisy, or the way the base of her throat colored when Daisy complimented her on the jacket she was wearing. It was obvious to everyone, including Daisy, that Al was attracted to her, and Daisy played on it, flirting up a storm whenever we all got drunk together. I don't know if it would ever have gone beyond that if Daisy hadn't kissed Al at the bar of the Students' Union. A barman she fancied was working that night, but other than a few polite nods, he'd barely given her any attention all evening. The kiss got his attention all right. It drew interested stares from several of the men in the line, but when Daisy pulled away from Al, locked eyes with the barman, and announced, "Emma's roommate's gone away so we're having a party! Want to come?" he merely shrugged and turned back to the till. Al looked stunned—by the kiss or Daisy's sudden decision to throw a party, I wasn't sure—but when Daisy grabbed her hand and said, "Your loss. C'mon, Al," and pulled her away, she willingly followed.

The impromptu "party" was a complete flop—just me, Leanne, Daisy, and Al, plus two guys from the flat next door who we ran into on the stairs. They helped themselves to my roommate's half-empty bottle of wine in the fridge, drank it, and then, with no other booze on offer, went home. Leanne went back to her dorm about fifteen minutes later, and with Daisy straddling Al on the sofa and noisily kissing her, I made my excuses and went to bed. Any hope Al may have had of turning their one-night stand into a relationship was dashed the next morning when, hungover and wrapped in a blanket on the sofa, Daisy nudged Al and, with her most winning smile firmly fixed in place, said, "I got a bit carried away last night, didn't I? Naughty me. Sorry, darling, it won't happen again." I was so angry with her, I had to leave the room.

"And Daisy introduced Al and Leanne to me," I tell Frank.

"Right." He nods. "And you've all kept in touch since?"

"Sort of. We all live in London now, but I don't see the other two as much as I see Daisy. We used to live in each other's pockets."

"Used to?"

"I think we might have outgrown each other." I can't believe I'm telling him, a total stranger, the truth about our friendship, but it's oddly liberating.

"They do say people come into our lives for a reason, a season, or a lifetime. Maybe what you need is to invite some new people into your life and see what happens." He steps closer to me.

I take a purposeful step back. There's no one on the patio doing yoga, and the back door is shut. There's no one in the orchard or tending to the veg patch either. The goats bleat noisily from the pen, but no one is tending to them.

"It's been lovely talking to you, Frank, but I should get back. The others are probably wondering where I—"

"Have you seen Paula?" He touches me on the arm. "The short redhead who works with the goats."

Paula. She was the one Isaac and Cera were talking about in his study when I was eavesdropping. Cera was worried about her telling us something, but Isaac reassured her that she'd be okay after her detox, whatever one of those is. I could tell Frank what I overheard in Isaac's study, but there's something about him that makes me uneasy.

"Paula? Yeah, I…um… No, no, I don't think I've seen her today."

"She's disappeared." Frank grips my bicep so tightly I squeal in shock. "I've been looking for her for a few days now, and there's no sign of her."

"Frank." I look pointedly at my arm.

"Sorry." He lets go but makes no effort to widen the distance between us. "I've asked a few people if they've seen her, and it's always 'Oh, you just missed her' or 'I'm sure I saw her in the meditation room a minute ago.' Have you seen her? Think. Did she sleep in the girls' dormitory last night? Was she there this morning? Any night recently that you can remember?"

"I…I don't know." I take a step up the bank, toward the safety of house. "I tell you what. I'll look for her this evening. I'm sure she's fine. She'll be flattered that you—ouch!" I'm yanked back down the bank by my wrist. "Frank, stop it! You're hur—"

"I need you to come with me." He strides off down the riverbank, dragging me behind him. "If Paula is still in Ekanta Yatra, then she's locked up in one of the huts. It's the only place I haven't looked."

"Okay." I try to lean back, to dig my heels in to slow Frank down, but I'm wearing flip-flops, and they skid and slip on the wet mud. "Let go of me, and I'll come with you. There's no need to—"

"No." Frank spins around. "I'm not stupid, Emma. I saw you looking at the house. You want to run away. Being 'weird,' am I?"

"No, I swear, I—"

"It was like that at work. All the secretaries and assistants gathering together in the coffee room to laugh and gossip about me. Freaky Frank." His voice goes an octave higher. "That's what they called me. They thought I couldn't hear them, Emma, but I'm not deaf, and despite what they might think, I do have feelings."

"Of course you do. I totally understand." I ignore the thud-thud-thud of my heart and put my free hand over Frank's. If I can unhook one finger, the rest of his grip will loosen and—

"No, you don't." He continues to drag me toward the bridge. "You don't have feelings. Not real ones, not genuine feelings for genuine people. Don't think I haven't noticed the way you've turned your nose up at me when I've tried to be friendly. Don't think I haven't watched you fawn all over Isaac and Johan just because they're tall and good-looking. I thought you were different, Emma. When you stood up to Isaac about Ruth's death, I thought you were someone I could relate to, someone I could admire—like I admire Paula—but to see you fawning over Johan last night—'Oh, Johan, you big, hunky Swede'—'Oh, Johan…'"

As Frank continues to mumble to himself, hauling me behind him like a sack of potatoes, I scan the riverbank for something, anything, I can use as a weapon. There are a couple of planks of wood left over from the pyre, but they're soft, crumbly, rectangular lumps of charcoal. I try to grab a branch from a walnut tree as Frank continues to drag me through the orchard, but they're too high, and my fingers brush air.

"Help!" I shout as we approach one of the huts. "Somebody help me!"

I drop to my knees, using the force of my body weight to pull my wrist from Frank's grip, and crawl back toward the bridge. I feel a hand on the neck of my T-shirt, and I'm yanked back onto my feet.

"Stop it!" Frank shouts as he wraps his arms around me, pinning my arms to my side. "You're being hysterical. I just need your help."

"Help!" I shout again. "Hel—"

A hand across my mouth muffles my cry.

Frank presses the side of his face against mine, his stubble scratching my cheek, his sweat smearing my skin. "Calm down, Emma. I'm not going to hurt you. I just want your help. I am looking for Paula." He speaks slowly and deliberately. "When I find her, when *we* find her, you can help me confront Isaac. He listens to you, Emma."

"Mmm." I nod my head beneath his hand. "Mmm."

"I'm going to have to gag you." He rips the scarf from the waistband of my shorts and wraps it around my mouth. "If you scream, they'll come running, and we'll never find Paula. You understand that, don't you?"

I nod.

"Now stand up." He puts his hands beneath my armpits, grunting as he gets to his feet. "Walk!"

He prods me in the back, and I take a step forward, toward the hut.

"You know what I thought?" he asks from behind me a few minutes later. "When I got here and I saw those huts? I thought they'd make excellent little fuck pads."

When I don't react, he prods me again. "They're all at it. You know that, don't you? They're all fucking like rabbits, the dirty hippies. Your friend Daisy has fucked half a dozen of them—I've heard the men talking about her. Even that skinny bird you're friends with has put out a couple of times. Everyone's getting some. Everyone apart from me and you, Emma. Doesn't that piss you off?"

We're within feet of one of the huts. The edge of one of the massage "beds" is just visible through the door standing ajar. I clench my fists as Frank pushes me toward it.

"You're different, Emma. You won't put out for just anyone. I sensed that about you the first time I saw you. You're different, special. You recognized that in me too, didn't you? That's why you were so coy. You wanted me to chase you, to pursue you. That's what I was told. That's what—"

I hit Frank in the jaw as hard as I can. He reels backward, and I fall toward him, the force of the punch unbalancing me, and I hit him again, in the throat this time, and then land on top of him as he collapses to the floor. I roll away before he can recover, tearing the scarf from my mouth, scrambling to my feet, and then I start to run. I run as fast as I can back through the walnut trees, back over the bridge, heading for the waterfall, toward the other women, toward safety, towar—

My right foot slips out from under me, and I hit the ground.

"You fucking bitch." Frank is on top of me. I hit out at him, at his angry, red-cheeked face, at his small, beady eyes and his wet, open mouth, but this time he grabs my wrists and pins them on either side of my head with his hands. He uses his full body weight to pin me down as he lunges toward me and tries to press his lips to mine. I whip my head from left to right, but he grabs my chin and holds it still. He lowers his face toward mine, and then I feel his wet lips and his slimy tongue parting my teeth. He twists his tongue around mine, then plunges it deep into my throat, making me gag.

My mind goes into hibernation. It crawls into a dark place and waits. Then Frank's hand is between my thighs, cupping me over my cotton shorts, and my body jolts back into action. I bounce my heels against the bare earth and arch my back, pressing up and down with my hips, and I wriggle and twist and try to build up the momentum to throw him off me, but he growls into my mouth and claws at the waistband of my shorts, yanking them over my hips, ripping them down over my thighs. My underwear go with them.

Frank is breathing quickly, his forehead dripping with sweat, his jaw hanging open, a pool of saliva gathered beneath his bottom teeth.

I can't move.

I can see him. I can feel him. I can smell him. And I can't move.

I'm not even sure I'm breathing anymore. I try to turn my head to the left, to the right, to close my eyes, to block out what's about to happen, but I can't. I can't do anything but stare up at Frank as he leans over me, holding my arms above my head as he puts a knee between my thighs to force my legs apart. He is going to rape me, and there's nothing I can do to stop him. The crickets continue to chirp, the river continues to roar, and the women at the waterfall continue to laugh, and something inside me dies.

And then there is a roar and the sound of branches breaking and a *thump-thump-thump* that seems to go on forever. And then there is silence.

25

I t's been two days since Chloe's school fair. Shortly after Chloe
told us what "the lady in the blue hat" had said, Will took
her to find her mom, then he drove me back to Green Fields
to pick up my bike. Neither of us said a word the whole way. I
could sense his anger bubbling inside him like lava, but whenever
I attempted to say something to defuse the situation, the words
dried on my tongue.

What could I say? That I was terrified that whoever had been
sending me messages had been watching us? They knew I was in
a relationship with Will and that Chloe was his daughter.

The Facebook messages hadn't come from Daisy's original
account, which featured the four of us in the cover photo—me,
Daisy, Al, and Leanne in some club or bar in London, with our
arms around each other and drinks in our hands.

But the messages hadn't been sent from that account, and other
than a dwindling number of "RIP Daisy" and "We still miss you,
Daisy" comments, it hadn't been updated since before we left the
UK. No, whoever sent the messages from Daisy had set up a new
account for her, same profile photo but no friends information, no

cover photo, nothing. The only information on it was her name and her location—Annapurna, Nepal.

I didn't reread the messages as Will's car pulled away from Green Fields. I waited until I'd checked that every door and window was locked, then I closed all the curtains, poured myself a glass of wine, and only then did I read them again.

Help me, Emma!

It's so cold.

You never came back for me.

I don't want to die alone.

They must have been sent within seconds of each other, one after the other.

I read them over and over again, then sat down at my laptop and Googled her—Daisy Hamilton. I clicked through page after page of newspaper articles, all basically saying the same thing the *Daily Mail* had said: that four friends had gone on vacation, and only two had returned. There was no news report saying Daisy had been found alive and well and nothing indicating her body had been found either. There was no way she could have survived what happened. Or was there?

As I sat in the dark with the best part of a bottle of wine inside me, I played what if. What if she's alive? What if she's spent the last five years looking for me? What if it's Al? Some kind of sick joke? She's the only one who knows about my Jane Hughes Facebook profile. Maybe she hasn't forgiven me for my reaction to the article she wrote, but my anger was justified. She sensationalized everything that had happened at Ekanta Yatra. The article made it sound like Daisy, Leanne, and I had willingly taken part in orgies and bought into Isaac's spiritual bullshit, and that Al had had to rescue me from it all. She said the journalist had twisted what she'd said, but there was so much detail in the article, Al had to have told her.

One other possibility occurred to me last night. What if Will was pretending to be Daisy? He'd been fiddling with his cell phone moments before my phone bleeped. One thing I learned in Nepal is that people who seem harmless on the surface can have the cruelest streaks. It might be a sick game to him, a way to pay me back for not trusting him enough to tell him about my past. No, I rejected the idea the second it popped into my head. It was ridiculous, and after a bottle and a half of wine, so was I.

~

"Hi, Jane!" Angharad waves at me from across the room. Seven aluminum bowls are laid out side by side on the counter in front of her, each of them filled with dried dog food. "I thought I'd get started on the food. That okay?"

For someone who potentially stole my letter, she seems remarkably unruffled. I'm not one hundred percent sure she took it, though, so I need to play this situation carefully.

"Of course." I glance at the medication sheet on the wall to my left. "Have you done the meds too?"

"For Stella, Willow, and Bronx? Yeah, I've put it in the food." She points at each of the first three bowls in turn.

"Great. I'm going to get started on the cleaning. I'll do Jack, Vinny, Murphy, and Chester, if you could do the other three?"

"Of course."

"Jane!" she calls as I reach the doorway.

"Yes?"

"Are you feeling better now?"

"Yes, thanks."

"That's good. I think Sheila was a bit worried about you. She said being locked in the cupboard at that old lady's house had given you a flashback." She gives me an inquiring look. "That must have been scary."

"I'm fine now."

"Did it happen a long time ago, the thing you had the flash-back about?"

"I'd rather not talk about it, if you don't mind."

"No, of course, of course." She bends to pick up the dog food sack.

"Oh, Angharad?"

"Yes?" She looks up.

"I don't suppose you knocked into my dresser when you came by my cottage on Friday, did you?"

"Knocked into it?" She frowns. "No, I'm pretty sure I didn't. Why?"

"Some documents were... One of my documents has disap-peared. If the dresser was knocked, I'll have to move it to look underneath, but it's very heavy. You didn't see anything flutter to the floor when you came in? A bill or a"—I look her straight in the eyes—"letter."

"I didn't see anything." She smiles prettily. She's either a really good liar, or she's got no idea what I'm talking about.

"You're quite sure?"

"Yes." She nods. "Would you like me to help you move the dresser? I could come over later, if you'd like?"

"No, thank you." I hover in the doorway as a thought hits me. If Angharad was able to let herself in because the door was unlocked, then anyone could have come in. Someone else could have slipped into my kitchen before her and...

All the hairs on my arms prick up, and I shiver.

"Everything okay?" Angharad asks. "You've gone awfully pale."

"I'm fine." I rub my hands over my forearms. "I just had one of those moments."

"Like when someone walks over your grave? I have those all the time."

~

The rest of the day passes in a blur of scrubbing, hosing, feeding, walking, and inoculating. I'm so tired that everything takes twice as long as it should, and when I nearly gave Murphy a booster shot instead of Chester, Angharad insisted I sit down and rest for five minutes while she made me a cup of tea. I was expecting her to leave at lunchtime but forgot I'd agreed for her to sit in on a potential adopter interview today.

Now we're both sitting at a table in the small interview room in the main building. Angharad's beside me, with Mr. Archer opposite, bent over the form he was given in reception, scribbling intently. He's a hulking giant of a man, midthirties, with close-set eyes and doughy cheeks.

"Here you go." He pushes the form across the table toward me, then sits back in his chair and folds his arms across his broad chest.

"Thank you." I scan the form and smile brightly at him. "So, Mr. Archer."

"You can call me Rob." He's got a broad London accent. You don't hear many of those around here. It reminds me of Al.

"Okay. Rob. Could you tell me why you'd like to adopt a dog?"

"I'm unemployed, and I need the company. And I like dogs. I've always liked dogs. And I'd rather rescue one, help it out, you know, rather than get a puppy." The words come out machine-gun fast.

"Right. Great." I flip over the form and note down his answer on the back. "So you'd be able to spend a lot of time with the dog."

"Yeah."

"Would there be any periods when you'd have to leave the dog on its own?"

"Nah." He shakes his head. "Well, when I go to the job center, but I don't go there often." He laughs dryly and runs a hand over his forehead. It's warm in the room, and he's sweating lightly.

"Okay, that's good. We don't like dogs to be left on their own for too long. Some of them have abandonment issues."

"Right. Right."

"Where do you live, Rob? House? Flat? Is there a yard?"

"Nah. I'm in a block, but there's a park nearby. I could walk the dog there."

"Great." I smile reassuringly and write on the form again. He's surprisingly nervous for such a big man, but a lot of people find this situation uncomfortable; it's called an interview for a reason, and no one wants to be rejected. "Do you have any experience looking after a dog?"

"Um..." He gazes at the table and tweaks his left ear. "Yeah. I had a dog as a child, a Staffie named Alfie. Do you have any of those?"

I don't know if it's the way his eyes just shifted from right to left, or the fact that he's been repeatedly tapping the floor with his right foot since he said the word "Staffie," but an alarm just chimed in my head.

"Is it only a Staffie you're after?"

"Yeah." He nods repeatedly and runs a hand over his thinning hair.

"And if I told you we don't have any?"

The table judders up and down as his tapping increases. "I heard you had some."

"We've got—" Angharad pipes up, but I silence her with a glance.

"Can I have a look around?" He glances toward the door. "The woman I spoke to on the phone said I could have a look at the dogs after I'd filled in the form."

"We need to do a home inspection first."

"What?" He looks genuinely surprised. "What's the point of doing that if there ain't any dogs here I want?"

"It's a new policy," I say, desperately hoping Angharad won't chime in and contradict me. "Only approved adopters can see the animals—less chance they're disturbed by repeated visits that way."

Mr. Archer rubs the back of his neck and stares down at the table. He seems torn. "So there's no way I can see the dogs today?"

I shake my head.

"And you definitely ain't got no Staffies?"

"No."

"Right, then." He rubs his palms on his thighs and stands up. "No point me being here. Thanks for your time." He reaches forward, shakes my hand, and then, without another word, strolls out of the room and turns left toward reception.

"What was that about?" Angharad whispers as his footsteps retreat into the distance.

"I don't know," I say, "but I've got a bad feeling about him."

26

saac?"

He's sitting a couple feet away, his arms wrapped around his legs, his forehead pressed to his knees. In one hand is a rock, slick with blood. I reach for my shorts, still down around my knees, and pull them up. The action is automatic—I am half-naked and I should cover myself up—but I barely register what I am doing.

"Isaac?"

Frank's body is on the ground behind him, his head turned away from us. The hair is matted, a pool of blood circling it like a red halo.

"Isaac?" I wince as I crawl toward him. There's something wrong with my right arm. I can't move it. "Are you okay?" He flinches as I touch him. "What happened?"

He raises his head and looks at me. His face is pale, his pupils dark. There is a graze on his left cheek, his lip is split open, and his left eye is bloodshot.

"Is he…"

We both watch as Frank's chest rises and falls.

"He…" The shaking starts in my hand, then continues up my

arm, across my chest, and into my jaw. My teeth chatter against each other. "He was…"

"I know." Isaac shifts himself toward me and wraps an arm around my shoulders. "I know."

I press my head into his T-shirt. It smells of sweat, jasmine, musk, and warmth. Neither of us says a word, then he gently peels himself away from me and cups his hands to his mouth. A piercing whistle fills the air, cutting through the cicadas' chirping and slicing through the river's roar. The sound of laughter from the waterfall stops abruptly, and then there's a new sound—the slap, slap of feet on mud—and then they appear: Isis, Cera, Daisy, and Leanne. They stop short, a good thirty feet away from us. Daisy's eyes grow big and scared as she stares at Frank's prostrate, bleeding body.

"What happened?" Isis asks, but she's interrupted by the crashing arrival of Kane, Jacob, and Kieran.

"Frank's hurt. I need you guys to take him to the basement"—Isaac nods toward Frank—"then go get Sally to check him over and patch him up."

"He looks like he should go to the hospital," Daisy says, but Isaac shakes his head.

"It's not as bad as it looks, and Sally's a trained nurse."

The men rush into action, dipping down to haul Frank up from the ground, his torso supported by two of the men, the third holding his feet. They rotate him around so his head's pointing toward the house, then set off, carrying him away.

"Emma?" Daisy takes a step toward me, her face contorted with indecision, and just for a second, I see her—old Daisy, university Daisy, the Daisy who'd sit on my bed and stroke my hair and make me imagine the sun on my face and the sea at my feet.

Please, Daisy.

She looks back toward the house. Frank and his human ambulance are tiny figures in the distance now, stick men, wind-up toys.

Help me.

Leanne exchanges a look with Isaac, then takes a step forward and loops her arm through Daisy's. She leans close and whispers something in her ear.

"But…" I sense Daisy's resolve slip.

"Daisy." Isaac holds her gaze for one second, two, three. "Emma will be fine."

Isis and Cera wander away without so much as a backward glance. As they head toward the bridge, Leanne trails after them, her arms crossed over her narrow chest. After a moment's hesitation, Daisy follows them. She pads after Leanne, calling her name.

"Come." Isaac reaches for my hand.

I take one last look at Daisy as she crosses the bridge, then put my hand in his.

~

I falter as Isaac opens the door to the hut and inclines his head, indicating that I should go inside. My hand, still in his, feels sticky with perspiration.

"It's okay." He opens the door wider so the interior is flooded with light. There's a pile of rugs on the floor, a small table in one corner, and a metal bucket, covered in a towel, in the other corner. I didn't notice the bucket when Kane gave me my massage. That feels like forever ago now. "I just want to talk to you somewhere that we won't be disturbed."

I step inside and press myself up against the wall as Isaac squeezes past me and closes the door. The hut is immediately plunged into darkness.

"It's okay," he says again. "I'll light a candle."

The white-painted floorboards creak as he crosses the room, then I hear the whir of a lighter being flicked. The darkness lifts gradually as a tiny flame dances from the end of the lighter to the large, white church candle on the table.

"Sit." Isaac reaches for something on the table, then settles himself on the pile of rugs and pats the space beside him. "Sit down, Emma."

My knees creak as I lower myself to the floor. Isaac hands me a bottle. There is no label and no seal on the lid. A dark liquid sloshes around inside as I tip the bottle left then right. "What's in it?"

"Rum. Drink it. It'll help take the edge off the shock."

I unscrew the lid, then raise the bottle to my lips and sip. The alcohol stings then warms the back of my throat as I swallow. I take another sip and another and another. When I put the bottle back down, it's half empty.

"Joint?" His eyes don't leave my face as he hands me a lit joint.

My thumb brushes his as I take it, but I barely register the sensation. All I can feel is the sharp tang of rum in the back of my throat. I raise the joint to my lips and inhale. I take another swig of rum. Suck on the joint. Repeat.

The candle flickers on the table, and shadows dance on the white wooden walls of the hut. I lean back and close my eyes.

"How are you feeling?"

His whisper fills the hut. The low tones wrap around me like a blanket.

"Emma? How are you feeling?"

I reach into myself for an answer, but there's nothing there.

"Emma?"

I try to shake my head, but the movement feels too powerful, so I stop.

"Emma?" Isaac asks, his face creased with worry, and a cloud of paranoia so dense, so acrid that I instantly forget how to breathe, engulfs me. The rug slips from beneath me, and I plummet down through the base of the hut, down through the hard soil beneath it, and then I'm floating through blackness—grasping, reaching—but there's nothing to hold on to. My mind has gone into free fall. And I can't breathe. I've forgotten how to breathe.

"Emma!" I feel hands on my face. "Emma, look at me. You're having a panic attack. Emma, look at me. You need to slow down. You need to breathe. Breathe with me, Emma…"

His face is inches from mine, his pupils huge, the tip of his nose lightly dotted with open pores, his top lip speckled with sharp, spiky stubble. I feel like I'm looking at him through a microscope.

"Emma, breathe. Inhale. In…one…two…three."

I try to do what I'm told, but the breath keeps catching in my throat.

"Out. Exhale, Emma. Slowly. For as long as you can, push the air out."

My breath escapes in raggedy gasps.

"Just keep looking at me, Emma. Just keep breathing."

In. One-two-three. Out. One-two-three.

After a couple of minutes—or a couple of hours, I can't be sure—I reach up and touch Isaac on the arm. I can breathe, but I'm still spinning. I need to root myself to the floor.

"I need…I need to lie down."

"Okay." He gently guides my elbow as I lower myself onto the rug, then unwraps the sweater from his waist and fashions it into a pillow. He gently slides it under my head.

"Close your eyes," he says softly.

And I do.

~

I wake with a jolt, slamming one hand against the wooden wall to my right, the other against something soft to my left. The candle is still burning on the table in the hut, but it's only a couple of inches tall now. Isaac is asleep beside me, facing away, his shoulders curled, his knees bent. I stirred at some point in the night and reached for him, but he'd gone. I was too tired to care, so I fell back asleep. He must have returned while I was sleeping.

"Isaac?" I put a hand on his back. "What time is it?"

He rubs a hand over his face and slowly uncurls, propping himself up on one elbow. "I don't know."

"Shouldn't we get back to the oth—" I stop speaking as a memory floats lazily to the surface of my mind.

"What is it?" He sits up. "Do you feel ill again?"

I shake my head.

"Emma, talk to me."

"Where's Paula? Frank said she was missing." I push myself up into a sitting position, then drag the rug off my legs and stand up. "Is she? Or was he lying?"

Isaac stands up too. He inclines his head to the left and groans with relief as his neck cracks. "Paula's not missing. She's in the hut next door."

"Why?"

"She's detoxing. She'd lost her way a bit," he adds before I can ask what detoxing means, "and she needed a bit of time to center herself, to find her way back."

"To what?"

"To contentment."

"Is she locked in the hut?"

"Yes."

I push the door open. It's pitch-black outside, the only light the soft haze of the moon, swathed in cloud. It's still nighttime, even though it feels like I've slept for hours.

"You can run back to the house and sound the alarm if you want to, but Paula *wanted* to be locked in the hut."

I can feel the heat of his body as he stands behind me and

the cold of the night air on my face. The house is dark apart from a dull light flickering in the meditation room. Isaac told the men to take Frank to the basement. I have no idea where that even is.

"What's going to happen to Frank?" I ask.

"We'll look after him until he's well enough to leave, and then I'll escort him to the gate myself."

I look back at him. "What if someone attacks him on his way back down the—"

The unfinished question hangs in the air. Isaac says nothing, but the edges of his mouth twitch upward ever so slightly. *Do you care, Emma?*

"Take me to see Paula," I say.

~

"I wouldn't normally interrupt someone's detox," Isaac says as he reaches into his back pocket, pulls out a key, and inserts it into the lock, "but Paula was due to return to the house today anyway, so…" He shrugs and pulls at the handle.

The stench of feces and urine hits me the second the door opens, and I cover my nose and mouth with my sleeve.

"It's just me"—Isaac steps into darkness—"and Emma. She wanted to check that you were okay." He looks back at me. "Wait here for a second."

The door closes behind him, and I'm alone, standing in the darkness outside.

There's a creaking sound, like floorboards being stepped on, then nothing for a couple of minutes. Finally, I hear the low rumble of a male voice and the shrill peel of female laughter.

"Come in, Emma," Isaac says.

I push gently at the door.

"I'm sorry about the smell," Paula says as I step inside.

Her voice is bright, but her words are slurred, pooling together like spilled mercury. It takes me a while to adjust to the gloom, but then I see her, sitting cross-legged in the corner.

"I'm sorry." I twist away, shielding my view with a hand. "I didn't realize—"

"It's fine. I'm comfortable with being naked." She pauses. "Sorry, I forgot you're an outsider. You can look now."

When I turn back, she's clutching a blanket to her chest. Isaac is standing beside her, his back to the wall, smoking. The scent of tobacco does little to mask the smell emanating from the bucket at his feet.

"Is there anything you'd like to ask Paula, Emma?" He asks the question casually, but there's a tension to the way he's standing— ramrod straight, with one arm crossing his body, gripping his side.

"Are you okay?" It's feeble, but it's the best I can manage.

"I'm fucking wonderful!" Paula laughs again.

"Did you agree to be locked in here?"

I expect her to look at Isaac. Instead, she stares me straight in the eye. "Yes."

I stare into the gloom, unsure what to say next. Even if she didn't come here of her own volition, Paula is not about to admit that to me with Isaac listening in. His presence fills the hut.

"Don't look at me like that." Paula stands up suddenly and lurches toward me. The blanket falls from her body, but she doesn't stoop to pick it up. "Don't pity what you don't understand."

"I don't. But you're right; I don't understand what's going on."

She glances down at my hands, knotted together in front of me. "That's because you're still rooted in your old life. You're still hanging on to the thoughts, feelings, and values you think are normal but actually make you desperately unhappy. How old are you, Emma?"

"Twenty-five."

She takes another step forward until her face is almost

202

touching mine. "And for how many of those years have you felt truly content?"

I fight the urge to cover my nose with a hand. I can smell alcohol on her breath, but there's something else too, a rancid scent I can't identify.

"Some."

"Some?" She smiles, her teeth and the whites of her eyes dull and gray in the darkness. "Or none? Because you can lie to yourself all you like about the value of friendship and the importance of family, but you will never know true contentment until you let go of your attachments."

"That's enough, Paula." Isaac puts a hand on her shoulder. "Sit back. Sit back and relax." He eases her back down to the floor and wraps the blanket around her, tucking it across her chest and under her armpits like a parent settling a child at nap time. "Emma only came here to check that you're okay."

"I should go." I take a step backward, toward the cool, fresh air outside.

Isaac reaches for the joint behind his ear, then gently lifts one of Paula's hands and puts it between her fingers. She takes it and places it between her lips as he sparks his lighter.

And that's when I see it: the violent red mark that circles her right wrist like a snake.

27

Take a seat." Isaac angles me toward the armchair in the corner of his study, and I've got no choice but to sit down. It's 5:00 a.m., and the sound of the gong being banged in the meditation room next door carries through the wall. If Isaac tries anything, people will come running if I scream.

I watch as he crouches down beside the threadbare rag-rolled rug that occupies the floor space between the bookshelves and his desk and rolls it up, exposing a square hatch about three feet wide in the center of the floor. He pulls on the cylindrical iron ring in the center and yanks it open, then places his hands on either side of the hole and lowers his head.

"Kane? It's me."

There's a hollow shout in reply, then a creaking noise, like a rusty ladder being climbed, and Isaac sits back on his heels as Kane's scruffy head pops up through the hole. He grins up at Isaac, but when Isaac nods his head toward me, the smile fades instantly.

"How's Frank doing?" Isaac asks.

"Came around about two hours ago. We gave him some water, then he started complaining that he'd hurt his arm. He thinks it's broken."

"What does Sally think?"

"She's not sure. There's no bits of bone sticking out; it could be a strain, maybe a fracture, she said."

"Can he move it? Rotate his shoulder? Wiggle his fingers?"

"Yeah, well, he could until we…" Kane glances at me. "Should she be in here?"

"She's fine. Look, stay with him until tomorrow, then we'll make a decision. I don't want him left alone, not even for a minute. Do you understand?"

"Sure. We done?"

"Yep."

Kane's head disappears back down into the hole, the ladder creaking under his weight as he descends into the basement. Isaac watches him go, then folds the hatch back, shakes out the rug, and places it on the floor, smoothing out wrinkles or creases with his hands.

"You okay?" He glances at me. "I know this looks weird, but there's nowhere else we can look after him and make sure you're safe too. There's lighting and a camp bed and bedding and other stuff we store down there."

I nod to indicate that I'm fine, but it's not true. I don't know what to think about any of it, and I feel sick with exhaustion. I don't care what happened to Paula. I don't care that Frank is locked in a basement under my feet. I just want to be a long, long way away from here. If it weren't for the weather and Al's ankle, I'd leave now.

"You are safe. You know that, don't you?" Isaac holds out a hand and pulls me to my feet. "It's important to me that you feel safe, Emma. More important than almost anything else. Now, why don't you go grab a bit of breakfast, then go have a nap."

I can tell the dining room is packed before I set foot in the room. The metal clang of cutlery scraping against tin bowls and the sound of people laughing and talking fills the hallway and obscures the soft *flip-flop* of my feet on the wooden floor. Word will have spread about what happened last night with Frank, and the second I walk into the room, all eyes will be on me. What's the alternative? Creep away to the girls' dorm and spend time alone with the memory of what happened? No, I can't do that. Not yet.

I take a step closer to the door, then stop as Daisy's laughter cuts through the hubbub. The sound feels so foreign, like the memory of another life. How can she laugh after what happened to me? She saw how upset I was. She must have guessed something awful had happened to me. Why isn't she with me, supporting me? We've been there for each other through everything, and yet the one time I needed her most, she walked away. She wanted to comfort me, I know she did, but whatever Leanne whispered in her ear changed her mind. I can't, I won't let that go. Not again.

~

Silence doesn't descend the second I step into the dining room. Rather it's a gradual hush—a dropped spoon, a silencing glance, a raised hand, a meaningful look. Conversations drop away one by one, chairs scrape on the floor as they're turned toward me, eyebrows flash and then furrow.

Al, Leanne, and Daisy are sitting together at the table on the right-hand side of the room. Isis, Cera, and Jacob are opposite them. Raj and Sally are seated with Johan at the large table to their left with half a dozen women. On the far left of the room is a table occupied solely by men. For the longest time, no one says a word, and then I hear it, a muttered "bitch." It came from the table of men, all of whom are staring at me with looks of undisguised disgust on their faces. Daisy shakes her head, Al looks down at her bowl, and the smallest of smirks crosses Leanne's lips before she bursts suddenly and unexpectedly into tears. Daisy wraps an arm around her and pulls her into her chest.

"Lying bitch."

This time I catch who said it. It's a dark-haired man. I don't know his name. He works with the animals and keeps himself to himself.

"Yeah, you heard me. People like you shouldn't be allowed here."

A cold chill runs through me. "I don't know what you're talking about."

"No?" He raises his eyebrows. "Maybe we should ask Frank."

"What's going on?" I look at Jacob, who shakes his head. "Isis? Cera? What's going on?"

They return my gaze, their faces expressionless, their eyes wide and blank. Neither of them says a word.

My hands start to shake. The sensation travels up my arms and then engulfs me. Every part of me quivers with fear. Why will no one talk to me? Why are they all staring at me like I just killed someone? "Daisy? Al? Please. Someone. Someone tell me what's going on. I don't understand. I—"

The silence is broken by the sound of a chair being pushed back, and Al stands up. She doesn't say a word as she crosses the dining room. She raises a hand as she approaches me, and for one terrible second, I think she's going to hit me. Instead, she grabs me by the wrist and pulls me out of the room.

~

She doesn't say a word to me until we're halfway down the yard, then she releases my wrist and turns sharply so we're facing each other.

"I need you to tell me the truth, Emma." Her cheeks are red, and there's a sheen of sweat in her hairline.

"Of course."

"Did you lie about Frank attacking you?"

"What?" I instinctively glance toward the patch of riverbank where it happened. "No! Of course I didn't."

"Are you sure? Because someone's pretty certain you did."

"Who said that?"

"Someone who saw what happened. They said they saw you and Frank walking hand in hand along the riverbank. You kissed—apparently you were all over him—then you both lay down, and you were about to have sex when you saw Isaac coming and cried rape."

A gasp catches in my throat. "That's not true. Frank attacked me."

"They said you led him on, Emma."

"They're lying. Daisy was there. Leanne too."

She shakes her head. "All they saw was you sitting on the ground, Frank unconscious and bleeding, and Isaac sitting beside him."

"Al, you know I'd never lie about something like that. You know!"

She looks at me steadily, and at last, her brown eyes soften in concern. "Of course I do."

"Oh my God." I stumble backward, and she has to grip my hand to stop me from falling. "Why would you do that? Why would you put me through that?"

"Because"—she gestures for me to sit on the grass, then lowers herself down too, her hand still on mine—"Leanne is convinced. I don't know who told her, and she refuses to say, but they did a bloody good job of convincing her it's true. She said she can never forgive you, not after she shared what happened to her as a teenager. She can't believe you'd lie about something like that."

"But I didn't! I can't believe she'd start a rumor about that without talking to me first."

"Actually"—Al lets go of my hand and runs her fingers back and forth in the grass—"Daisy started the rumor."

"What?"

"She's acting like the two of you are competing to 'get Isaac.'" She makes quotation marks in the air with her free hand. "She believes you were getting it on with Frank, and then, when you saw Isaac coming, you pushed him away. She didn't actually say you cried rape, but..."

I can't take it in. It doesn't feel real. Daisy's my best friend, *was* my best friend. She knows me. She knows everything about me. She can't believe I'd do something that awful, that immoral. I can't believe it. I won't.

"Did you actually hear her say that, Al?"

"Yeah..." Al touches me on the shoulder. "Emma, Daisy's not herself. She's bought into Isaac's philosophical crap about attachment and detachment, and she's taking it out on you. I don't know why, but she's got it into her head that you're the reason she's unhappy and that she needs to distance herself from you. The sooner we all get out of here, the better. My ankle's nearly better, and Johan reckons the worst of the monsoon is almost over. We can try to leave again in a couple of days—we're due to leave soon, anyway. Things will have died down a bit by then."

"No." I stand up. "I'm not waiting that long."

"What do you mean?"

"I'm going to get Isaac to tell everyone exactly what happened."

"Don't! You'll stir things up even more." She reaches out a hand to stop me as I turn to go back to the house, but I walk straight past her.

"Emma!" she shouts as I start to run. "Emma, don't! You'll make things worse."

28

I jolt awake the second I hear my phone. It's the fourth night I've slept on the sofa with the lights on, and everything aches as I sit up and reach for my cell phone. The room is still dark, there are no chinks of light escaping between the curtains, and the world outside my windows is quiet.

"Hello?" I press the phone to my ear. "Sheila? What time is it?"

"Two. Listen, I'm sorry to disturb you, but there's been a break-in, and the police are here."

I sit up sharply. "At Green Fields? Are the animals okay?"

"They're fine. Look, could you come up? The police want to ask you a couple of questions. Sorry, Jane, I know it's the middle of the night. I'd come collect you myself, but—"

"No problem. I'll jump on my bike. I'll be there in ten minutes."

~

It's so dark outside, I have to use the light of my phone to find the hole in my bike lock. I push the key in and turn it. Thirty seconds later, I'm on the road. The weak, amber glow from the light on the front of my bike illuminates a few feet in front of me. Everything else is cloaked in shadow. I call it the main road, but it's so narrow there are shoulders every hundred yards or so where cars are forced to pull in to let vehicles coming the other way pass. The hedges on either side are overgrown, and I'm forced to cycle down the center of the road to avoid being scratched. It's a clear night. The moon is large and round, and the Big Dipper and Venus twinkle overhead.

My head is still hazy from sleep, and I take deep breaths of the cold night air to try to clear it as my feet pound the pedals. I lean forward as I approach the hill that leads to Green Fields. I was the last person to leave tonight. Did I lock everything up? I mentally run through my normal routine—check all the dogs are in their enclosures, ensure they've all got water for the night, lock the dog compound, do the same for the cats and the small animals, check on Freddy and the pigs, enter the main building through the back, lock the back door, do various checks, lock the front doors. Walk to the side entrance of the animal enclosure—the entrance the gardener and tradesmen use—and check that's locked too. A pulse of panic passes through me. Did I do that? Angharad was with me as I locked up. She was talking to me as we walked through reception, asking what my parents did for a living. I was trying to throw her off, giving her some half-baked reply about them being retired, and then she walked off to her car, and I went to check the side entrance. Or did I? Did I hurry to my bike instead, keen to check my phone for the umpteenth time that day?

Something small and dark leaps across my path, and I squeeze the brakes and jolt to a stop, nearly tipping over my handlebars. A tiny rabbit lollops across the road and disappears into the bushes on the right. The leaves rustle, then fall still.

Shit.

I press a hand to my heart, then put my feet to the pedals and start cycling again. It's harder now that I've restarted midway up the hill, and my thighs ache as the wheels revolve slowly and the bike creeps upward. Just another third of a mile or so and I'll be there. I grip the handlebars and stand up, leaning my weight into the downward press. Will told me off for cycling like this. He says it's a really inefficient way of getting up a hill. According to him, you should raise your saddle and stay seated. That's fine for him to say; he's got thighs like tree trunks, while mine—

My train of thought is interrupted by the distant rumble of a car engine. It's coming from behind me, so I tuck my bike as far left as I can and keep cycling. My rear light is on, but in my haste to leave home, I forgot to grab my high-visibility jacket or helmet. All I could think about was getting to Green Fields to check that the animals are okay. The car driver should see me in good time; there are some tight bends up here, and if they're local, they'll slow down.

The sound of the car engine grows louder. The gears crunch as they slip down from third to second as the hill takes its toll, but they're speeding up, not slowing down. What if they're not local? What if it's a bachelor party that's been camping down on Griffiths' Farm, and they're drunk after a night out in town? The car revs its engine, and I speed up. I rock from side to side, and my thighs burn as I climb, climb, climb up the hill. There's a side road down to a farm about a hundred yards away. I can pull in there, and then—

The first thing I feel is a jolt, and for a split second, I think I'm okay—the car just clipped me and I've managed to stay upright—but then my hands feel as though they're ripped from the handlebars, and my stomach falls away as I'm lifted into the air. High, high, high in the air. I hang there forever, and then...

And then the air is knocked from my lungs, and there's a searing pain in the side of my face, and everything goes black.

⌣

"Jane? Will's here to see you, sweetheart."

Someone strokes my left hand, and I peel open my eyes. My right eye is still sealed shut, so swollen from my fall that I can't see through it. I peer at Sheila through my left eye.

"Will?" I croak.

"I called him. I thought you'd want him to take you home rather than me."

"Hello, Jane."

His face is clouded with worry as he crosses the room and stoops to kiss me. "You look awful."

I try to smile, but it hurts. "Thanks."

"I'll give you some time alone." Sheila pats my hand. "And don't you worry about Green Fields. It wasn't your fault. The police are checking the CCTV. They'll catch the buggers."

"Thanks, Sheila."

"Will said he'll take you home. You rest up, and I'll pop by to see you tomorrow. Drink, if you can." She pours me a glass of water from the jug by the bed, presses it into my good hand, then scoops up her enormous handbag from the chair and breezes out of the room.

Will, still hovering by the left side of the bed, takes her seat and pulls it close. "How are you feeling?"

"Bruised."

"Is there anything I can do?" He glances at the full cup of water in my hand. "Do you need a straw?"

I try to shake my head and grimace.

"Sheila told me about the break-in," Will says. "Thank God none of the animals were hurt."

Not for the want of trying. The police found bolt cutters by the fence and evidence that they'd been used on at least three dog cages. Fortunately, the intruders weren't able to make more than a few small holes before the frenzied barking of the dogs woke Sheila and she realized what was going on. Lucky her house is so close. The cages were mended, she told me, but it's taking forever to remove the graffiti from the walls. Whoever broke in sprayed *BASTARDS* in at least five or six places, Sheila said.

One of the cages the intruders tried to get into was Jack's, and I've already spoken to the police about the conversation I had with his owners last week and the weird interview yesterday with Rob Archer, the man who wanted to adopt a Staffordshire bull terrier. I'm convinced one or both of them must have had something to do with the break-in. Sheila also said she saw two people in balaclavas, probably men, run off and jump into a car, then speed away. Everyone assumed that was the car that hit me, but there was no way. According to Sheila, they turned left out of Green Fields and headed toward the lake. I was coming up the hill from the right and, unless they did a loop and were returning to Green Fields, it's highly unlikely it was them who'd struck me.

I was lying on the grass shoulder when I came around. I don't know how long I was unconscious, but when I opened my eyes—my left eye, at least—it was still dark, my bike was in the bushes, and my left arm and shoulder ached when I moved. Sheila and a policeman were standing beside me. They'd heard the impact and the screech of the car's wheels on the road as it had sped away. Fifteen or twenty minutes later, an ambulance arrived. The paramedic was concerned that I felt nauseated and light-headed, and according to Sheila, I hadn't made any sense for the first couple of minutes after I'd come around, so he insisted on taking me to the emergency room to get checked out. He was also fairly certain I'd dislocated my left shoulder. I was seen very quickly after I arrived at the hospital and was sedated before a doctor reduced my shoulder and put my arm in a sling. Then I was moved to the observation ward to wait for a CT scan. The results came back clear an hour ago. I just need the doctor to officially discharge me, and I'm free to go home.

"Did you manage to get my phone?"

Will laughs. "Bloody hell, Jane. You're addicted to that thing. Yes, I've got it." He digs into the messenger bag he's wearing across his body and hands me my cell phone. "Most people would ask for a change of clothes and a good book, but no, you need to check Facebook. Or is it Twitter you're addicted to?"

I look at the screen. There are no new Facebook notifications, but there is a new text message. It's from a number that isn't registered in my phone...

"Chloe says hello," Will says as I click on the message icon. "She wanted me to find out if you've got to have your arm in a cast, because she thinks the pink ones are really coo—Jane? What's the matter? Why are you crying?"

I turn the phone around so he can see it.

"'*Only the good die young,*'" he says, reading the text message aloud. "'*That'll explain why you're still alive, then.*'" He stares at me, his mouth agape. "What's that supposed to mean?"

I flinch as he wipes a tear from the scratched, swollen side of my face.

"Jane? What does it mean?"

29

Emma!" Isaac stands up from his desk and steps toward me, his arms spread wide. "Good breakfast?"

I'm breathless from running through the yard to the house without stopping, and I push him away as he attempts to hug me. He smells of cigarettes, incense, and deodorant.

"What's going on?" He glances at Al, hovering behind me. She shrugs in response, then reaches down to rub her ankle. She hobbled after me all the way back to the house, still trying to convince me not to talk to Isaac about the Frank rumor. She said she'd talk to Daisy and Leanne for me, but it's not enough. I won't have people think I'm the type of girl to lie about an attempted rape. Isaac saw what happened; everyone needs to hear it from him.

"I'd like to know what's going on too," says Leanne from the doorway, her expression unreadable.

"Good," I say. "You need to hear this."

A wry smile crosses Isaac's face as he looks from Leanne to me and back again. "What's going on?"

Leanne crosses her thin arms over her chest and leans against the doorway as though she needs its support in order to stay upright.

She's steadfastly refusing to return my gaze. Whoever told her I lied about the attack must have been very persuasive.

I glance behind her, but the hallway is empty. "Where's Daisy? She needs to hear this too."

I move to go look for her, but Isaac grabs my hand before I can leave the room. "Daisy's tidying up after breakfast. Just tell me what's going on, please. Leanne, come in and shut the door."

She steps into the room, shutting the door behind her, and then sits down on the rug. Al gives me a look that says, "This doesn't mean I believe her," then joins her on the floor.

"Okay then." Isaac gestures for me to sit as well, but I choose a chair instead and perch on the edge of it. Isaac slumps into his desk chair. He swivels idly from side to side, the wheels swiveling back and forth on the thin rug that covers the entrance to the basement. "Hit me with it. What's going on?"

"There a rumor going around that I lied about Frank attacking me."

"Is there?" He stops swiveling and cups his chin with his hand. "And who started this rumor?" He rolls the word "rumor" on his tongue as though he enjoys the sound it makes.

Al and Leanne both shake their heads.

"Leanne knows," I say.

"Do you?" He rests his elbows on his knees and leans toward her.

When she shakes her head, Al leans away from her, a look of surprise on her face. "Yes, you do! You said you'd been sworn to secrecy."

"No, I—"

"Okay, okay. Forget who started the rumor." Isaac holds up his hands and sits back in his chair. His gaze shifts toward Leanne, just for a split second, then returns to me. "I'll put this right, Emma."

"Tell them!" I point at Leanne and Al. "Tell them Frank

217

attacked me and that's why you hit him. Tell them I didn't lie about it."

"Emma!" He wheels his chair toward me, then puts a hand on my shoulder. He squeezes it as he leans toward me and hisses in my ear. "I said I'd put this right, and I will."

"But…"

"You need to trust me, okay?" There's a finality to the way he says "okay" that stops me from objecting again.

"Right, let's have a drink, shall we?" He rolls his chair back to his desk, then reaches into the bottom drawer and pulls out four bottles of Budweiser.

None of us have had real lager since we got here. Daisy's vodka is long gone, and so are the bottles of wine the rest of us brought. We've been here twelve days now, and the only alcoholic drink available is Raj's vile homemade beer. We were supposed to be leaving in a couple of days to go on a jungle adventure in Chitwan. The trip Leanne never got around to booking. Those plans feel like they were made in another lifetime.

Isaac flips off the metal lids and hands us each a bottle in turn. "I'm sorry I haven't spent as much time with you guys as I would have liked. Obviously, Leanne's come to a lot of my seminars"—he smiles warmly at her—"but Al and Emma…I feel like I need to get to know you guys a bit better." He gives Al a lingering look, as though he hasn't quite figured her out yet.

"So, Emma." He sits forward in his chair, puts his own bottle between his knees, and reaches into his back pocket for his tobacco tin. "Tell me a bit about yourself."

"There's nothing to tell."

He opens the lid of the tin and pulls out a packet of rolling papers. "Humor me."

"Um…I'm twenty-five. I'm from Leicester. I've got two brothers and a sister. My parents are both doctors, and—"

"Boring." He licks two rolling papers and presses them

together, then sprinkles tobacco along the length of paper. "Tell us what matters to you. Tell us what you care about."

"Family. Friendship." I shrug. "Loyalty. Trust."

"Okay." He sprinkles some weed on top of the tobacco and rolls the joint back and forth in his fingers. "What else?"

"I've always loved animals. I wanted to be a vet until I did badly on my exams."

"Did you also want to be a Miss World contestant? Come on, Emma, you can do better than that."

I shift in my seat, aware of Al and Leanne silently watching. "I don't know what you want me to say."

"I want you to tell me something you care about that's going to make me sit up, something raw and honest."

"Fine. I care about people being straight with each other. I care about honesty."

"Better." He lights the joint and inhales deeply. "What pisses you off?"

"Injustice, racism, homophobia."

"You've gone back to being Miss World."

"Okay." I take a swig of my beer. "I get pissed off when people don't give up their seats for old people on the train, or when they believe everything they read in the papers. I can't stand spineless and weak people. And as for Jerry Springer—"

"Stop!" He hands me the joint. "Now I want you to tell me how many of the things that piss you off you actually do."

"None of them."

"Really?"

"Well, I don't watch Jerry Springer, if that's what you mean." I laugh, but no one else joins in. Leanne has her eyes closed.

"I imagine you give up your seat for old people too," Isaac says. "But what about the rest?"

I know what he's getting at. He wants me to admit to some weaknesses.

"I'm a people pleaser," I say. "I do and say what other people expect so they like me. I hate that about myself."

"Cool." Isaac nods. "Good."

I raise my beer bottle to my mouth, and I'm just about to take a swig when he grabs my hand. The bottle rattles against my top teeth.

"If you could kill anyone right now and get away with it, who would you kill, Emma?"

"What?"

"You heard me."

"Yes, I did, and it's a ridiculous question."

"I still want you to answer it."

"Right, well, I wouldn't kill anyone."

"Liar!"

"I'm not lying."

"Yes, you are. Nothing you've said since you walked in here has been honest. Everything is measured; everything has to be carefully thought out before you say it. Even when you admitted to being a people pleaser, other weaknesses and faults occurred to you first, but you rejected them because being a people pleaser is a more socially acceptable answer. You're not *living*, Emma; you're pretending to live. Your whole fucking life is a lie. It isn't other people stopping you from being you: it's you. Now tell the truth. If you could kill anyone, who would you kill?"

"I've already answered the question, Isaac, and you're not listening to my answer. I would never kill anyone, whether there were consequences or not. I would never take someone else's life."

"Liar!"

The bottle flies from my hands as he lunges toward me and knocks me off my chair. My head smacks against the wooden floor, and then he's on top of me, straddling my waist, his hands on my wrists, pressing them to either side of my head.

"Get off me, Isaac!"

"Isaac!" Al shouts his name, but he ignores her.

"Who would you kill, Emma?"

"I wouldn't."

"Liar! Who would you kill?"

"No one!"

He shuffles forward so he's sitting on my chest. I'm struggling to breathe now. Al pulls at his arm, but she's not strong enough to dislodge him.

"Who would you kill?" Isaac shifts his weight down to my pelvis, his face dips to meet mine, and I know what he's about to do before he does it. I open my mouth to protest, and then his tongue's in my mouth. My instinct is to bite down, and I'm about to clench my teeth when Isaac grabs my jaw with his right hand, preventing it. I try to free my left arm to push him away, but he presses his knee into the crook of my elbow, pinning it to the floor.

He pulls back to ask again, "Who would you kill?"

A wave of panic engulfs me, and the room seems to spin.

"Who would you kill, Emma? Tell me!"

I close my eyes, but the tears force their way through my closed lids and roll down my cheeks. "Frank. Okay? If I had to kill someone, I'd kill Frank for trying to rape me. I want him to feel as terrified and defenseless as I did, the evil, fucking bastard."

"Who else, Emma?" I hear a small, almost imperceptible click, but I can't turn my head, because Isaac still has his hand on my jaw. "Who else is causing you pain? Who else has hurt you? Who else would you kill if there were no consequences, no judgment, no remorse? Who would you kill?"

The last twelve days flash through my mind like scenes from a silent film. Al and Leanne openmouthed, laughing hysterically as Daisy makes fun of me. Daisy's heel grinding against the gecko, the bitterness in her eyes when Isaac talked to me at the welcome meeting, the sneer on her face when she said "Hunt the Cunt," the submissive tilt of her head when Isaac sent her back to the house after Frank attacked me, and her smug expression when one of the men called me a bitch when I walked into the dining room for breakfast.

This trip was supposed to be an adventure, the vacation of a lifetime, but I've never felt more lonely, more isolated, or more disliked in my life. And it's all down to her. She could have defended me, but instead she actively turned people against me. All the confusion, all the resentment, all the pain of the last few days burns in my chest, and I open my eyes. "Daisy."

There's a gasp. But it's not from Al or Leanne. It's from someone else, standing in the open doorway. Someone who just heard every word I said.

30

I know who is standing in the doorway, even without turning my head. The energy in the room changes; the air doesn't grow cold, but it does still. I can no longer hear Al's slow, heavy breaths or Leanne's light nasal whistle. Even Isaac, still astride me, his right hand cupping my chin, is silent.

"Well, isn't that charming?"

"Daisy, I didn't mean it. I just... I was..."

As I try to explain, Isaac vaults off me and crosses the room to the doorway.

"Daisy." He puts a hand on her arm as he whispers her name. "Can you come back later?"

"Actually, darling"—she glares at me, her blue eyes glittering with anger—"I'd quite like to stay."

"We were having a session. I'd like you to come back later, please."

Daisy continues to stare at me for what feels like forever, her eyes narrowed, her lips a thin slash, then she takes a step backward. The hem of her long, scarlet skirt swishes around her ankles as she turns and walks toward the kitchen. Her flip-flops slap against the wooden floor.

"I'd like you two to go too, please," Isaac says.

"Us?" Leanne points at her chest.

"Yes, please."

She rises silently from the floor and, without so much as a glance at me, drifts out of the room and into the hall. Al remains where she is, sitting cross-legged on the rug. Her nostrils flare as Isaac looks down at her and raises an eyebrow as if to say, "Now you need to leave too."

"I'm not leaving Emma alone with you."

"I'm not going to hurt her." He looks at me. "I promise. I just want to talk to her. I want to explain why I did what I just did and how it will help her."

"Emma?" Al looks at me. "What do you want to do?"

The sound of raised voices drifts through the open door of Isaac's study. Daisy and Leanne are arguing in the dining room. There's no way I'm going to walk straight into that. The second I leave this room, Daisy will fly at me, and I can't deal with that, not now, not after everything that's happened. If I stay here for a few more minutes and give her a bit of time, she'll calm down. Then I'll try to explain what just happened— not that I really know myself.

There's something so uncomfortable, so unbearable, about the way Isaac pressures you to answer his questions that the only way to make it stop is to say what he wants to hear. I understand now why Leanne told him about being raped as a teenager, not because she was desperate to share it with him but because she needed to say something, anything, to stop his constant questioning. There's no way I'd ever harm Daisy, but I am angry with her. I haven't felt like this since I was a teenager. The rage I can deal with, but the hurt is unbearable. I've always known Daisy could be cruel, but to have that cruelty turned on me feels like the ultimate betrayal. It's as though the last seven years of our friendship have meant nothing.

"Emma?" Al asks again.

"I'm going to stay. I want to hear Isaac out."

"Okay." She says the word uncertainly as she twists onto her knees and stands up. "All right. I'll be in the dorm if you need me."

She stands in the doorway for several seconds, shoulders back, chin raised as she locks eyes with Isaac.

"If you touch her again, you'll have me to answer to. Right?"

Isaac's lips twitch as though he's trying to suppress a smile. "Got it, Al."

"Good." She steps into the hallway, closing the door behind her.

~

"Okay then." Isaac collects the beer bottle he'd knocked out of my hands and tosses it into the trash, ignoring the puddle of spilled beer on the floor, then picks up an ashtray from his desk and lies down on the rug. He closes his eyes and stretches himself out like a cat, bathing in the wide, warm triangle of sunlight that streams in through the window. He lies there, perfectly still, for several seconds, then reaches into his shirt pocket for his tobacco tin, opens his eyes, and props himself up onto his elbow.

"Want one?" He flips open the tin and tosses a ready-rolled cigarette toward his mouth. He catches it between his lips, then nudges the tin toward me.

I don't even deliberate. I take out the lighter and a cigarette, light it, and then offer the flickering flame to Isaac. He puts a hand on mine and guides the flame closer to his cigarette. The tip sparks orange, and he lets go of my hand. The weight of his touch remains, the imprint of his fingers still warm on my skin.

"Thanks." I puff on my cigarette, drop the lighter back into the tin, close the lid, and nudge it across the rug toward him.

Isaac exhales slowly, then nods toward his shirt pocket, indicating that I should put the tin back in there. I shake my head.

"Why did you attack me like that?"

"I didn't attack you."

"No? So you didn't knock me off my chair and hold me down?"

He looks at me lazily, the cigarette dangling from his lips. "Why do you think I did that?"

"I don't know."

"Yes, you do."

I shift away from him and lean back against the wall, taking another puff on my cigarette. He's playing games with me.

"Why are you so afraid to get angry, Emma?"

"I'm not."

"Someone taught you to suppress your anger. Who was it?"

I exhale slowly, aiming the smoke toward the motes at the window. They twirl violently as it engulfs them.

"No one taught me. I'm not an angry person."

"I disagree."

"That's because you don't know me."

"Really? It's all very well being, as you call it, a 'people pleaser,' someone you think people want you to be, but when faced with real jeopardy, your true character is exposed. I saw that yesterday, after Frank attacked you. The person I talked to in the hut, that was the real you."

I take another puff on my cigarette. "We didn't do arguments in my house, growing up. We'd run off to our rooms to sulk instead. There was a lot of running off to other rooms in my house. We never slammed the doors, though. If you were going to sulk, you had to do it silently."

"Then what would happen?"

"We'd slope back into whatever room the rest of the family was in and pretend nothing had happened."

"Your parents would pretend nothing had happened too?"

"Yeah."

I'm telling him too much. He's feeding me questions like he fed them to Leanne, but there's a part of me that wants to answer him. I don't know if it's because Daisy and I aren't speaking so I haven't got anyone to confide in apart from Al, or because there's a tiny part of me that's flattered that Isaac's showing an interest.

"Did anyone ever stand their ground instead of running off?" he asks.

"No. If you did that, you'd be ignored. Dad would pick up the paper, and Mom would close down emotionally. No conversation, no eye contact, no warmth. It was like being shut out in the cold."

"So you learned that, in order to be loved, you should remain agreeable."

"Pretty much."

Isaac rubs a thumb over his cheekbone and gazes at me thoughtfully. "You mention your mom as having a reaction, but not your dad."

"She was the one who'd discipline us. Dad would keep quiet. I don't think he liked being on the wrong side of her either."

"And you wanted her to be proud of you, to love you?"

"What child doesn't? My brothers and sister—George, Henry, and Isabella—they made her proud with their sporting achievements and their dancing and their acting, but I wasn't good at any of those things. There was a space in our family for 'the intelligent child'—we already had sporty, beautiful, and funny—and I tried to fill it. I worked really, really hard. I wasn't being Miss World when I told you about loving animals and wanting to be a vet. The plan was to get three As on my exams and then study veterinary science at the university. Then I got pregnant, and it ruined everything."

"You got pregnant?"

My cigarette has gone out, so I lean over and flick the butt into the trash. "I was seventeen. I'd had the same boyfriend, Ben, for a year, and we got drunk one night and didn't bother with a condom. I took the morning-after pill the next day, but...it didn't work."

"So you had a baby?"

"No. I wanted to, but my mom insisted I have an abortion. She said I'd ruin my future, and she wasn't going to sit back and let that happen. She made me an appointment at a clinic, but I didn't go; I hid at Ben's house, but she came and got me. She told me I'd have to leave the family home if I didn't get an abortion. I couldn't bear it. I couldn't bear the way she was looking at me, at the deep, deep disappointment in her eyes. All I'd ever done was try to make her proud, and—" I take a deep breath and gaze up at the ceiling. The plasterwork is rough, and there's a deep crack running from one corner of the room to the other. "So I did it. I had the abortion two weeks before my exams."

"Wow." Isaac raises his eyebrows.

"Yeah. I had my first panic attack in my biology exam. I knew it, I knew the answer, and I was about three hundred words into my essay when my chest tightened and I felt like I couldn't breathe. The room shrank, and then I was aware of everyone staring because I was gasping, really gasping, and then Miss Hutton started running toward me, and—"

"It's okay." Isaac rolls toward me and touches my hand. "It's okay, Emma. You're not there now; it's not happening. It was in the past. It's gone. It's over."

He keeps hold of my hand as I take deep breath after deep breath.

"Okay?" he asks when I finally exhale steadily and reach for the tobacco tin. "You all right?"

I nod. "Yeah."

He releases my hand and watches silently as I slide a rolling paper from the packet, sprinkle tobacco into it, then roll it into a tube and lick the glue. When I've finished, he picks up the lighter, strikes it, and holds it toward me. I light up and take a deep puff on the cigarette.

"Have you ever wondered why you became Daisy's friend, Emma?"

"Not really. It just happened. We were freshmen together. She chatted with me. It was just one of those things."

"You don't think she subconsciously reminded you of your mom—a woman with a strong personality and a need to dominate?"

"God—I've got no idea." I take another puff, blowing the smoke away from us both.

"The reason why I did what I just did"—Isaac props himself up on his elbow again—"was to help you. You might think it was cruel, in light of what happened with Frank—*particularly* in light of that—but I had to do it. I had to make you relive the trauma in a safe environment to give you the opportunity to be honest with yourself. You don't want to kill Daisy, not deep down, but you're carrying around a lot of anger about that relationship. Do you suffer from eczema or asthma, Emma?"

I shake my head.

"Psoriasis?"

"I get flare-ups when I'm stressed."

"There you go. Asthma, eczema, psoriasis, IBS—they're all outward symptoms of issues that are going on in your psyche that you're trying to repress. They're your subconscious manifesting itself in a cry for help—not to the outside world, but to your own consciousness. Ninety-nine percent of illnesses are caused by stress, and where does stress come from?" He taps the side of his head. "If you can sort out what's going on up here, you can sort out everything else. You don't need your antianxiety pills to prevent your panic attacks, Emma; you need to address the cause of them."

"I know, but—"

"God, Emma." Isaac tips his head to one side and looks at me in wonderment. "If you could see the look on your face right now. The light in your eyes is..." He shakes his head. "Wow."

"Don't." I reach for the ashtray and grind my cigarette into it, spending longer than necessary ensuring the glowing tip is ground out. I'm prickling with embarrassment, and I can't meet his eyes.

"You have no idea, do you? No idea at all how beautiful you are? The first time I saw you, walking toward the gates of Ekanta Yatra, with your shoulders folded in, your head down, I wanted to shake you. You were trying to hide, because you felt big and awkward and unattractive compared to Daisy, and you didn't want me to notice you."

"That's not true."

"Isn't it? You think she's more attractive than you, but you couldn't be more wrong. Women like her are ten-a-penny. She wears her sexuality like a beacon, blinding men with the intensity of it, stunning them into submission. But there's a reason why she's still alone, Emma—why she's so desperately unhappy: she thinks, deep down, that she's an ugly, worthless human being. Why else would she be so desperate to get men into bed to validate her self-worth?"

"But they still sleep with her."

"Because she's available, because she makes them feel good about themselves. But the light Daisy emits isn't real, Emma. She can switch it on and off like a lightbulb. Yours is real, but you hide it."

For a while, I say nothing, thinking about his words.

"Emma." It's only as Isaac puts his hand over mine that I

realize I am still grinding the cigarette butt into the ashtray. And there it is again, the hot, weighty sensation of his skin on mine.

"Have you slept with her?" I ask without looking up. There is a raspy tone to my voice that wasn't there a few seconds ago.

"No."

"Because she wants to sleep with you, you know."

He smooths a hair back from my face, then lets his hand rest on the curve of my jawbone. His eyes are narrowed, intense, scanning my face, returning again and again to my lips. I'm not stupid. I know he's pulled this seduction routine with dozens, hundreds of other women.

"Daisy is jealous of you, Emma. You know that, don't you?"

I move his hand from my cheek. "Now you're being ridiculous."

"It's true. Why else do you think she's stolen so many men from you in the past? She's in competition with you, and she wants to win. Daisy isn't your friend, Emma. She's been silently leaching your confidence for years without you even noticing."

"You're wrong." I shake my head. "She's got her faults, but she's been there for me when I've needed her."

"Has she?" I jump as he grabs my hands between his. "Or has she used your moments of weakness to make herself feel stronger? Daisy needs you all right, Emma, but not in the way you think."

I yank my hands away and press them to the floor. My head is spinning, but the more I try to anchor my thoughts, the more they spin away from me. Do I feel weak, directionless, and fractured because I've been comparing myself with Daisy and found myself wanting? Is he right? Has she been reinforcing that belief since we met?

"I'm sure she spread the rumor that I lied about Frank attacking me."

"Why do you think that is?"

"I don't know. I know she can be cruel and—"

"Emma." Isaac pulls himself onto his knees and crouches in front of me. "Daisy's lashing out because she's trying to walk her own path and she doesn't know how to deal with it. But that's not your issue anymore. You need to let go too. The reason you're so confused is because you're trying to hang on to a friendship that wasn't good for you. It wasn't good for either of you. Don't worry about Daisy. And don't worry about what happened with Frank; I'll deal with it."

I think of Frank in the basement below us, hidden away beneath the hatch, and the pain of what happened washes through me again.

"Emma." He lifts the curtain of hair that's fallen in front of my eyes and leans forward so his face is only an inch from mine. "I believe in you. Why don't you?"

I don't know whether it's loneliness, desire, or his relentless questioning, but instead of answering, I put my hands on either side of his face, and I kiss him. He kisses me back—hard—his hands in my hair. He pulls at my clothes, grabbing the straps of my tank top and yanking them down over my arms so they're pinned to my sides, then he presses his lips to my neck, my collarbone, my cleavage. I wriggle out of my tank top, pushing it down to my waist, and clutch him to me so we tumble to the floor, knocking over a pile of prayer mats that scatter beneath us.

I grab at Isaac's T-shirt, forcing it up toward his throat before he knocks my hands away and yanks it down. "It stays on."

My bra is the next to go. Then Isaac's shorts. My shorts. My underwear. We are partially naked and sweaty, grabbing at each other, grappling, kissing, biting. For the first time since we got here, my head is empty. Isaac fucks me, over and over again, one hand twisted in my hair, the other on my collarbone. His shoulder-length hair falls over his face, but he keeps his eyes locked on mine the whole time. He doesn't once look away or close his eyes.

"It'll be okay," he breathes as he collapses on top of me. "I promise."

31

W ho sent you this?" Will hands the phone back to me, the message still on the screen:

Only the good die young. That'll explain why you're still alive, then.

I navigate out of the text messages. "I don't know."

"Surely you must have an idea." He perches on the edge of the bed.

A fly buzzes at the window, a cart is wheeled past the door, and somewhere farther down the ward, a woman groans as a nurse takes a blood sample.

"Jane." Will touches me on the arm. "You need to trust me. Tell me what's going on."

"I can't. I…"

"You don't trust me." His jaw clenches, and his hand falls away from my body.

"I do. I want to. But…"

"But what? Jane, I want to help you, but I can't if you won't talk to me. For God's sake." He presses his hands to his face and takes several deep breaths.

"You don't have to stay."

I regret saying the words even as they leave my mouth.

"Okay." He stands up wearily and turns to go. "If that's what you want. If I hurry, I'll catch Sheila in the parking lot. She'll drop you home."

"No." I reach for his hand. I can't let him go. I can't deal with this on my own anymore. I have to trust him. I have to trust someone. "Please. I'm sorry, Will. Don't go."

He sighs resignedly and grips the back of the bedside chair with his hand. "Are you going to tell me what's going on?"

I nod. "Yes. Yes, I will."

～

Will listens in silence as I tell him everything that happened at Ekanta Yatra. He audibly gasps several times, and his eyes widen with horror when I tell him what happened with Frank. When I get to the part about Al selling her story, he holds up a hand for me to stop speaking.

"Okay, I know that part."

He stares at me for the longest time, shock, worry, and concern written all over his face. When he does finally speak, it's a single word.

"Fuck."

"Yeah." I pull the hospital sheet farther up my chest. It's not cold, but I feel exposed, and not just physically. "That's why I wanted to start a new life."

"And you think the text message is from someone who knew you as Emma?"

"It's not just the text message. I received a letter at Green

Fields last week. They said they knew my name wasn't really Jane Hughes. A day later, an email came through the website at work saying Daisy's not dead. Then, when we were at Chloe's school fair, I got some Facebook messages pretending to be from Daisy, saying she was cold and I'd left her for dead. Then the woman in a blue hat talked to Chloe about me, and then"—I hold out the phone—"this."

"Do you think Daisy could be alive? You didn't see her body, did you?"

"No, but…"

"I know." He purses his lips. "It doesn't seem likely. And Isaac and Leanne are definitely dead?"

"I think so, yes. If Daisy's dead, then Isaac must be too, and as for Leanne… Al got in touch with her mom several times after we returned to the UK, but she said she hadn't heard from her, so…"

"You think she died in the fire at Ekanta Yatra?"

"Yeah. I don't know whether it was arson or accidental, but the whole place burned down when everyone was sleeping. They think it happened a few nights after we escaped. The Nepalese police found bodies everywhere, some of them so badly burned they couldn't be identified. There were people there who'd cut all ties with their friends and family, and they'll never know if they're alive or dead."

"Shit."

"I know."

"So that just leaves Al."

"Yeah, but why would she suddenly start sending me horrible messages? Yes, she stalked Simone after they split up, but that was a reaction to being dumped. We argued after she sold her story, but she never threatened me. We fell out and drifted apart, nothing more macabre than that."

"Maybe she's been holding a grudge because you left her behind on the mountain."

"To get help!"

"Maybe she sees it differently. Things have escalated since you sent her a message on Facebook. Did she ever reply?"

"No, but"—I shake my head—"it can't be her. She was my friend."

Will raises his eyebrows. "So were Leanne and Daisy."

I turn my head away as my eyes fill with tears. I can't let myself believe Al is behind this. Whoever ran me off the road could have killed me.

"Jane." Will touches my hand. "You need to go to the police; you know that, don't you?"

~

Officer Barnham listens intently as we take our seats in the police station interview room and I tell him everything that's happened recently, pausing every now and then when he chips in, asking me to confirm certain details so he can write them down in his notepad. I tell him who I really am and why I decided to reinvent myself as Jane Hughes, but I don't mention what became of Daisy and Isaac. Instead, I feed him the line that Al and I agreed on five years ago: that they mysteriously disappeared. I can't break the promise I made to her, not until we've spoken. After everything that's happened, that probably sounds naive, but I owe Al. If it wasn't for her, Leanne might not have been the only one who died in the fire.

When I get to the end of my story and reach for the glass of water another policeman has brought for me, Officer Barnham sits back in his chair and looks at me thoughtfully. He can't be much older than twenty-seven, twenty-eight, but his hairline is receding. It looks incongruous against the pitted acne scars on his cheeks. I don't think he's the same policeman I spoke to immediately after my accident, but I was feeling so groggy when I first came around that I barely remember who I saw.

"First off," he says, "I'd like to reassure you that we're doing everything we can to find the person responsible for the hit-and-run. We're following up on all the details you and your boss gave us at the hospital this morning, and we've put a board up at the scene of the accident, asking for eyewitnesses, but no one has come forward yet. We've also examined the CCTV footage from Green Fields, but the camera range doesn't cover the road, so we were unable to get a shot of the car as it passed. I'm afraid we've got very little to go on at present."

I take a sip of my water. "I understand."

"As for the notes and messages you've received"—he glances at his notepad—"we do take stalking very seriously these days, and someone is obviously trying to unsettle and unnerve you, and keeping their identity secret is part of the intimidation. There haven't been any obvious threats of violence, but"—he circles something on his pad with his pen—"the most recently received text message does sound as though it could have been sent by the person who knocked you off your bike, and that's something we need to take seriously, since, if the two are connected, that could mean an intent to harm, or even attempted murder. I'm going to talk to my sergeant about your case and whether we should pass it on to CSI, and then…"

I don't hear the rest of his sentence, because two words are repeating over and over in my head. *Attempted murder.* I've spent the last twelve hours trying to convince myself that what happened was an accident, that it was a drunken bachelor party driving too quickly through unfamiliar roads in the dark.

"Jane?" Officer Barnham waves his hand across my line of vision. "Are you okay?"

"Yes, sorry. What were you saying?"

"That we won't offer police protection at this stage, but I would like you to think about all the people who might hold a grudge against you or want to harm you in some way. If you could let me have that list as soon as possible… I'd also like you to continue to log and save every text, online message, and written note, and keep a diary of any unusual activity. You might want to consider carrying a personal safety device and installing a security alarm in your home. If it makes you feel safer, you might also want to consider asking your boyfriend to move in with you until that's done. William Smart, did you say his name is? Or maybe you could stay with him?"

"I could ask." If I moved in with Will now, I could still be there at the weekend when Chloe comes to visit. I don't know how he'd feel about me sharing his bed, especially since as far as his daughter is concerned, we're just friends.

"Or a friend?" the officer asks, as though he's just read the expression on my face.

I can't bring myself to tell him that I don't have any close friends in the area. There's Sheila, but she's also my boss, so I couldn't possibly impose on her. I don't reply but nod in vague agreement.

"Here's a leaflet that may be of help," he says, pushing one toward me. "There's a number for the National Stalking Helpline on the front. There's information about personal and cyber safety. You could get your computer checked to make sure that key-logging software hasn't been installed and that your antivirus software is up to date. If any more messages come through via your work website, you could try contacting your web hosting company to see if they can help."

"Thank you." I reach for my bag with my good arm and slip the leaflet inside, then pick up my cell phone, lying on the center of the table between us, and put that in my bag too. My hands are shaking so much it takes three attempts to get it into the inner pocket.

"Are you sure you're okay?"

"I'm fine. I just… It's a lot to take in."

"You've got someone waiting for you? Someone you can talk to?"

"Yes."

"Good." He stands up and holds out a hand. "We'll be in touch. Try not to worry; we'll do everything we can."

~

Will is waiting for me in his car outside the police station. He opens the passenger door as I draw near.

"Well, how did it go?"

I try not to wince as I climb in. I was discharged from the hospital five hours ago, and every part of my body still aches from where the car hit me. A huge black-and-green bruise covers most of my right thigh, and the palms of my hands are scratched and pitted from where I hit the road before I rolled onto the shoulder. The scratches on the left side of my face are tender, although thankfully the swelling has gone down, and I can see through my right eye now, even though it's still swollen and bruised. I'm still nursing my left arm in a sling, but it's a relief that the shoulder isn't dislocated anymore and it should feel better soon, according to the doctor.

"The officer asked me to write a list of anyone who might hold a grudge against me. He said there's a possibility that the accident was deliberate, that someone might intentionally have been trying to hurt me."

Will stares at me for several seconds, his lips parted, his eyes wide. "Well, that's decided, then."

"What is?"

He starts the engine and puts the car into first gear. "You're moving in with me."

32

The shower block is empty, but I still choose the stall farthest away from the dormitory. The solar panels have been temperamental for days, but it isn't the cold trickle of water that dribbles from the showerhead that makes me shiver.

I shouldn't have slept with Isaac.

I rub the soap over my face, hair, arms, and breasts, then I rub it over the soft flesh of my hips and between my legs. If anyone overheard us having sex, if anyone finds out, then word will get back to Daisy, and she'll feel completely justified in having spread the rumor about Frank and me. It won't matter if Isaac tells people what he saw; the suspicion will be there.

BANG!

Something solid smashes against the wooden floor of the dormitory and makes me start. I snatch my shorts and tank top from the top of the shower stall and yank them on, my body still wet. There's someone in the dorm.

My clothes cling to me as I silently step out of the shower, testing my weight against the creaking floorboards with each step. I should have left the shower running. Whoever's out there will have heard the water stop. They'll know I'm about to step into the dormitory.

My heart thuds in my chest as I peer around the door.

A tiny gecko, spread-eagled on the wall above the window, scuttles into the corner at the sound of my footsteps. Other than the scurrying creature, the room is completely deserted. Deserted, that is, apart from the metal figure of Kali, the Hindu goddess of time, death, and destruction, lying on her back in the center of the room. I've seen it before, on the table in the hallway. I snatch it up and sprint lightly to the doorway and out onto the walkway. Sally strolls out of the boys' dorm, a bundle of dirty bedding in her arms.

"Wait!" I run toward her, but she bounds through the hallway and into the kitchen like a startled rabbit. "Sally, wait! Have you seen anyone—"

I draw to a halt next to the hallway table as a low rumble of voices seeps from beneath the closed door of the meditation room. It sounds packed in there.

"Emma!" My name is shouted, clear as day, above the hubbub. It's followed by an explosion of male and female laughter.

I place the statue of Kali on the table, then just as I turn to walk back to the girls' dorm, I collide with something solid. My arms are pinned to my side as I'm wrapped in a tight hug.

"Tsk, tsk," Isaac whispers into my ear. "I really should chastise you for being late for meditation, Emma. But you're here now." He throws an arm over my shoulders and pulls me into him so we're standing side by side. "Shall we go in?"

~

A hush falls as we enter the meditation room. I try to pull away, but Isaac tightens his grip on my shoulder and steers me through the mass of cross-legged bodies. When we reach the altar, he releases me and steps in between Isis and Cera, so he's the focal point in the room. I turn. There's a small space to the left of one of the Swedish girls, two rows back.

"Here." Isaac indicates the floor to his right, where Cera is sitting.

I shake my head. I don't want to sit somewhere so visible. Not when Daisy, Al, and Leanne are all sitting together at the back of the room, pointing at me and talking among themselves. When I make eye contact with Al, she acknowledges me with the smallest nod of her head. It's a tiny movement, almost as though she doesn't want Daisy or Leanne to notice.

"Sit down, Emma." Cera inches to her right and taps the space between her and Isaac.

"Isaac—" I say, but he silences me with a look.

I squeeze into the space, pull my knees into my chest, and keep my gaze lowered.

"Okay, everyone," Isaac says. "Close your eyes and breathe in deeply through your nose."

I close my eyes too, but concentrating on my breathing is making me feel claustrophobic. Isaac stops speaking, and the room falls silent.

Someone is watching you, Emma. Someone has their eyes open.

I fight the thought, but the harder I fight it, the more powerful it becomes.

You need to open your eyes, Emma. You're in danger.

The darkness behind my closed eyes is suffocating. My skin is prickling, my breathing quick and shallow. I press my sticky palms to the floor to try to anchor myself, but it does nothing to stop the seasick feeling in the pit of my stomach.

Open your eyes, Emma. Open them NOW!

I don't recognize her immediately. Her hair has been washed and falls to her shoulders in soft waves, the dark shadows beneath her eyes have almost disappeared, and her slim body is engulfed in an oversize man's plaid shirt.

Paula is staring at me from across the room.

I smile at her—pleased she's no longer in the hut, relieved that it wasn't Daisy that was staring at me—but she doesn't return my smile. Instead, she shakes her head. It's a minute movement, but it's there, disapproval and something else. Another emotion I can't put my finger on. Her gaze flicks toward Isaac, and I instantly recognize the expression on her face. Envy.

33

saac refuses to let me leave his side, and I trail behind him like a shadow for the rest of the morning, from the dining room to the study, from the meditation room to the water- fall. He takes every available moment to touch, stroke, or kiss me. When we walked past Daisy and Leanne practicing yoga on the patio, he stopped walking, pulled me into his arms, pressed his lips to mine, and stuck his tongue down my throat. I put my hand on his chest to try to push him away, but he held me fast. Daisy's mocking laughter followed us all the way down the yard and across the bridge to the animal pens.

I want to talk to her. I want to apologize and explain, but there's no reasoning with her when she's like this. If I can talk to Al, if I can get her on my side, then maybe she'll talk to Daisy with me, and we can work out how we're going to get out of here. I have to leave—rain or no rain—and I need to know if she wants to come with me. We're officially supposed to be leaving the day after tomorrow, but with Leanne and Daisy both ignoring me, I've got no idea whether that's still happening or not.

I spot Al strolling into the kitchen for dish duty after lunch. With Isaac waylaid by Johan in the dining room, I slip in after her. She heads for the sink and turns on the taps; they squeak into life, dribbling water into the rusty sink as the ancient heating system rumbles and chugs to life.

I pick up a pile of dirty plates from the stack on the side-board and carry them over to the sink. Al doesn't acknowledge me as I lower them into the bowl. Instead, she reaches for the grubby dishcloth and dips it into the bowl of salt that masquer-ades as dish liquid.

"Al. Don't say anything. Just listen to me. It's important. I didn't mean what I said about Daisy earlier. I don't want to kill anyone; it was just a figure of speech. Isaac forced me to say it, the same way he—"

"What are you doing?" Isaac clamps a hand on my shoulder.

"Washing the dishes," I shout above the noise of the taps. "It's my turn to help."

"Get someone else to do it."

"But I need to—"

He yanks me out of the room before I can finish my sentence.

Al, her arms submerged in a dark, greasy pool of water, doesn't say a word.

~

The next time I see her, it's late in the evening. She didn't go to Isaac's afternoon talk about fasting to enhance willpower and spirituality, nor the early evening meditation. Daisy nudged Leanne when they walked in and spotted me sitting beside Isaac. They stopped walking and stood stock-still in the entrance, silently staring at me until Daisy burst out laughing, grabbed Leanne's hand, and took a seat at the side of the room. I hope against hope that when I do find Al, she tells me that neither of them want to leave with us the day after tomorrow.

Now, everyone is gathered in a circle on the patio, drinking Raj's home brew as a goat slowly rotates on a spit above the fire in the center. Isaac, Isis, Cera, and I are sitting nearest to the house. Al, Daisy, and Johan are on the other side of the circle, staring silently at the fire, the flickering flames illuminating their faces. I stare at Al, willing her to look at me, but it's Johan who senses me watching and looks up.

I look away, toward the river where Paula and Sally are skinny-dipping, their naked bodies visible in the moonlight, pale against the blackness of the water, their laughter and screams cutting through the low murmur of voices around the patio. The air is thick with the scent of cooked meat, joints, and Raj's home brew. The smell reminds me of something, and I tap Isaac on the arm to ask him what it is.

"Yeah?" he asks without turning to look at me. He and Cera are deep in conversation about how much longer Raj can stretch the remaining meager food supplies without another trip to Pokhara.

I don't answer him. I've remembered what the smell reminds me off. The night we "said good-bye" to Ruth.

I reach for the cup of beer at my feet and swig at it. It tastes of yeast and vinegar, but I swallow it back.

"I need a refill," I say.

Isaac makes no move to stop me, so I stand up, wander back to the door leading to the kitchen, and refill my cup from the barrel outside the doorway. When I look back toward the fire, Leanne has taken my place. She doesn't make space for me as I draw closer, and I'm forced to sit on the edge of the group.

Across the circle, Al rises. She stretches her arms above her head, then cranes her neck to one side, then the other, as though stretching. Our eyes meet, and she angles her head to the right again, only this time the movement is more deliberate—a sharp sideways nod toward the river. She wants to talk to me.

She disappears into the darkness before I can respond.

I move to go after her, but Isaac grabs my hand and yanks me toward him. "Is someone feeling a bit left out?"

Leanne squeals as I trip over her and land in his lap. I try to get back to my feet, but he has his arms around me, nuzzling my cheek with his lips.

"Please." I push at his chest. "I need to go the bathroom."

"I'll tell you when you can go to the bathroom." His voice is light as if he's joking, but there's no denying the unspoken threat. He moves his lips to my mouth and kisses me fiercely as I wriggle desperately in his arms. I need to go down to the river. If I don't, Al will think I don't want to talk to her. She'll think I stayed with Isaac through choice.

"You're no fun." He shoves me away so I tumble against Leanne. Cera laughs. There's a malicious edge to the sound that makes the hairs on my arms prickle.

If she says something, I don't hear it. I'm too busy squinting into the darkness, scanning the riverbank for any sign of Al. "What's the matter?" Isaac slaps my bare calf.

"Nothing."

"No, it's not. You're lying to me. Why? Why are you lying to me?" He peers at me, then looks away, a frown creasing his brow as he surveys the group sitting around the fire. Raj catches his eye and waves, but he ignores him and looks into the distance, toward the river. Did he see Al signaling at me to go down there? Does he know?

"I'm fine, Isaac. I swear. I'm—"

"Don't talk." He presses a finger to my lips and continues to look around. His frown deepens as he glances back toward the house, but when he looks back at me, his expression is jubilant.

"It's Frank, isn't it? You're scared I'm going to let him out of the basement because of the rumor Daisy's been spreading?

Jesus." He bangs himself on the side of his head with one hand. "You told me this morning that you wanted to kill Frank, and I didn't give it a second thought, because I was so focused on getting you to give voice to your negative emotions, and you've been suffering in silence ever since." He pulls me into his arms, crushing me against him. "I'm sorry, Emma."

The scent of musk and sweat on his T-shirt makes me feel sick, but I wrap my arms around his waist and try to relax as he rocks me from side to side.

"I'll make it up to you." He pulls away sharply, his hands on my waist. "I promise."

"What do you mean?"

He shakes his head, a small smile playing on his lips. The sick feeling in my stomach grows, but he strides away, heading for Johan on the other side of the circle before I can say another word.

A gentle tap on my shoulder makes me look up. It's Leanne.

"I'm going to look for Al. I think I saw her head down to the river."

I say nothing. If I speak, I'll cry.

"Emma." Her fingers brush my forearm. "I know you slept with Isaac this morning."

"How?"

"You don't need to know that. But you might want to consider leaving before Daisy finds out."

"I can't go anywhere. The weather's too bad."

"That's a shame." She smiles sweetly. "Because it's not safe for you to stay either."

She drifts away, the hem of her skirt silently sweeping the ash on the patio as she moves.

I got Leanne wrong. She's not a tick bird pecking at a rhino's hide. She's a sea horse—harmless, unusual, cutesy—drifting through our friendship without disturbing anything or anyone until she's right up beside me, and then *snap*, she attacks. What she just said wasn't a dig, and it wasn't a subtle put-down. It was a threat. And I'm not waiting around to find out what it means.

34

I sit up slowly, the beginning of a hangover pulsing in my temples, and push my hair off my face. The air smells of bonfire smoke, meat, and sweat. Leanne is asleep on the mattress next to mine, a white church candle between us, spluttering and spitting as the wick fights to stay lit in a deep pool of wax. Al's asleep on the other side of her, the hood of her sleeping bag pulled up over her head, her mouth ajar as she snores softly. Daisy is spread-eagled on the next mattress along, still wearing her clothes, her sleeping bag rolled up at the end of the bed as though she passed out where she fell. She looks doll-like in her sleep, her long lashes splayed on her cheeks, her short stubby fingernails pressed to her mouth.

Leanne looks so tiny and frail. Without her enormous black-framed glasses, her face looks small and mole-like. Black roots have appeared at the base of her pink bangs. I crept away from the party after her "kindly" word in my ear last night and returned to the girls' dormitory. I crawled into my sleeping bag, still wearing my shorts and tank top, and pulled up the hood, and then I lay awake for hours, sweating beneath thick layers of nylon, polyester, and wool as excited screams and raucous laughter taunted me from the patio.

How had our vacation gone so wrong? We'd arrived at Ekanta Yatra as friends, friends with issues rumbling beneath the smiles and excitement, but ours was a friendship that had outlasted university and survived relocation, jobs, and relationships. Or so I thought. And yet the bonds I'd believed to be so strong were only ever superficial, and like a game of Jenga, all it took was one false move, and everything collapsed.

I reach for the water bottle beside my mattress and shake it. Empty. I wriggle out of my sleeping bag and pad across the dorm to the walkway. The water in the shower block isn't suitable for drinking, and I'm thirsty.

~

I step from the walkway into the hall, the only sound the soft slap of my bare feet on the floorboards and the low rumble of snores emanating from the boys' dormitory, the only light the soft glow of the candle on the table Al overturned last week. It feels like far, far longer than that. I head for the kitchen and the scent of cumin, cardamom, and cinnamon, then pause and glance back toward Isaac's study. The door is wide open, the room deserted. The desk has been pushed back against the window, the rug piled in a crumpled heap beside it. Books, papers, and shoes litter the floor, haphazardly framing a dark hole in the ground to the left of the desk.

My breath catches in my throat and I freeze.

The hatch door is open.

I want to look away, but I can't. I can't do anything other than stare at the black square less than ten feet away from me.

Where's Frank?

From the state of the room, he either left in a hurry or there was a struggle getting him out. The curtains beyond the hatch billow into the room as a gust of wind from the open window lifts them into the air, and several sheets of paper skid along the floor and settle by the open doorway. Without thinking, I take a step forward and reach out for the one nearest to me. My hands are shaking so much, it takes me two attempts to pick it up.

It's an email from Leanne to Isaac, dated April 15, three and a half months before we came out here.

> Dear Isaac,
>
> I've written this email half a dozen times and then deleted it and started again. This time I'm going to write what I feel and just send it; otherwise, I'm never going to reply to you, and I can't do that, not when it's taken me so long to find you.
>
> Isaac, I spent my whole childhood feeling lost and unsettled, like a piece of me was missing. Of course, I couldn't verbalize it like that as a child. I just felt "sad" a lot.

I glance up, half expecting to see Frank looming at me through the shadows, but the study is still deserted, the hatch an empty hole in the ground. I try to lick my lips, but there's no saliva in my mouth.

> To find out I had a half brother made sense. It explained everything—the void in my chest, the pang of loneliness that seemed to follow me about everywhere I went, and the abiding feeling that my whole family was keeping a secret from me. I don't think Mom would ever have told me if she hadn't been drunk. I won't repeat her exact words, Isaac, because I don't want to hurt you, but she was maudlin and angry, and she thought it would hurt me.
>
> She was wrong. By telling me about you, she

gave me a gift. A brother. A brother she'd given away because my asshole of a father couldn't deal with the fact that Mom had been with someone else. Mom didn't—wouldn't—tell me where you were, but I got in touch with the Salvation Army, and they helped me trace you. One of your friends in Aberdeen told them you'd started a retreat in Nepal called Ekanta Yatra. I cried when I saw the website and there was no photo of you.

Isaac, I can't begin to tell you how sorry I am, how angry, how much I hate...

I stop reading and grab the other piece of paper by my feet. It's another email from Leanne to Isaac; this one is dated May 12.

Dear Bro (sorry, I know it's cheesy, but I love being able to call you that),

Amazing to hear from you, as always. I can't begin to tell you how ridiculously excited I am about my trip to Nepal. You asked if I could bring some friends with me so they can help spread the word about Ekanta Yatra when we get back. My God, I'd love to! I definitely want Al to come; I think she'd get a lot out of the experience. Daisy too. I think you'd love her. She's so effervescent and fun that...

I want to read more, but it's too risky to stay here. I dart into the study and scoop up more pieces of paper, never looking away from the hatch for more than a split second, then sprint back out of the room and slip into the kitchen. I keep the door ajar to let some of the candlelight from the hall into the room, but it's gloomier in here, and I have to squint to make out what's written on the pages.

Dear Isaac,

Me again! You wanted some background info about my friends to aid their sessions with you. My pleasure!

Al's twenty-five. She's from Croydon, and she works in a call center. She used to have a brother named Tommy, but he died in a motorbike accident when he was eighteen and she was fifteen. She feels really guilty about it, because she came out to their parents the day before, and they reacted really badly, so she ran away. Tommy went after her, but he was driving too fast and was hit by a car pulling out from a T junction. They took him to the hospital, and for a while, they thought he might pull through, but it wasn't to be. He spoke his last words to Al—"I'll always love you, Sis"—and that means a lot to her. She's quite a spiritual person in her own way—she believes in ghosts and psychics—but she's very dismissive about organized religion and even yoga and meditation, which she thinks is "hippie bullshit" (sorry, I'm sure you can convince her otherwise!).

My other friend is Daisy. I think you'll love her! She's twenty-five too, and she's the poshest person I've ever met. Like Al, she's lost a sibling—that was the thing that really drew them to each other, when they realized they'd both suffered a loss—but her situation was very different. She was five when her one-year-old sister Melody died. They were sharing a bath together, and her mom popped out of the room to get a towel from the laundry basket in the master bedroom. I don't know what happened. Sometimes, when she's drunk, Daisy says that Melody reached for a toy on the other side of the bath and slipped and banged her head on the taps and fell into the water. Sometimes she says she was trying to teach Melody how to swim underwater, and she didn't realize her sister had stopped holding her breath. Sometimes she says she got out of the bath to try to find her mom, and when they returned, they found Melody facedown. I think that, deep down, Daisy does know what happened to Melody, but she's fabricated different scenarios either to assuage her guilt or increase it. As if what happened wasn't terrible enough, her mother blamed her for Melody's death. She accused Daisy of being jealous of the new baby and deliberately hurting her. Six months later, Daisy's mom killed herself. I don't know why, but I can't help thinking that, deep down, Daisy's always blamed herself for that too. Oh, Isaac, it's so heartbreaking. To meet Daisy, you'd never know she'd been through something so awful. She's so cheery and full of life, but she's carrying a terrible burden.

The other person you'll meet is Emma. Emma is Daisy's best friend. Theirs is a friendship I've never really understood. They're like chalk and cheese. While Daisy is the life and soul of the party, Emma is the killjoy in the corner pointing out that people have been putting out cigarette butts in the potted plants.

Fucking bitch. At least I mingle at parties, unlike Leanne, who clings to Al and Daisy as though her life depends on it. I stifle my indignation and keep reading.

Emma's a weak, needy person with no backbone, and she can't make a decision without running it past Daisy first. But whereas Daisy has tried to put her tragic past behind her, Emma wears her "tragedy" like a badge. She takes antianxiety pills for the panic attacks she's had since she had an abortion when she was seventeen, and doesn't everyone know it. She says the pills keep the panic attacks in check, but weirdly, they seem to stop working whenever she needs attention. I've lost count of the number of times Daisy's canceled nights out with Al and me because Emma needs someone to sit at home with her and stroke her back while she pretends she's having trouble catching her breath. I'd like to see what would happen if someone chucked her bloody pills in the trash and forced her to...

The letter ends suddenly, midsentence. I turn it over, but it's blank on the back. The second half of the email must still be on the floor in Isaac's room.

I sneak out of the kitchen, cross the hall, and step back into the Isaac's study. I crouch down to pick up a sheet of paper on the floor near the bookcase.

Dear Isaac,

I can't wait to join you at Ekanta Yatra. There's nothing here for me anymore and, other than Al and Daisy, no reason to stay. I know they'll want to stay too once they get there. Your community sounds like the kind of family I've been looking for all my life. It sounds like the kind of life we've all craved...

I pick up another sheet of paper, then another, then another. More emails from Leanne, earlier than the last one, telling him about her life and her dreams and ambitions. Another one telling him about their mother and her alcoholism. From the dates on the emails, it looks like she was writing to Isaac for over six months, at least three emails a week. There are no replies from him. Given that there's no Internet connection here, he must have trekked down to Pokhara every week or couple of weeks, logged on to the Internet at a café, and printed out all his emails.

There are still four or five pieces of paper scattered among the books and magazines at the far end of the room, next to the window. To read them means passing the hatch. I glance back into the hallway, then dart forward. I pick up two, three, four print-outs, and then I hear it, a low, rattling cough, too loud to originate in one of the dormitories. I toss the emails away, then slip behind the curtain and press myself up against the open window as the *slap-slap-slap* of flip-flops on wood reverberates through the hallway.

Please don't let it be Isaac. Please don't let it be—

"What the fuck?"

It's a man's voice. A man standing in the doorway of the study. But it's not Isaac. It's Johan.

~

I drop silently out of the open study window and press myself up against the house, my heart thudding in my chest, my fingertips vibrating against the stone wall. The study floorboards creak, and I take the smallest of steps to my left. If Johan looks out of the window now, he'll see me. A small circle of light, barely visible between the trees, bobs jerkily from side to side down by the huts. I step toward it, then stop. What if it's Frank? What if he escaped, and the light is his flashlight? A gust of wind courses through the yard, bringing with it the low, muffled roar of men shouting. One of the voices is Isaac's. Above me, Johan swears under his breath, and I make my decision. I run.

I sprint across the patio and head down the bank toward the

orchard. I slow down as I pick my way through the trees, stepping carefully to avoid knotty roots and sharp stones, then duck down behind a thick, thorny lavender bush when I spot a group of men standing on the bank of the river. There are four of them: Isaac, Kane, and Gabe have their backs to me, and Gabe is shining a flashlight on the fourth man—Frank, who's on his knees in front of them, his hands bound behind his back.

"You're fucking insane!"

His shout drifts over, carried by the wind.

He shouts again, his head turned toward Isaac. "You can't just lock someone in your basement. That's false imprisonment. It's kidnapping. It's illegal!"

"So's attempted rape."

"Bullshit it was rape! This place is a fucking whore house. She was up for it."

There is a loud thump, like the sound of a football being kicked, and Frank topples to his left. He lies still for a couple of minutes, the side of his face pressed into the mud, then he wriggles and twists his way back onto his knees.

"Fuck you, Isaac."

Thump! Isaac kicks him again. This time, when Frank gets back onto his knees, a slow stream of blood flows from his temple to his jaw.

"Say that again," Isaac says, lifting the ax in his right hand. The blade glints in the light of Gabe's flashlight.

Frank shakes his head.

Thump! Isaac kicks him again. "Talk! Come on, Mr. Mouthy. Share your fucking insightful thoughts with the group!"

This time, Frank doesn't bother getting up. Instead, he twists onto his back, spits toward the river, then looks up at Isaac as a dark shape speeds toward them from the bridge. Gabe raises the flashlight as the man draws near. It's Johan.

The tall Swede steps between Isaac and Frank and holds up his hands. "I just came from your study. Whatever you're planning on doing, don't."

Isaac steps around him as though he's invisible. "Come on, then, Frank. If you're such a fucking expert on the way we do things, why don't you share your observations with us?"

Frank shifts into a sitting position and nods toward Johan as though thanking him for his intervention. "Fine. If you want to know, Isaac, I'll tell you. This place isn't a retreat. It isn't some idyllic haven for eco-warriors. It's a fucking joke and a sham. What's up, Isaac? Got small dick syndrome, have you? Is that why you need everyone to suck it? I know what you do to the girls. Don't think I haven't seen the marks around Paula's wrists, and you've got the nerve to call me a fucking rapist!"

Isaac flies at him, but Johan grabs him before he can reach Frank, scooping Isaac up around the middle and lifting him off his feet.

"Get your fucking hands off me, you Swedish twat." Isaac twists in his arms and punches him in the side of the head, forcing him to let go.

"I'm going to the papers," Frank continues, "as soon as I get back to the UK. They'll have a fucking field day with you, and then MI5 or Scotland Yard or whatever fucking establishment deals with scum like you will come over here and drag your lying, kidnapping, violent ass to prison."

Gabe angles the flashlight from Frank to Isaac. He's standing sideways to the group now, a wide smile on his face.

"What makes you think you're going to go back to the UK, Frank?"

"Because I'm not staying here, you twat." Frank squirms back onto his knees, and the light flashes back to him. There's more blood on the side of his head now.

"That's funny, because you don't look like you're going anywhere in a hurry."

"Isaac." Johan shoots him a warning look, then takes a step toward Frank. He crouches down in front of him, his elbows on his knees, his hands folded under his chin.

"You won't say anything, will you, Frank? You'll just quietly find your way back to Pokhara and disappear."

Frank peers up at Johan through his good eye. A second passes, then another. Finally, he clears his throat.

"Fuck you!" He spits straight in Johan's face. "Fuck all of you."

"Move," Isaac says.

Johan turns toward him but stays crouched.

"I told you to fucking move."

"No." He stands up and takes a step toward Isaac. The two men stand face-to-face, barely an inch separating them.

"If I have to take you out, Johan, I will."

Gabe and Kane say nothing. They stare silently, their shoulders hunched with apprehension. Gabe's arm is outstretched, the flashlight in his hand pointing toward the two founding Ekanta Yatra members, their silhouettes haloed with light.

"Let me go, you fucking prick," Frank shouts from the ground, "or I'll fuck that skanky skeleton of a sister of yours too."

Isaac moves like a blur. One minute, Johan is in front of him; the next, he is sprawled on the ground, unbalanced by a shove to the chest. Isaac leaps forward, the ax raised in the air. As he lands, he brings the ax down, and Frank screams.

It is the sound of an animal being slaughtered.

His body reels backward, and he slumps in the mud, his head turned to one side, a deep, black pool of liquid fanning out around him. His face is black too, his features obscured by the blood gushing out of the gaping hole in the side of his skull.

"You fucking asshole." Johan springs to his feet and launches himself at Isaac, toppling him with a rugby tackle around the waist. The two men hit the ground with a thump, then Johan is up again, astride Isaac, and he's punching him in the head—once, twice, three times—and Isaac's head rocks from side to side, but his right hand reaches for the ax, and he lifts it into the air. My gasp of horror is masked by Kane's shout.

As the two men freeze, Kane rips the ax from Isaac's hand.

Isaac leaps to his feet and holds out his hand. "Give it to me."

Kane shakes his head. "You fucking killed him, man." He grabs Gabe's wrist and points the flashlight at Frank's body. "He's dead."

"And?" Isaac takes another step toward Kane, his hand still outstretched. "If you've got a problem with what just happened, you know where the front gate is."

Kane shakes his head. "I just didn't want you braining Johan, Isaac, that's all."

"Good." Isaac reaches for the ax and takes it. He looks at Johan. "What about you?"

"You shouldn't have killed him."

"And what should I have done? Let him go down to Pokhara and contact the authorities? Let that dick weasel bring Ekanta Yatra to its knees?"

"No. But I could have talked him out of it. I just needed to get him on our side. A few joints, a few beers, a few chats; ask one of the girls to fuck him. I could have turned him."

Isaac laughs dryly. "Like you did with that fat dyke, you mean?"

He's talking about Al.

"She's still here, isn't she?"

Isaac shrugs. "Until the next time she tries to leave. And how many people will she take with her then? I don't like her, and I don't trust her. And if she smashes anything else up, I'll kill her myself."

"We need her, Isaac. You said yourself that we need more members."

"Not if they're going to cause trouble."

"So what's the plan? Are you going to send her to Pokhara like you did Ruth? Is that what happens to women who won't sleep with you? You get Gabe to—"

"Don't fucking go there, Johan."

"Guys!" Kane raises his hands. "Let's not—"

"Tell you what," Isaac says as Johan crosses his arms over his chest and heads in the direction of the house. "You keep fucking who I tell you you can fuck, and keep your dick out of my business." He raises his voice as Johan moves into the distance. "I'll let you know when it's your turn with Emma."

It's all I can do to keep breathing.

"Right, then." Isaac strolls over to Frank's body and prods his head with the end of the ax. It flops onto his shoulder, and something thick and viscous oozes out of the wound in his skull. "What are we going to do with this fucker? I suggest we chop off his head and bring it to the next meeting. Tell everyone he tried to escape and the Maoists lopped it over the fence?" He laughs. "Who wants to do it?"

Gabe reaches for the ax. "Me."

35

I t's been a week since I was knocked off my bike, and other than the yellowing bruises on my face and body, it's starting to feel like a remote, horrible nightmare. Will insisted I stay in bed for twenty-four hours after we drove back to his house, and he and Chloe took turns bringing me drinks, snacks, and entertainment. He even popped over to my cottage to pick up my TV and DVD player so he could install them at the end of the bed.

"Now you can finish watching *Battlestar Galactica*," he said, whipping the DVD out from under his jacket and making me smile for the first time in what felt like forever.

He insisted that I hand my cell phone over to him.

"You'll drive yourself mad," he said as he tucked it into his back pocket, "checking and rechecking it to see if there's been any new messages or texts. The police said they'd be in touch once they've traced where the messages originated from."

"But—"

"If the police call, or you get any weird messages, I'll give it back to you. And if there's anything really dodgy, we'll call Officer

Barnham. I promise. But I don't want you to worry, Jane. I just want you to get well. We both do."

At first, I welcomed the warmth and safety of Will's cozy home and the weekend filled with continuous replays of *Frozen* and lessons in how to create loom bracelets, but after a week, I found myself yearning for Green Fields Animal Shelter. I missed my dogs. I missed the clean, feed, and walk routine of my days. I missed the freedom of walking them through the fields and the feeling of fresh air on my face and in my lungs. I started to feel stifled, as though whoever was responsible for the texts and messages had succeeded in taking me away from the one thing that made me feel content and fulfilled.

Will was resigned when I told him I was going back to work—he'd seen it coming—but he insisted on dropping me off on my first morning back. Not that I have any other choice—my bike was trashed, and the alternative is a four-mile walk from Will's house.

"You'll take it easy, won't you?" After parking outside Green Fields, he leans over and kisses me on the cheek. "If you feel unwell, just give me a call, and I'll come collect you."

"I'll be fine. And if I'm not, don't worry: Sheila or one of the others will run me home. Look, there's Angharad." I gesture at the black VW Polo pulling into the yard. "I'd better go." I open the passenger door, then look back at Will. "And thank you, for everything."

"Least I could do. We both love you, you know." He glances away, his cheeks coloring as he registers what he just said. It's the first time either of us have used the word "love." Neither of us says anything for several seconds. "Anyway"—he turns the key in the engine—"I'll pick you up later, Jane. Have a good day."

"You too." I slam the door shut, and he pulls away.

I continue to stare after his car long after it's turned the corner and disappeared back down the lane. He's not the sort of man to use a word like "love" in a throwaway context, but ten days ago, before Chloe's summer fair, he was asking for space—some time to process everything. If I hadn't had my accident, would we even be talking now? There have been moments, countless moments over the last week while he's been looking after me, when I've felt perilously close to telling Will that I love him. But I'm too scared. Not because I think he's got anything to do with the accident or the messages, but because it's been so long since I truly trusted anyone. My barriers have been up for so many years that I don't know if I'm even capable of bringing them down anymore. There's a part of me that thinks it was wrong of me to accept Will's offer to stay with him and Chloe. If Officer Barnham is right and the person who ran me off the road was deliberately trying to harm me, then I'm putting Will and Chloe at risk.

I turn away from the road and return Angharad's wave as she gets out of her car.

~

"Have you got a minute, Jane?"

I stop typing and glance around. Sheila is peering around the door of the staff room. "What's up?"

"Nothing urgent. I just want a chat, that's all."

"Do you want to read the ad I just wrote for Willow for our Facebook page? I'm desperate to find her a home. She's been here too long."

"I know. I'll take a look at it in a second." She nods toward reception. "Could you come with me? It won't take long."

"Okay." I wheel the chair back from the desk and stand up. "Is this about the dry food order? I was going to put it in this morning, but I needed to—"

"It's not about the food." Sheila takes me by the elbow and

guides me down the corridor toward reception. I stop short when a dozen beaming faces stare back at me from across the counter. "It's about you and how we wanted to do something to help after your accident."

"Sheila—"

"No, don't say anything." She scans the crowd of faces in front of us and frowns. "Where's Angharad?"

Everyone looks around blankly. Several people shrug their shoulders.

"Never mind," Sheila says. "We'll have to start without her. So, Jane." She squeezes my elbow. "We know how much you loved your blue bike, so we took up a collection, and, well, it's not exactly the same, but we hope you like it." She waves at Barry, who's standing outside the glass double doors. He disappears around the corner, then reappears pushing a beautiful blue mountain bike. Claire opens the doors for him, and the crowd parts as he pushes it into reception.

"I put it together myself," he says proudly. "It's one of those kit bikes you can get. Made one for my grandson last Christmas. They're very sturdy."

"Barry, Sheila, everyone..." I press my hand to my mouth and inhale deeply through my nose to stop myself from crying.

"It's okay." Sheila clasps my shoulder and pulls me into her side. "You don't have to thank us. We just wanted you to know how much we appreciate what you do for Green Fields, and it really hasn't been the same without you over the last week. We have missed you, you know—especially Barry." She winks lasciviously, and everyone laughs.

"I missed you too, Barry," I say, and everyone laughs again. "Seriously, thank you all so much."

"Take it for a ride!" someone shouts.

"The bike or Barry?" someone else shouts, and as the room explodes with laughter, Sheila lifts up the reception counter, and Barry wheels the bike toward me. Thirty seconds later, I'm riding around the yard, being applauded like a five-year-old who's just had their training wheels removed. Sheila has the biggest smile on her face as I ride around and around, but there's tension in her cheeks and worry in her eyes. She told me when I came in that Gary Fullerton and Rob Archer both have alibis for the night that Green Fields was broken into but that a car had been found abandoned in a pull off on the outskirts of town. It had been stolen earlier that evening. Whoever broke into Green Fields that night is still out there.

~

My ears ring with the sound of applause and laughter as I walk back through reception and down the corridor, but it's the worried look in Sheila's eyes that haunts me. I was *sure* Gary Fullerton or Rob Archer must have been behind the break-in.

"Oh!" I stop short in the doorway to the staff room, and Angharad, sitting in the chair in front of the computer, visibly jumps, then, lightning fast, shuts down whatever file she was looking at, snatches something from the USB drive, and twists around to look at me.

"Sorry, Jane. I was just... I was..." Her gaze flits around the room. "I was just checking my email. I...I...um...I've been waiting to hear back from a job I applied for, and with all of you out in the yard, I thought...I..."

"But you know employed staff are the only ones allowed to use the computers, don't you? It's Green Fields's policy. Sheila will have explained that to you in your induction."

"She did, and yes, I do; I do know that. But I was just passing, and the computer was on and..." She pauses and looks down at her hands. "I'm sorry, Jane. I was desperate. I haven't been able to concentrate all morning."

Her phone is on the table next to the mouse. It's a top-of-the-line Android model. I remember her showing it to me on her first day when she was telling me what great photos it takes.

"Couldn't you have checked your email on your phone? I thought you had 3G. That's what you said."

"I have but"—she reaches for her phone and shoves it into her pocket—"I'm out of data for this month."

"There are some very sensitive files on the computer, Angharad. Case histories, evidence for court, reports from the animal behaviorist, that sort of thing. We can't let just anyone—"

"I know, and I only accessed my Yahoo mail. I promise." She jumps up from the chair and crosses the room toward me. "Please, Jane, don't say anything to Sheila. It was a one-off. I promise."

She holds out her hands imploringly. Her cheeks are flushed and her eyes shining—either with excitement or adrenaline, I can't be sure.

"I don't know, Angharad." I shake my head. "I really have to say—"

I'm interrupted by the tinkling tune of my cell phone. I reach into my pocket and pull it out as Angharad continues to step from foot to foot, wringing her hands in front of her. The call is from an unknown number.

"Hello?" I press the phone to my ear.

There's a pause, then, "Emma, is that you? It's Al."

~

"Al?" The world stills, and the only thing I'm aware of is the banging of my heart in my chest. "*Al?*" A look of curiosity crosses Angharad's face, and I wave her away. "I'll see you back in the compound in five minutes. The blankets and dog toys need washing, if you could do that."

"But…"

"Five minutes."

I step into the staff room and gesture for her to leave. She hesitates, then slips past me, her eyes trained on the phone in my hand as she leaves the room. I close the door behind her.

"Sorry," Al says in my ear. "Do you want me to call back in five minutes or something?"

"No, no." I cross the room and drop onto the desk chair as my legs give way beneath me. "Fuck, Al. I can't believe it's you."

"I know." She laughs dryly. "It's been a long time, Emma."

"What... How... Did you get my Facebook message?"

"Yeah, literally five minutes ago. I haven't used my Facebook account in years, and then... What the fuck's going on, Emma? Someone from CSI called me this morning; that's why I checked it. They said you'd been involved in an accident, and they wanted to know where I was in the early hours of Tuesday morning last week. They asked if we'd been in touch. I said I hadn't spoken to you for years."

"Someone ran me off the road," I say. "I was on my bike, and a car hit me. They think it might have been deliberate."

"And they think I did it?"

"No, I... They asked me to give them a list of people who might have grudges against me, and I..." I run a hand over my face. "We fell out about the article you sold, and—"

"Oh, for fuck's sake, Emma." She sighs heavily. "That was four years ago. Four years! I told you, the journalist twisted my words. You don't seriously think I'd try to hurt you because of an argument we had four years ago?"

"No, of course I don't. I—"

"And what's all this shit about Daisy being alive? Emma..." She sighs again, only this time, she sounds exhausted. "I've tried so hard to put all that behind me. I've got a new life in Brighton. I'm with an amazing girl, Liz. We got engaged last month. I've got a good job with Amex, and I don't totally hate it, and life is...

It's okay. It's good. That's not to say I don't think about what happened. I do. But sometimes I forget too. And it feels good. I feel good. I feel..."

"Normal," I say.

"Yeah."

Neither of us says anything for several seconds.

"Someone's been pretending to be Daisy," I say. "They've been sending me messages on Facebook. They said they were cold, that I'd abandoned her, that I'd left her for dead. Then, after the accident, I got a text message from someone saying 'Only the good die young. That'll explain why you're still alive, then.'"

Al says nothing.

"Al? Are you still there?"

"Yeah, I heard what you said. I was just... Emma, has it occurred to you that maybe it's some sick Internet troll? You hear about this sort of thing all the time—people writing sick things on the memorial pages for people who've been murdered or died tragically. They do it to get a reaction, and you're giving them that."

"I haven't."

"So you didn't reply?"

"Well, yes. I asked who it was and why they were doing it."

"So you reacted. And then they upped their game a bit and found your cell phone number on the web and sent you that text."

"How could they have found out my cell phone number? I changed it when I came here, and I've never put it on the Internet. Apart from in my direct message to you, which was private."

"Doesn't matter. There are sites that you can pay to get some-one's details. They masquerade as a service to help reunite you with long-lost family, but it's basically a stalking service. If you've got someone's name and date of birth, that's all you need."

"How do you know this?"

She sighs. "Remember Simone? How do you think I found out

where her girlfriend lived? If you've got the money, Emma, you can find pretty much anyone."

"But I didn't receive any text messages until after the hit-and-run. It seems too much of a coincidence to get a text message about dying young on the same day as I'm knocked off my bike. "

"Coincidences happen."

"The police don't seem to think so."

"That's because it's their job to take this kind of shit seriously. Can you imagine the backlash in the press if something did happen to you and they'd dismissed your concerns? Listen, Emma." Al lowers her voice. "You need to be careful about what you say to the police, especially what you say to them about me. I did what I did to protect you." Her voice is little more than a whisper.

"I know."

"Some sicko is trying to freak you out, and they're succeeding. You're jumping at shadows. The police have started asking questions, and who knows where this will lead? I don't want to go to prison, Emma."

"But this person knows where I work! They know my cell phone number. What if they know where I live too?"

"So leave. Move."

"I can't."

"Why not?"

I want to tell her that I don't want to leave because I like my life here. I like being Jane Hughes. I like working at Green Fields, and I... The sudden realization twists my heart: I love the life I'm building with Will. If I leave, I'll have nothing. I'll be nothing. I'll have to reinvent myself and start all over again.

"I want to help you," Al says, and there's steel in her voice, "but you need to calm down. Everyone who might possibly want to hurt you is dead."

"And you're sure of that?"

"Yes."

She's so convincing, so sure, and I want to believe her. I so desperately want to believe her.

"Give me a call on this number if anything else happens," she says. "Okay?"

"Okay."

There's a long pause, and then she says, "Ever wish you could rewind time, Emma?"

"Every day."

The line goes dead, and I sit still for the longest time, gazing at the floor, then twist around in my chair and move the computer mouse with my hand. The screen flickers to life, and almost as though on autopilot, I move the cursor to the Start button and then to the list of recent documents. I scroll down the list, looking for the last document I was working on, before realizing with a start that it's not at the top of the list—it's midway down. Above it are at least half a dozen documents I didn't open, including JaneHughesCV.doc, JaneHughesAppraisal.doc, and StaffContactList.doc. Angharad wasn't just checking her email; she was checking up on me.

36

A l! Al! Wake up!" I shake her shoulder gently. My lips almost graze her ear. Her hair smells of bonfire, cigarettes, and beer. Less than half a yard away, Daisy is lying on her back, snoring softly. The girls' dormitory is littered with comatose bodies, some of them still in their clothes, their sleeping bags bundled up as makeshift pillows under their heads.

"Al." I nudge her again. She moans softly and swipes at my hand, then rolls over.

There's a bang, somewhere in the depths of the house.

"Al!" I put my hand over her mouth and pinch the fleshy skin on the back of her arm. "Al, you need to wake up."

She wakes with a start and grabs at my hands.

"It's just me. It's Emma." I take my hand away from her mouth. "I need to talk to you."

"Emma?" Her voice is groggy with sleep.

"Shh!" I press a finger to my lips as she sits up, and then I point toward the door to the shower block.

She understands and rises slowly, climbing out of her sleeping bag and grabbing a hoodie from the pile of clothes draped over her backpack, and then she makes her way toward the door. I follow, picking my way through slumbering women. When we reach the entrance to the shower block, Al pauses. I point toward the stall at the far end of the block, and she nods.

"What the fuck's going on?" she whispers as I shut the stall door behind us. "I thought you were trying to suffocate me." She pulls her hoodie over her head.

"We need to get out of here."

"Why?" She glances toward a gap in the corrugated roof. There's a smudge of scarlet light beyond it. The sun is coming up. In less than half an hour, it will be daylight, and we'll stand no chance.

"They killed Frank."

"What the fu—"

I press a hand over her mouth for the second time. "Shh. Shh. Promise me you won't shout again."

She nods, and I let go.

"They…" I fight to keep my breathing steady. "They had Frank on his knees, tied up. He was mouthing off about how he was going to go back to the UK and report them to the authorities. Isaac kept kicking him and kicking him. Johan tried to stop him, but then Frank made a comment about Leanne, and Isaac hit him. They decapitated him with the wood ax, Al. He's out there now, on the banks of the river. There's blood everywhere."

"Jesus." Her eyes are wide with fright.

"Listen." I grab her shoulder. "We need to go. Isaac said something to Johan about telling him when it was his turn to 'have a go' at me, and they said something about you too. I don't know what Isaac's planning, but we have to leave. Fuck the mud and rain. We have to get out."

"How do I know I can trust you, Emma?"

"What?"

She inches away, toward the stall door, keeping her back against the planks. "You slept with Isaac."

"I know, and I regret it."

"You regret it? That's it? A little shrug of the shoulders and 'Oh well'? Emma, have you seen Paula's back?"

I shake my head.

"Isaac whipped her. He tied her up in a shed, whipped her, and called it a detox. How can you not know this? Have you been walking around with your eyes shut the last two weeks?"

"I knew she was in a hut, and I saw the marks on her wrists, but—"

"You slept with him anyway?"

"Yes! No! I didn't know—"

"Stop." She presses her hands to her head and closes her eyes. "This place is doing my fucking head in. Leanne's telling me one thing, you're telling me another, and Daisy's just fucking hysterical."

"That's the other thing. I just found some emails between Leanne and Isaac. She's his half—"

There's a loud creak from the dorm, and I shoot Al a warning look. We stare at the closed stall door and listen. Someone in the dorm coughs, and there's another creak, then the almost imperceptible sound of a door squeaking on its hinges.

I barely notice the smell at first, and then it's everywhere—smoke, sweat, musk, and blood. I look at Al. She stares back at me. Her face is pale, the circles under her eyes purple bruises against her white skin.

"Isaac," I mouth.

Two things happen at once: the stall door slams open, and Al launches herself at me. She kisses me violently, pressing me against the stall wall. I try to wriggle away, but she pins herself against me as her hands roam over my waist and hips. I feel her tug at the pocket of my pants, and something sharp presses against my right hip. She yanks my hand away as I reach for it.

"Well, well, well." Isaac's laugh is dry. "Now there's something

I didn't expect to see." He yanks Al away from me. "Dirty dyke!" he chastises, waggling a finger in her face, a dangerous smile on his lips. "You need to wait your bloody turn. And you"—he slips his hand underneath my hair and grips the back of my neck—"I've got something I want to show you."

I catch a glimpse of Al, peering out of the shower stall as Isaac angles me toward the doorway to the girls' dormitory.

"I trust you," she mouths.

37

T hat wasn't what it looked like." I try to twist away from Isaac as he leads me through the girls' dormitory and out onto the walkway, but his grip on the back of my neck is viselike.

"What did it look like?" he asks, steering me through the hallway and out of the back door.

I don't know what to say, so I say nothing as he marches me across the patio, down the yard, and through the orchard. I don't know how to explain what just happened, because I don't understand it myself—although, from the sharp pain in my right leg, a pain that increases each time I take a step, I'm fairly certain the kiss was a way to mask the fact that Al slipped something into my pocket.

As the waterfall roars in the distance and we approach the river, I'm gripped with a new terror. What are we doing down here? Does Isaac know I saw what happened with Frank? Did he see me run away?

"Are you ready?" he asks as we cross over the bridge.

"Ready?"

"For your detox."

My leg spasms with pain as he pulls me toward the huts, and I plunge a hand into my pocket to press my thigh, where the pain is the worst. Instead of feeling the soft yield of my cotton shorts, my fingers close over something else. Something cold and hard. The knife Al put there.

~

"Isaac, no." I lean back, jamming my heels into the ground, the skin around my wrist twisting as I try to wrench it out of his grip. "I don't want to."

He turns the key in the lock. "You don't know what's going to happen yet."

I cry out as he throws open the door to the hut and yanks me inside, but the sound only lasts as long as it takes for him to clamp a muffling hand to my mouth. He holds me against him as he turns the key in the lock with his free hand.

"Emma," he says as I twist and wriggle and pull and push and attempt to unbalance him. "You need to calm down. I don't want to hurt you, but I will if I have to."

"That's it," he says as I stop fighting. He holds me tightly for several seconds, then slowly lets go of me and angles me so he's standing with his back to the door and I'm in front of him. The door is ajar behind him, a sliver of sunrise lifting the gloom of the hut. "Are you calm now?"

I nod, but my hands are clenched at my sides.

"Light the candle." He hands me a lighter and watches as I turn and light the large white church candle on the table to my right.

As the gloom lifts, he pulls his T-shirt over his head and drops it to the floor.

He looks at me steadily, almost daring me to glance away. His chest, his arms, and his stomach are striped with scars— thick, thin, long, short, raised, flat. There isn't a patch of skin on his upper torso that hasn't been cut, slashed, hacked, or carved. So that's why he wouldn't let me take his T-shirt off when we had sex.

"Are you shocked?" His voice is barely louder than a whisper.

"Yes."

"Would you believe me if I told you it didn't hurt? Because it didn't, you know." He takes a step closer to me and reaches for the string at the waist of my cotton shorts.

"I'll do it," I say, untying the string and slipping my shorts down to the floor. I step out of them, picking them up and keeping the ball of material scrunched up in my hand.

"It's a natural progression," Isaac says, dropping to his knees and pushing my underwear to my ankles. "Once you've lost your attachments to people and things, the next step is to learn how to detach from your own body. It's incredible"—he kisses my belly—"to be able to mentally overcome pain. Absolutely incredible. You'll be blown away, Emma, by how much your mind can accomplish."

His lips travel from my stomach to my hip bone then to the top of my thigh.

I fumble with my balled-up shorts, searching for the knife. They feel too soft, too yielding. Where is it? Did it fall out when I was trying to get away from Isaac outside? I partially unfold the shorts, but there's nothing but soft cotton in my hands.

"Before the pain, a little pleasure." Isaac plunges his fingers inside me, and I stumble to my right, smacking the shorts against the table as I try to keep my balance. The fruit knife slips from the bundle of material and clatters onto the surface. It spins around and around in slow motion.

Isaac looks up. His eyes widen as he spots the knife, and he reaches a hand toward the table.

I grab it first and, without pausing to think, bring it down against the side of his head. It slips from my hand as it makes contact with his cheekbone. As he roars with pain and reels to the side, I leap for the door.

There are lights on in the house now. People are awake.

"Oh, no you don't."

The air is squeezed from my lungs as one arm grips me around the stomach and the other around the throat, and I am pulled back into the hut. Isaac lifts me as though I'm weightless and then spins me around before forcing me against the back wall, facing the rough wood. One by one, he grabs hold of leather bonds and uses them to attach first my left wrist, then my right wrist to the metal hoops in the corners of the ceiling.

"Isaac, stop! Stop!" I pull at the restraints, but they are bound too tightly—leather cuffs buckled around my wrists with strong brass clasps and attached to the metal hoops. My ankles are strapped too. I am spread-eagled against the back wall of the hut, my face pressed against the cold wood.

"You stupid bitch." He touches the side of his head. There's a dark mass in his hairline. He scratches at it, digging in his nails until the blood runs free again and dribbles down the side of his face. He swipes at it with his palm, then slowly, deliberately, wipes his hand over my face. My nostrils are flooded with the scent of iron and salt.

"You had to make this difficult, didn't you?" he asks as he steps out of my line of sight, and I hear what sounds like a metal box being dragged across the floor. "Ah, well." He sighs deeply. "It looks like we'll have to do this the hard way."

I hear the crack of the whip before I feel it. At first there is nothing—no discomfort, just the sharp sensation of being slapped on the back—then the burn bites at my skin, and I howl with pain.

He cracks the whip again.

I screw my eyes tightly shut, curl my toes, and clench my fists. To begin with, I count the strokes—one, two, three, four, five—and then I focus on the candle, flickering violently on the table whenever he raises the whip in the air.

38

There's a creak as the hut door opens, followed by the low rumble of a man clearing his throat. I don't turn my head to see who it is; I don't even open my eyes. I stay where I am, huddled in a heap on the floor, pressed against the back wall. My wrists have been released from the leather bonds, but they burn as if I'm still tied up.

"Is she good?" the man asks as an icy blast of air hits me.

"Finished about half an hour ago."

"So can I have a go?"

"On the whip or her?"

Isaac and the other man laugh. I don't understand why, and I don't care. They may as well be a million miles away.

"What are you doing here?" Isaac asks.

"Isis said something about another Pokhara run. You didn't mention it to me."

"Didn't I? Must have forgotten."

"What about her?"

"Emma? You're lucky if I let you shag anyone ever again after the shit you pulled with Frank."

"You promised I'd be next, Isaac."

"That was before you threw a fist in my face."

"You said there would be no more deaths."

"Fuck off, Johan. We've already talked about this."

"Yeah, but—"

"You heard what I said. I'll let you know when she's ready, you dirty, fucking Swede. Haven't you got turnips to fertilize or something?"

There is a click as the door shuts, and then everything goes black.

~

The next time I open my eyes, Isaac has gone, and it's pitch-black inside the hut, apart from a shallow pool of light at the base of the door. I crawl toward it, retching as I pass the bucket Isaac left there. My lungs fill with the stench of vomit, piss, and shit.

When I reach the door, I tilt my head to one side and press my lips against the half-inch gap between the bottom of the door and the ground. The air smells sweet and fresh. I gulp at it, filling my lungs, inhaling until they feel fit to burst.

"Help!" The word scratches at the back of my throat. I try to swallow, but there's no saliva in my mouth. "Help! Please help! Somebody help me."

The gap is too small for me to see more than the tiniest patch of grass, so I press my ear to it instead. All I can hear is the whirl of the wind and the roar of the waterfall.

"Help!" I drag myself onto my feet and pound at the door with my fists. The wood is weatherworn and cracked. Splinters drive themselves into my skin, but I keep on thumping, smacking, and hammering at it. The door shakes but remains on its hinges. I kick at it, steadying myself by pressing my hands to the sides of the hut. It holds fast, so I turn and kick backward like an angry mule.

Nothing.

My legs buckle under the weight of the table as I pick it up and hurl it toward the door. It hits the wood with a thump, then bounces back. One of the legs catches me in the stomach, and I reel backward. My heel hits the bucket, and I trip. Urine, vomit, and feces swirl around me as I fall to the floor.

39

A chorus of excitable barks greets me as I approach the dog compound. I dip the soles of my shoes into the antibacterial wash outside and then step inside and close the door quietly behind me. Only Jack is in his bed; the other dogs are in their runs outside. A low rumbling sound accompanies the cacophony of barks. The washing machine and tumble dryers are on. I head down the corridor toward the laundry room, stepping carefully so my shoes don't squeak on the floor. Jack raises his head as I pass and then lowers it again when I don't stop to greet him. I can see through to his run, beyond his indoor bed area and the dark patch of wire where Derek the handyman has done his best to patch up the hole the intruder made with wire cutters. Attempts were made to reach several of the other dogs—all of them the more dangerous breeds—but the largest hole was in Jack's cage. I hate to think what would have happened if they hadn't triggered the alarm. Jack would have been taken, of that I'm sure.

Another sound joins the hubbub as I draw nearer to the laundry room—a woman talking in hushed tones. Angharad has her back to me. Her neck is cricked to the right, holding her cell phone between her ear and shoulder, and she grabs armfuls of bedding and towels from the plastic bin at her feet and lifts them into the machine.

"Yeah... Yeah... No, not yet. It's definitely her, though... What? No, I've tried, but she's a cold fish. It's going to take me a bit longer than I thought. I reckon I'll have everything I need by the end of next week... Okay, all right. I'll talk to you then. Bye."

"Angharad."

She snaps around at the sound of my voice, and her phone slips from between her ear and shoulder, landing on the tiled floor with a clunk.

"Jane! You scared me." She ducks down to retrieve it, tucks it into her pocket, then scoops an armful of blankets into the washing machine. "I'm nearly done with the blankets. The load in the tumble dryer is nearly finished, and most of the toys have already been—"

"Angharad."

She turns slowly.

"I think we should have a little chat with Sheila. Don't you?"

~

"Everything okay, Jane?" Sheila gives me a warm smile as I walk into reception with Angharad trailing behind me. I haven't said a word to her since we left the laundry room.

"Could we have a word? In the staff room, if it's empty?"

Sheila's smile fades as she registers the look on my face. "Sure. I'll just grab Anne to cover. One second."

Angharad and I stand in silence as we wait for Sheila to return with Anne, her deputy, from one of the back rooms, and then the three of us troop into the staff room, and I close the door behind us.

"Would you take a seat, please, Angharad." I gesture to a chair. Sheila frowns but says nothing as she sits beside me on the opposite side of the room. Angharad smirks and tucks a strand of hair behind her ear. For someone who's on the verge of being asked to leave the volunteer program, she looks remarkably composed.

"So." Sheila looks from Angharad to me. "What's all this about, then?"

"I think Angharad should explain, don't you, Angharad?"

"Actually"—she sits up straighter in her chair—"I think you should explain, Emma." She pauses for long enough for a cold shiver to run down my spine. "Sorry, Jane. I forgot your name there for a second."

She holds my gaze just longer than is comfortable, and I instantly understand. She wants there to be a confrontation, and she wants it to be in front of Sheila.

"Sorry, Sheila." I stand up. "I've just realized that… Angharad, could you come with me for a second?"

Sheila looks at me blankly. "I thought you needed to talk to me. I just put Anne at reception."

"I know." I open the door and gesture for Angharad to follow me. "I'm sorry to mess you about, Sheila. I just realized something urgent that we forgot to do."

~

"Who are you really?"

We're standing outside the main doors of reception, on the edge of the parking lot. It's cold and blustery, and I rub my hands over my bare arms. It's too cold to be working without a sweatshirt.

"I could ask you the same thing, *Jane*."

"I'm not playing games with you, Angharad. I know you

were looking at my documents on the staff computer, and I'm pretty certain you stole a private letter from my cottage too."

She crosses her arms over her chest, a self-satisfied grin on her face.

"Nice. I bring you a cake and do all your work when you're off sick, and this is the thanks I get."

"What do you want from me?"

"Paranoid, aren't we, Emma?"

"Who are you? Tell me! Tell me who you are."

She slips on her coat, buttons it slowly and deliberately, and then puts the strap of her handbag over her head and slips it across her body so it sits on her right hip. "It's been nice working with you, Emma. I'll be in touch."

"No!" I hurry after her as she crosses the yard at a pace and takes her car keys out of her pocket. "Angharad!" I grab her arm as she points the key fob at her Polo. "Tell me who you are."

"Don't you dare." She snatches her arm away from me, but the anger in her voice belies the fear in her eyes. "Don't you dare touch me."

"I didn't...I..." I take a step back, palms out, and that's when I see it: a blue knitted hat on the backseat of her car. "It was you. You were the woman at the fair at Chloe's school."

Angharad shakes her head and reaches for the door handle. "No idea what you're talking about."

"Yes, you do. How did you know we were at the fair? You followed us, didn't you? Then you waited until Chloe was alone, and you approached her." I snatch my phone out of my pocket. "I'm calling Officer Barnham."

"No." Angharad reaches out a hand. "Don't."

"Then *tell me* who you are."

"Okay, okay. Fine. Put the phone away."

"Tell me who you are first."

She takes a deep breath, then exhales slowly. "My name is

Angharad Maddox. I'm a journalist at the local paper. I saw your photo in the *Post* about six months ago when we ran a feature on Green Fields's fundraising, and I thought I recognized you. You've lost a bit of weight, your hair's a different cut and color, but your face hasn't changed much: you look virtually identical to the photo in the *Daily Mail* article from four years ago. I knew from digging around that you've always refused to talk to journalists and wouldn't talk to me if I approached you directly, so…" She shrugs.

"So you pretended to be a volunteer, you followed me, you talked to my boyfriend's daughter, you stole a letter, and you looked at private files on the work computer."

"Whoa!" She shakes her head. "I didn't steal anything, Emma."

"Yes, you did. You stole a letter addressed to me when you dropped off the cake—the letter you wrote to try to scare me into talking to you."

She shakes her head again. "I don't know what you're talking about."

"Yes, you do. The letter arrived the day before you started. A bit of a coincidence, isn't it? I get a letter intended to freak me out, and then, all of a sudden, I've got a new volunteer who asks me all kinds of personal questions."

"I didn't send you anything, Emma."

"No? So you didn't set up a fake Internet profile either? You didn't pretend to be Daisy?"

Her eyes grow wide. "Daisy, your friend who disappeared in Nepal? Really?"

"Don't pretend you don't know what I'm talking about."

"So either Daisy's back in the UK, or someone's pretending she is?" She glances away, toward the road. When she looks back at me, there's a light in her eyes. "Is this connected to your accident in any way? Sheila said something about a CSI investigation. I thought she'd gotten confused, because CSI wouldn't get involved unless there was something a lot more serious going on, like…attempted murder." She takes a step toward me; she's standing uncomfortably close. "Has someone been making death threats, Emma?"

I can almost hear the cogs whirring away in her head. She can't have gotten much of a story up to now—Emma Woolfe becomes Jane Hughes, animal shelter worker, girlfriend to a local teacher, virtual hermit—but this is something new. This is something her editor would be very interested in. I can see it in her eyes. She's either a first-class actress, or she genuinely wasn't behind the letter, the text, or the Facebook messages.

"Talk to me, Emma. This all sounds really scary." She gazes at me with doe eyes, her face the picture of genuine concern. "Tell me your story. There's been a cloud hanging over you since you returned from Nepal five years ago, what with all the specula-tion concerning Daisy's disappearance and Leanne's death, and this could be your chance to set the record straight. Our readers would be ever so sympathetic, especially with everything that's happened recently."

"No." I back away. "I'm not interested."

"It's all going to come out anyway, Emma. You know that, don't you? Sheila, Anne, Barry, Derek, they're all going to find out who you really are. You may as well put your side across. I know the local community would be completely understanding of your pretense if they knew what you've been through."

"No." I take another step backward. "I told you. I don't want to speak to you, and I want you to go." I gesture at her car. "Go, or I'll call Officer Barnham," I say through gritted teeth.

Angharad sighs, a resigned look on her face. "I'll go, I'll go. But if you change your mind, just give me a ring at the *Post*. I'll handle your story sympathetically. Despite what you might think, I do actually like you." She turns and opens the car door, then slips inside. The tires crunch on the gravel as she reverses out of her parking space, then straightens up and drives out of the yard.

I press a key on my cell phone, then hold it to my ear. "Officer Barnham, please."

40

Emma," a female voice says. "Emma, sit up."

I remain where I am, curled up on my side on the floor. At some point, someone must have left me a blanket, which I've pulled around my shoulders, but it's sodden and uncomfortable. I push it back and cover my eyes with my hand as light floods the hut. Someone has opened the door.

"SIT UP!"

The light disappears as a female shape steps into the hut, blocking the doorway.

"Jesus," another voice says. "It fucking stinks in here. Fucking Isaac; he should do his own dirty work."

I try to push myself up with my arms, but they buckle beneath me as I blink up at the woman. She crouches beside me. A scarf is covering her nose and mouth, but I recognize her eyes. "Cera? What's going on?"

She shakes her head and hooks a hand under my armpit. "You need to stand up, Emma. You need to take a shower and get changed."

"What day is it? How long have I been in here?"

"Emma." There is a warning tone to Cera's voice. "You need to stop asking questions and do what you're told. Do you understand?"

I nod, looking beyond her now, transfixed by the tree outside the hut, bending and swaying in the wind.

"Isis!" Cera shouts. "I'm going to need a hand."

Isis appears from out of nowhere, darting into the hut with a bundle of cloth in her arms. She looks me up and down and sighs.

"Put your arms up, Emma."

I do as I am told, and a soft cotton dress is pulled over my head. When she lets go, the hem drifts to the floor and tickles my ankles.

"Step into these." She crouches down and holds out some underwear, and I obey.

"Flip-flops." She reaches into a cloth bag slung diagonally across her body and pulls out some sandals. I slip them on. I feel like I'm a doll being dressed by a rough-handed young girl.

Isis looks at Cera, who shrugs her shoulders. "That'll have to do until we get her down to the waterfall for a wash."

"Right, Emma." Cera takes me by the shoulders and turns me to face her. "We're going to take you down to the waterfall so you can have a wash. Then we'll have a little picnic so you can get a bit of food and water in you"—she glances at the bucket and screws up her nose—"then we'll take you back up to the house."

"Where's Isaac?"

The women exchange a look and laugh.

"Busy," Cera says.

Isis puts my arm over her shoulder and nods to Cera to do the same.

"Can you walk?" she asks. "Try to take a few steps."

I take a step forward, toward the light and air outside. My legs wobble, but I take another step.

"That's it," Cera says. "Now remember, if anyone asks where

you've been, you're to tell them you've been detoxing and that it was the most amazing experience of your life."

The tree outside is buffeted to the right. It bends so sharply I think it might snap, but then the wind drops, and it rights itself.

"Who gave you the knife?" Isis asks as I step outside the shed and breathe in a lungful of fresh air.

I shake my head. "I don't know what you mean."

"The knife you attacked Isaac with. Sally said it's one of the kitchen knives, and only people who work in the kitchen could have had access to it. Leanne and Al were working with Sally and Raj. Which one of them gave it to you, Emma?"

Isaac's clearly on a witch hunt and wants to pin the knife incident on Al, Sally, or Raj. Why? To use it as an excuse to get rid of them?

Or maybe he already knows who gave me the knife. Leanne's his half sister, but she's also Al's best friend. Where does her loyalty lie now? She's already sold Al out by telling Isaac about her brother Tommy and then lying about it when Daisy and I were trying to get to the bottom of Isis's "psychic" reading. What was it she said—she'd never tell anyone about Tommy, because it was too personal? She saw how distraught Al was, and yet she said nothing. I know exactly where her loyalties lie.

"Emma?" Isis asks again. "Who gave you the knife?"

I look her straight in the eye. "No one. I stole it."

~

Cera and Isis don't leave my side for the rest of the day. Everywhere I go, they go too—to the girls' dorm, to dinner, to the meditation room, to the bathroom. The first time we see another member of the community—Sally, down by the waterfall, washing her clothes—they both stiffen. Sally looks up as we approach, a pink T-shirt in one hand, a gray rock in the other. Fear flickers in her eyes.

"Hello, ladies." Her smile barely registers on her lips. "How are you?"

Cera throws an arm around me and pulls me toward her. Her nails dig into the top of my arm. "Emma's just come out of her detox."

Sally's gaze flicks from Cera's hand to my face. "Congratulations! I'd hug you, but I'm up to my arms in muddy clothes. The vegetable patch won't weed itself." She laughs, but there's a hollow ring to it.

"Are you coming to the party tonight?" Isis asks.

"Party?"

"Yeah. Isaac's organized a Pokhara run for tomorrow. It hasn't rained for a couple of days, and the ground's a bit firmer than it was."

"Do you know who's going?"

"Gabe, of course," Cera says, "and…nope, can't tell you. Isaac's going to announce it at the party. He wants it to be a surprise."

"It's not Raj, is it?" Sally asks. She cups her hand to her mouth, but it's too late. Her question hangs over her like a flashing neon sign.

"Would it matter if it were?" Cera leaves my side and takes a step toward her.

"Of course not."

"Are you quite sure about that? The two of you spend a lot of time together. People are talking."

"Oh, come on." Sally shakes her head airily. "We're all starving. Who could blame me for hanging around the chef? The only thing I'm attached to is his dal bhat."

Isis and Cera laugh as though she's just told the funniest joke in the world. Sally laughs too, but the knuckles on the hand that's clutching the rock whiten as she tightens her grip.

"Is it me?" A wave of hope courses through me, and I touch Isis lightly on the arm. "Am I going to Pokhara with Gabe tomorrow?"

She stops laughing and places her hand over mine. "I don't think Isaac's going to let you go anywhere. Do you?"

⌒

We are walking back to the house when I see a tall, hulking figure crossing the patio. I clutch hold of Cera, too terrified to speak.

"Emma." Cera pulls at my hand. "Let go; you're hurting me."

"Emma!" Isis pulls at my fingers, peeling them off Cera's arm. "Stop it. What's the matter with you?"

"Johan." My arm shakes as I point toward the patio, where he's dragging a felled tree toward the woodpile at the front of the house.

Johan interrupted me when I was reading Leanne's emails in Isaac's study. I threw them onto the floor when I jumped out of the window. Oh my God. A cold shiver courses through me as the memory of my first night in detox comes flooding back. It was him. He was the one who came into the hut.

"What about Johan?" Cera snaps.

"He asked Isaac if he could sleep with me."

"So?" Cera shrugs. "It's no big secret. It was all around the dining room last night."

Isis laughs. "Kane was really pissed off. He didn't even know you'd gone into detox."

"Kane?"

"He wanted to sleep with you after Isaac, but Johan asked first."

I stare after Johan as he drags the tree around the side of the house and disappears. The front gates have been locked since Gabe came back from the mountain with Ruth's body. The key is in Isaac's room somewhere. I need to get it. I need to escape, but Cera and Isis are watching my every move. Even now, they're studying my face intently. I have to pretend that everything's fine, that the detox was a good thing.

"Why do you think Isaac locked Frank up in the basement?" Cera laughs lightly. "He didn't wait his turn!"

So it wasn't because Frank was raping me; it was because he dared to try to have sex with me before Isaac.

"And what if I don't want to sleep with anyone else?" I ask.

"Your choice. No one's going to force you, Emma."

"Really?"

"Jesus!" Cera stares at me in horror and tucks a loose dreadlock behind her ear. "What do you take us for? The guys have to register their interest in the new detoxers to prevent jealousy and competitiveness, that's all. You should be flattered, not freaked out. Who you sleep with is up to you."

"As long as you don't form a relationship with them," Isis adds, "because then attachment is inevitable, and that goes completely against the Ekanta Yatra ethos."

Her gaze flicks toward the orchard. Sally is hanging up her damp clothes on a clothesline strung between two trees. She senses us watching and raises a tentative hand in greeting. She's too far away for me to make out the expression on her face.

"So has everyone slept with Isaac, then? All the women who've had their detox?"

"Yes."

"What about Ruth? Did she?"

They exchange a look, then Isis looks back at me. "Ruth was a troublemaker."

"In what way?"

She reaches into the bag she's wearing over her shoulder and pulls out a bottle of water, unscrews the lid, takes a sip, then hands it to me. "Have you ever had a one-night stand, Emma?"

"Yes."

"How many?"

I shrug. "Four or five."

"And were you drunk when you slept with them?"

"Possibly." I wipe the neck of the bottle on my dress, then raise it to my lips. "Probably."

"Ever sleep with someone you didn't fancy particularly?"

I pause midsip. I want to say no, that I fancied everyone I've ever slept with, but that's not true. There were at least two men I've slept with that I wouldn't have gone near if I'd been sober, men I only took home with me because Daisy encouraged me to.

"That's a yes, isn't it?" Isis says when I don't answer. "Everyone's done it, Emma. You might have slept with them because you were drunk or horny or lonely or sad or bored, but you did it, you enjoyed it, and other than a hangover the next morning, it didn't do you any harm, did it?"

"It made me feel hollow."

"But you did it again?" She puts both of her hands on my shoulders so I'm forced to look at her. "All I'm saying, Emma, is that you might find life a little easier here if you let go a bit. Have a drink, have a smoke, and let go of your inhibitions. You can learn to view sex differently. It can be recreational, adventurous, comforting, or just a release. And if you can appreciate people for more than just their looks or how sexually attracted you are to them, you'll find it hugely liberating."

I want to ask her if she really believes that, if she never misses the intimacy of loving one person and being loved in return, of crawling into a cocoon of just the two of you and blocking out the rest of the world, but I know she'd never admit to it—none of them would.

"Johan's a very attractive man." She glances toward the patio, but he's long gone. "Kind too. You could do a lot worse, Emma. A lot worse."

~

"Okay, Emma." Cera points me toward the pile of beanbags in the corner of the meditation room. "If you could put the beanbags out, Isis and I need to go have a word with Raj."

She steps out of the room and, with Isis at her side, crosses the hallway toward the kitchen. She doesn't drift, as she normally does. Her head is up, her shoulders are back, but her arms don't swing at her sides. Each step is heavy, determined. She strides into the kitchen and gestures to Isis to close the door behind them.

What do I do? I could run down to the orchard to warn Sally that they've gone to speak to Raj about his relationship with her, but I don't know her well enough to predict how she'd react. She might thank me and head up to the kitchen, or she might get angry and deny everything. She might tell them that I spoke to her. She might tell Isaac. I can't risk it. I can't get involved.

I wince as I bend to pick up a pile of beanbags. The skin on my back is still tight and sore, and the cotton dress, a size too small, rubs at my wounds.

"And this is the meditation room." I look up at the sound of Isaac's voice. He steps into the room, followed by three women and a man I've never seen before. He glances over at me as the group, all clean and shiny in their cut-off shorts, walking boots, and anoraks, chatter excitedly, their faces shining with wonder and apprehension.

They remind me of us—Al, Leanne, Daisy, and me—on our first day. One of the women, a short blond with a wide face and a flat nose, is even wearing the same bracelet I bought from a blanket laid out with jewelry outside one of the refreshment stops on the way up the mountain, all jangly bells and cheap silver plating.

My heart twists in my chest as the flat-nosed blond hooks an arm through the tall, skinny girl's elbow and excitedly presses her head into her shoulder. They have no idea what they've just walked in to.

"Five beanbags, please, Emma."

I respond automatically, drifting back and forth across the room. I lay them neatly on the floor, one beanbag in front of the altar, the other four laid out in a semicircle in front of it. When I straighten back up, Isaac isn't looking at me; he's staring at the third woman—a short, curvy girl with long, dark hair to her waist and wide-set green eyes. She breaks off her conversation with the flat-nosed girl and smiles at him, the base of her throat coloring pink.

"Thank you, Emma," Isaac says.

The tall, thin man to my left laughs nervously, but I'm barely aware of him.

"Thank you, Emma," Isaac says again. This time he turns to look at me, but his gaze is cool and detached. The knife wound on his cheekbone has faded to a thin, pink scratch above his stubble. I barely grazed him.

"Hi, guys. Welcome to Ekanta Yatra!" He angles himself toward the group and holds his arms wide, a warm smile lighting up his face. Everyone looks up at him excitedly. I have been dismissed.

~

The door to the kitchen is still shut, but I can hear raised voices behind it.

"We know something is going on between you and Sally," Cera says. "You'd be doing everyone a favor if you just admitted it."

"I've told you, we're friends."

"You do know I'm going to have to go to Isaac with this."

"No, you don't, because it's bullshit." Raj raises his voice. I can hear the fear and desperation in his words. "I don't know who told you about Sally and me, but it's not true. It's idle gossip, nothing more. Someone's obviously got an ax to grind."

"We'll let Isaac decide that, shall we?"

"No! Cera, don't. I told you…"

I drag myself away and head for the dining room. I haven't eaten for days, and I can't bear the stabbing pains in my stomach a second longer.

I nearly walk straight back out again. Daisy, Al, Leanne, Kane, Shona, and the two Swedish girls are sitting in the corner. They're drinking tea and smoking rollies, a plate of dried crackers on a chipped plate in front of them. They glance over as I walk in. Daisy looks me up and down, then bursts out laughing. Al nudges her to stop, but she ignores her and twists to whisper something into Leanne's ear. Leanne glances at me, then starts to laugh too.

Does Daisy know who Leanne is? I'm pretty sure Al doesn't, or she would have told me—and I didn't get the chance to tell her myself before Isaac dragged me out of the shower stall. But Leanne and Daisy have been living in each other's pockets for days now. Would Leanne have told her?

I ignore them and head to the food table. With Raj trapped in the kitchen with Cera, no one has cleared the breakfast table, and I pounce on the scraps that are left. A piece of green mango goes into my mouth first, swiftly followed by a handful of walnuts and the tiny teaspoonful of goat's yogurt I scrape from a tin bowl. I flip open the door to the bread bin. There's half a slice of bread left. I grab it, and I'm about to put it in my mouth when someone knocks into me. The bread flies from my hand and falls to the floor. I squat down to reach for it, but a grubby foot gets there first.

"Whoops." Leanne grinds the bread into the floor with the heel of her flip-flop. "I'm so clumsy. Sorry, Emma."

"Leave me alone, Leanne."

"Or what?" She laughs again. Now that I know she and Isaac are related, I can see the similarity in their eyes. Isaac's and Leanne's eyes aren't the same shade of brown, but they're the same almond shape, framed with thick black lashes. "You have no idea how much has changed since your detox."

I want to tell her that I know her secret and that I think she's a total bitch for what she wrote in her emails to Isaac, but I have to bite my tongue. At least until I've told Al. "What's that supposed to mean?"

"You'll find out soon enough." She gives a small smile, then kicks the piece of bread under the serving table and drifts out of the room.

The second she's out of sight, I drop to my knees and reach for the bread. As my fingertips graze the crust, there's a clattering sound; half a dozen teaspoons spin on the floor beside me, and a woman swears loudly.

"Don't acknowledge me and don't look at me." Al crouches at my side. She picks up a teaspoon and peers under the table as though looking for the rest of the cutlery. "I know Isis asked you where you got the knife and you didn't give me up."

"Of course I didn't. Al, I need to tell you about Leanne. She's—"

"Shh." She presses a hand over my mouth. "You need to be careful, Emma. Isaac's started shagging—"

"Everything okay, Al?" Kane puts a hand on her shoulder and peers around her to look at me. His eyes travel up and down the length of my body, pausing as his gaze reaches my breasts. "I thought you were supposed to be helping me kill the goat for the Pokhara party?"

"Yeah, I am." Al jumps to her feet, the teaspoons in her hand.

"Let's go, then." Kane spits on the floor. It lands inches from my hand. "There's nothing worth hanging around in here for."

I stare after Al as she walks out of the room with Kane, his arm casually slung around her shoulder.

41

N o one comes into the girls' dorm to tell me that the Pokhara celebration has started, but they don't need to. Shouts and laughter drift up from the patio, and the smell of cooked goat and a bonfire fills the room. With Isis, Cera, Raj, and Sally all shut in Isaac's study, it was easy for me to slip unnoticed from the dining room and into the girls' dormitory. My plan, after Kane ferried Al off to the goat enclosure, was to find all my stuff, pack my backpack, and hide it somewhere so I could grab it later. But it had gone. It had all gone—my mattress, my backpack, my sleeping bag, everything. There were three empty mattresses on the left-hand side of the room, presumably for the new guests, and all the other mattresses had been pushed together to make space for them. There was no gap between Daisy's and Al's things, no sign I'd ever slept on a mattress between them, no sign I'd existed at all.

I found my mattress, sleeping bag, and towel crumpled up in a corner of the shower block, sopping wet. My backpack had disappeared, along with my underwear and swimming things, but I found a pair of my shorts and a T-shirt poking out of the top of Daisy's backpack and a skirt, two T-shirts, and several pairs of socks under Cera's sleeping bag. I stuffed all my clothes into a dirty laundry bag I found in a corner of the dorm and squeezed it into the small gap between the ceiling and the cistern above one of the toilets.

My plan is to get Al on her own, then leave when everyone has passed out after the party.

I roll off her mattress and steal a bottle of water, a waterproof jacket, and a pair of walking boots from the Swedish girls. They're a size too small, but I'll tear up the soles of my feet if I go down the mountain barefoot. I hide my stash under Sally's sleeping bag, then head for the pile of backpacks propped up in the corner nearest Sally's mattress. They're so bright and new, they can only belong to new girls. I undo the clips of the first one I reach—a red one—and pull back the cover. I need food, some kind of first aid kit or medication, and with my 150 quid long gone, some money. A noise from the walkway makes me jump, and I yank the cover back down. I grab one of Sally's novels from the pile beside her mattress and prop myself up against the wall, the book in front of my face. A bead of sweat rolls down my temple and drips off my jaw. A second later, someone walks in.

"Hi!" I peer over the top of the book. It's one of the new girls—the curvy, dark-haired one Isaac was so captivated by. She walks toward me, swaying as she picks her way through the piles of belongings, and holds out a hand. Her cheeks are flushed, her eyes shining with excitement and home brew. "You were in the meditation room when we arrived. Emma, isn't it? I'm Abigail."

"Yeah, hi." I shake her hand.

"Ha!" She points at the book I'm holding in my other hand and laughs. "How drunk are you?"

"Sorry?"

"Your book's upside down!"

I glance at the open page in front of me, then flip the book around. "It's about Australia," I say. Abigail doesn't laugh; she's too drunk to get the joke.

"You should come down to the patio," she says as she crouches down beside the red backpack. "They've got an amazing fire burning, and everyone's playing I Have Never. You wouldn't believe some of the things Isaac's been drinking to."

Oh, I could guess, I think but don't say.

"It's brilliant here, isn't it?" She frowns at the unclipped cover of the backpack, then flips it back and reaches in. She pulls out a pale pink lip gloss and a thin, gray sweater. She yanks the sweater down over her head and shakes out her long, dark hair. "We were only going to stay for a couple of nights, but it's so lovely here, I think we might stay for longer. Everyone's so friendly, aren't they? They make you feel so welcome."

"Yeah."

"I just heard Gabe telling Isaac how much he's looking forward to doing the Pokhara run with Al."

"What?"

"I know, right! It was a bitch walking up all those steps. You couldn't pay me to do it again, especially not for fun!"

"What do you mean, fun?"

"That's what Isaac said. He told Gabe to have some fun with Al, and then Gabe said, 'Like I did with Ruth?'" She frowns and rubs a hand over her face. "Have I met Ruth? There are so many people here, I've forgotten all their names already."

The book falls from my hands. Masked attackers didn't kill Ruth. Gabe did. And now they're going to do the same to Al.

"What's the matter?" Abigail looks at me, her lip gloss wand poised over her bottom lip, the tip gloopy and pale. "Why are you looking at me like that? Are you okay?"

"No." I stand up. "I think I'm going to be sick."

I leave her crouched beside her backpack and sprint across

the bedroom and into the shower block. I throw up before I reach a toilet, spewing mango and water all over the tiles.

"Emma?" Abigail calls from the doorway. "Are you okay? Should I get someone?"

"I'm fine." I force the tremor out of my voice. "You go back to the party. I'll be out in a minute."

"If you're sure?"

"I'm sure."

"I could get Cera—"

"No, no, don't. I'll be fine. Honestly. I just had too much home brew."

"Okay…" There's doubt in her voice, so I force myself to stand up straight. I hang over the sink and turn on the taps. "See," I say as I splash tepid water over my face, "I'm fine. I'll be right out in a minute. I just need to fix my face first. A girl can't go to a party with mascara all down her cheeks, can she?"

I haven't worn makeup for weeks, but Abigail, with her lip gloss freshly applied, buys the lie.

"Okay then." She turns to go. "I'll see you in a bit, Emma. Nice talking to you."

~

I don't risk going through Abigail's backpack again. Instead, I grab the laundry bag containing my clothes from the top of the toilet cistern, then hurriedly stuff it with the waterproof jacket, walking boots, and bottle of water that I hid under Sally's sleeping bag and wedge it back into place above the cistern. When I walk back into the girls' dorm, I glance toward Al's mattress. Her backpack is empty, all her belongings strewn over the floor and her mattress. I shove everything back into her backpack as quickly as I can, keeping an eye on the door the whole time. As I slip her iPod into the zipped side pocket, something small and white in the bottom of the compartment catches my eye. I slide the small pack of pills out and turn them over in my hand so I can read the print on the foil side. Pregabalin: my antianxiety pills.

42

Oh, thank God that's over!" Will drops onto the sofa, then swings his legs up and over mine so he's lying fully stretched out. "I never want to go through another inspection again. I am planning on sleeping for the entirety of half term."

"That'll be fun for Chloe. A week in Cornwall with her dad asleep on the sofa."

"Who said anything about the sofa? I'm claiming the double bed." He reaches for my hands and pulls me toward him. "Come with us tomorrow."

"I'd love to, but I can't. I'm sorry."

It's Friday evening, and following my confrontation with Angharad on Tuesday and my realization that I'm putting Will and Chloe at risk by staying with them, I decided that I needed to be at home in my own cottage. Will resisted the move at first, but after I told him about the phone call with Al and the conversation with Angharad, he finally relented.

"Why not?"

"We've got volunteer training for the first half of next week,

and with Sheila away on vacation and two of the girls off sick
with the flu, I'm the only one who can do it. And one of the
inspectors is due to bring in six puppies that have been rescued
from a puppy farm."

"And you're okay with that?"

"What?"

"Being on your own?"

"I won't be on my own. Anne is Sheila's deputy, so she'll be
in charge. I'm just doing the training. It'll be fine, Will." I rest
my hand on his chest. "They've arrested Gary Fullerton's cousin
for the break-in. He's already been taken into custody, so I'm
not worried."

Will shakes his head. "That wasn't what I meant. Are you going
to be okay being on your own here, in the cottage?"

"At least without you here, I don't have to watch any more
Battlestar Galactica."

"I thought you liked it?"

"I do!" I laugh. "Seriously, Will, I'll be fine. Nothing's happened
since the accident. I haven't had a single text, Facebook message,
nothing. Well, other than a text from my mom saying that she hasn't
heard from me for a while, but I can't face talking to her, not now."

"And the police think Angharad was behind it all?"

"I don't know. Officer Barnham said he'd passed on what I told
him about Angharad the other day to CSI, but I haven't heard
anything more—from them or her."

"Don't you think you should chase them down?"

"Chase down the police? This isn't a bit of late homework!"

He doesn't laugh. "Jane, you were knocked off your
bike. You told me Officer Barnham said it might have been
attempted murder."

"Might have been. Or it could have been a coincidence. Will,
I've been on my bike, my new bike, half a dozen times since then,
and it's been fine. No one's tried to knock me off the road."

"But that doesn't mean—"

"No, it doesn't. But I can't live my life looking over my shoulder all the time. What kind of life would that be? Angharad has admitted at least some of her role in all this, and the more I think about it, the more I think that Al was right—that everything else was all down to some Internet troll trying to get their kicks. As soon as I stopped replying, they lost interest."

"What about the hit-and-run?"

"Exactly that. A hit-and-run. No big conspiracy. There isn't a single streetlight on the road between here and Green Fields, and I wasn't wearing my high-vis jacket. The roads are narrow and twisty, and if you'd had a drink or three—"

"I get it." He runs a hand over my head, stroking my hair. "I just worry about you, that's all."

I look up at him, at his big, warm brown eyes and the crease of concern running between them. "I know you do. But I don't want to be scared anymore. As soon as Sheila gets back from vacation, I'm going to tell her everything, and the rest of the staff at Green Fields."

"Everything?"

"Nearly everything."

~

"Call me if anything happens," Will says as he gives me one last hug good-bye the next morning.

"Nothing's going to happen."

"I mean it, Jane." He holds me at arm's length and looks intently at me. "Promise me that you'll call me if anything happens, no matter how trivial. I don't want you keeping it to yourself and stressing yourself out. You don't have to do that anymore. You know that, don't you?"

"Yes."

"Promise."

"I promise."

He smiles and turns to go, then wavers and turns back. "I should stay. Just say the word, Jane, and I'll cancel the vacation."

"You'll do no such thing. You deserve this break. And imagine how disappointed Chloe will be if you cancel right at the last minute. It wouldn't be fair on her."

"I know, but…"

"Please, Will. Go. I'll be fine, and I promise I'll call if anything happens."

"Really?"

"Really. Now please, go before I drive you there myself!"

"Okay, okay." His face sags with relief, and he stoops to kiss me.

I wave him good-bye as he ambles toward his car, the taste of his good-bye kiss still on my lips, then go back into the cottage and close the door behind me. I lock it twice—first with the Yale, then with the dead bolt. I wasn't lying when I told him that I didn't want to be scared anymore, but that doesn't make me an idiot. I still need to be careful. What I didn't tell him when I mentioned the half dozen times I've cycled down the lane from work was the number of times I glanced over my shoulder, or how, whenever I heard a car behind me, I jumped off my bike and pressed myself into the bushes.

I haven't heard from Angharad since our conversation in the parking lot. When she didn't show up for work the next day, I told Sheila that Angharad wouldn't be volunteering anymore. Sheila wanted to know why, but before I could reply, the phone rang. It was the police. They'd had a tip-off that Gary's cousin was responsible for the break-in, and when they searched his flat, they found the petty cash tin from reception. Sheila was so relieved that she announced she was going to take a week off. She'd been putting off going away, just in case the police needed to ask her anything more, and now she was going to "bloody well enjoy a week off in the Lakes." She didn't ask me any more about Angharad, and the conversation moved on. I'll tell her what really happened when she gets back. Of course, there's a risk that Angharad will publish her article before then, but I'll deal with that when, or if, it happens.

I wander into the kitchen and turn on the kettle. As I'm not working the Saturday rotation today, my plan is to do a bit of tidying up, then cycle into the village and put up a few posters for the Green Fields fundraiser next month, then come back and have a quiet evening watching National Geographic with a bottle of wine and a box of chocolates.

~

I'm watching a David Attenborough documentary about the African savannah, my hand hovering over the box as I deliberate between an orange crème and a dark chocolate truffle, when the phone rings.

"Hello," says a male voice. "Is that Jane Hughes?"

"Speaking."

"Hello, Jane. It's Sergeant Armstrong, from CSI. We haven't spoken before."

"No, no, we haven't."

"Sorry it's so late, but it's about your case. I've been chasing down some of the names Officer Barnham gave me, people you thought might have a grudge against you."

"Right."

"And you thought that several of the people were uncontactable because they'd disappeared, possibly feared dead. Is that right?"

"Yes," I say as my heart quickens in my chest. "That's right."

"Well, the thing is, Jane"—he pauses—"I've managed to track one of them down. A Leanne Cooper. I managed to trace her to the Royal Cornhill up in Aberdeen. It's a psychiatric hospital. She was a patient there."

"Leanne? Leanne Cooper?"

"Yes."

"But she...she died in the fire at Ekanta Yatra."

"Apparently not. She's been a patient at the Royal Cornhill Hospital for the last four or five years. She left three months ago. I've been trying to track her down, but I haven't had much luck. You gave me an address for her mother, but I couldn't get any information out of her either. Is there anyone else Leanne might stay with? Anyone she might contact? Can you think?"

"Um..." I rack my brain to try to think of someone, anyone Leanne might contact, but she was always so private about her life. "She had a boyfriend, years ago, before we went to Nepal. I think his name was Gerrit, but he moved back to Holland. She used to work at a beauty salon called MeTime, doing massage. You could try there? Or Al, Alexandra Gideon, but I spoke to her only this week, and she didn't mention anything about Leanne."

"Alexandra Gideon? You spoke to one of the people that you've listed as having a grudge against you?"

"Well, yes, she called me. But I never really suspected that—"

"Do you think that was wise, Jane, during the course of an investigation?"

"I—"

"Never mind." There's a weary tone to his voice. "I just thought I'd update you on what we know so far. I'll look into the business you mentioned and the ex-boyfriend. Everything okay? No more messages, no other communications?"

"No, nothing like that."

"Okay then. I'll speak to you soon, Jane. Good night."

The phone line goes dead, but the television continues to flicker and glow as David Attenborough carries on his voice-over, his dulcet tones describing the interplay between rhinos and the birds that pick the ticks from their backs.

"The relationship between rhino and ox picker was originally thought to be an example of mutualism, but recent evidence suggests that ox pickers may be parasites instead."

~

The phone is answered on the first ring. "Emma! I was just thinking about you."

Sergeant Armstrong's warning about being careful about whom I speak to chimes in my ears, but I block it out. I can't talk to Will about this. I can't talk to anyone other than Al.

"Emma?" she says again. "Are you there?"

"Leanne's alive."

The tinny sound of a TV crackles in the background. "What? What did you just say?"

"Leanne's alive. She's been in a psychiatric hospital in Scotland for the last four or five years. Did you know?"

"No." The background buzz of the television stops suddenly as she turns it off. "Fuck."

Neither of us says anything for several seconds. I glance at the TV. The documentary has moved on from rhinos and tick birds and is showing a slow-motion shot of a lion chasing down an antelope.

"Are you sure, Emma? Are you absolutely sure she's alive?"

"A detective from CSI just rang me. He said she's been in the hospital all this time. She left three months ago. He didn't say what she was in for, and he doesn't know where she is now."

"Has he tried her mom?"

"Yeah, couldn't get any sense out of her."

"Probably drunk."

We both fall silent again. Silent apart from the heavy, rasping sound of Al's breathing followed by the "pssst" of compressed air being released as she takes her inhaler.

"I shouldn't be talking to you," I say. "The sergeant told me not to, but I didn't know who else to call."

"You did the right thing. Fuck, I can't believe it. Five fucking years I've thought she was dead..."

"Do you think she could be behind this, Al? The messages? The text? The"—I pause, not wanting to say it—"hit-and-run?"

I hold my breath and pray that she says no, that she thinks I'm being paranoid, that no one in the real world holds a grudge for five years. Instead, she says, "I'm not sure. I want to say no, that she'd never do something like that, but she changed. We all did. What are you going to do?"

"I don't know, Al." I stand up, cross the room, and pull the curtains closed, blocking out the darkness outside. "I really don't know."

43

FIVE YEARS EARLIER

I wiggle the handle up and down several times, then put my shoulder to the wood and push as hard as I can, but the door to Isaac's study doesn't so much as creak. It can't be locked; it just can't. It's always open. I wiggle the handle one last time, then give up. I'm going to have to leave without my passport.

The patio is still crammed with people talking, laughing, dancing, and singing. Everyone is gathered in a circle around the fire pit, a goat revolving slowly on a spit above it. Hot fat drips into the fire, making it spark and crackle. The air is thick with the smell of meat, joints, and smoke. Kane and Shona are sitting to the left of the fire. He's wrapped around her, one hand on her bare thigh, the other around her waist. Shona rests into him, eyes closed, hands slapping against a pair of bongos that are gripped between her knees as Kane sings a Nepalese folk song I don't recognize. Beside them, Gabe and Raj are deep in conversation. As I watch, Gabe glances across the circle to where Sally and Isis are sitting together in silence. They're watching Paula as she twirls and spins around the fire, dancing to the beat of Shona's drum.

Sitting nearest the garden are three of the new arrivals. The flat-nosed girl has twisted her blond hair into a bun and adorned it with vibrant pink orchids. Her sparkly tank top looks out of place among the tattered T-shirts and faded combat shorts. So does her brunette friend's full face of makeup. They're both talking to the tall, slim guy who arrived with them, gesticulating wildly with their hands, touching him on the shoulder or the knee as they wail with laughter. He raises a cup of home brew to his lips and takes a sip, his eyes darting from one woman to the other as though he can't decide which one he likes best.

Sitting nearest the house is Isaac. He is flanked either side by Leanne and Cera. Daisy is on his lap, her arms twisted around his neck, her head resting against his shoulder, her face tipped up toward his. He holds her loosely, one hand gripping a drink, the other a joint. Daisy is midstory, her cheeks flushed, feet wiggling as she smiles up at him, but Isaac is only half listening. He nods at her every couple of seconds, then his gaze flicks back to the rest of the group and beyond them toward the orchard and river. Is he looking for Al too? I take a step backward, toward the house, but my heel catches on a metal bucket. It clatters to the floor, spilling water onto the patio.

Isaac twists around to see what the noise is. "Hello, Emma."

The smile slips from Daisy's face, and she pulls herself into him so she can whisper in his ear. He nods, then extends an arm and crooks his index figure, gesturing for me to approach.

A smirk plays on his lips as I walk toward him. Daisy reaches up a hand and caresses the side of his cheek, her eyes never leaving my face.

"Hello, Emma. We haven't spoken since your detox ended."

"No, we haven't."

"I've been busy." He gives Daisy a squeeze. She squeals with delight and nuzzles her face into his chest.

"The dress suits you." Isaac looks me up and down again. "It's very…simple."

Daisy snorts with laughter and presses a hand to her mouth. She's wearing one of Cera's long, turquoise skirts and a white tank top with no bra. An indigo head scarf is twisted in her hair.

"Did you enjoy your detox, Emma?" Isaac asks.

"Yes," I say evenly.

"Are you grateful?"

I grit my teeth and nod. The sooner he gets bored with this game, the sooner I can slip away and leave.

"Great. That's very good. Would you do anything for Ekanta Yatra, Emma?"

"Of course I would, Isaac."

He gestures toward the center of the patio with a nod of his head. "Would you put your hand over the fire, Emma?"

The fire crackles and spits as the goat revolves around and around and around. Its eyes are black holes, its jaw slack, tongue protruding. The skin on its face is red and crisp.

"Of course."

"Go on, then." As he points at it, Daisy tumbles from his lap and gives a snort of indignation.

"Okay."

I take a step toward the fire. Isaac isn't going to make me go through with this. He's just showing off. He's playing with me to amuse Daisy and Leanne.

"Hurry up!" he shouts, and I take another step forward. The flames leap and crackle, and then it hits me—a wall of heat so overpowering, I'm forced to retreat. As I step back, I smack straight into Leanne. She's twisted her hair into two tight buns on the top of her head. Her long, pink bangs hang over the thick, black frame of her glasses, but I can still see her eyes, piggy-small and dark behind the glass.

"Go on." She shoves me between the shoulder blades. "Do what you're told."

I take another step forward. The repetitive *bang-bang-bang-bang-bang* of Shona's drum and the wailing of Kane's song grow louder, drowning out the chatter. My eyes water as I approach the fire. The goat turns on the spit, the black sockets where its eyes should be gazing up into the dark sky, then at me, then down at the ground. There's a *crack*, then a *pop*, and its lower jaw drops to the ground. Paula stoops to pick it up, then squeals with pain, drops it, and dances away, her arms twisted above her head like the branches of a vine. I glance back at Isaac. Daisy is back in his arms, and they're both watching me, their eyes glazed with booze, their mouths twisted into amused smiles.

"Carry on!" Isaac shouts.

All I need to do is hold my palm between the goat and the fire for a couple of seconds, and then I can go. If I do it quickly, it won't hurt.

"Emma." Leanne moves so she's standing beside me, one hand shielding her face from the heat of the fire.

I reach out a hand toward the flames. They jump and dance toward the tips of my fingers. I instinctively curl them into my palm.

"I've only ever wanted us to be friends, Emma."

Time slows as I turn to stare at her. And in that second, that split second when I realize that she's lying, her hand reaches out, whippet fast, and slaps mine into the heart of the fire. Sparks fly, the fire roars, ash spills onto the floor, and I snatch my hand back.

At first, I feel nothing. And then it comes.

A wave of pain so violent my knees give way, and it's all I can do to stand upright.

The drumming stops, Kane falters midnote and falls silent, and everyone stops and stares.

Flat-Nosed Girl raises a hand to her gaping mouth and covers it. The guy beside her half rises, and the skinny brunette stifles a nervous laugh. Daisy, her arms still wrapped around Isaac's neck, meets my gaze. There's no compassion in her eyes, no concern, no regret. She regards me dispassionately, the same way she looked at the gecko after she'd stamped on it.

"She's okay." Leanne's voice cuts through the silence. "Just a bit drunk. Step away from the home brew, everyone. It's more lethal than it looks."

Flat-Nosed Girl snorts from behind her hand, the tall guy sinks back to his knees, and the brunette laughs openly.

"Come on, you." Leanne grips my elbow and yanks me away from the fire. "You need to have a lie down."

As she pushes me roughly out of the circle, Kane catches my eye. His tongue protrudes from his mouth, and he licks his top lip.

"Wait your fucking turn." A hand circles my wrist as Johan yanks me away from Leanne. He half walks, half marches me toward the door and plunges my hand into the metal bucket I kicked over. There's barely any water left in the bottom, but the relief is immediate.

"Thank you," I gasp as he crouches beside me. "Thank you."

His lips part as though he's about to reply, but then he shakes his head and looks away, his hand still gripping my wrist.

"Ladies, gents!" Isaac rises to his feet. "Now the town drunk is receiving medical attention, I thought I might say a few words.

"Abigail, Lesley, Caroline, and Mason, I can only apologize for the meager meals we've served you today. We might have the best chef in the whole of the Annapurna range"—he nods toward Raj, and Kane gives a solitary clap—"but he can't work miracles when we're running low on food. Not to worry, though, because we're going on a Pokhara run tomorrow. I say we, but I actually mean Gabe and Al."

The new girls cheer drunkenly, totally oblivious to the concerned looks being passed between the established members of Ekanta Yatra.

"Any questions?" Isaac asks, his arms crossed over his chest, daring someone, anyone, to ask the obvious question about Gabe and Al's safety. When no one speaks up, Isaac sits back down, and

Daisy leans in to him and kisses him hard on the mouth. A second later, the drumming, singing, and chatter resume, and Johan stands up, tugging me onto my feet. The instant my hand leaves the water, my palm pulses with pain.

"So you'd do anything for Ekanta Yatra, would you, Emma?"

He pulls me away from the group, toward one of the smaller fire pits that lights the steps down to the garden.

"Please." I try to dig my heels into the soft earth, but he's too strong. "Please, don't make me put my hand in the fire again. Please, Johan. Please."

He reaches into the back pocket of his shorts and hands something to me. "It's Al's passport. Throw it into the fire, Emma."

I look at the small maroon book in my good hand. Al's passport isn't just her way out of the country; it's proof of who she is. Without it, they could dispose of her as easily as they disposed of Ruth.

"Do it, Emma."

I look past the patio to the gate. Without the key, my only way of escaping is to go over it. There's a broken ladder patching up the goat enclosure. If I could find a way to untie it, it might still be usable.

"Now!"

I was going to take Al with me, but then I found my pills in her backpack. Why would she do that? I thought I could trust her, but then I thought I could trust Daisy too.

"Throw the passport in the fire now, or I'm taking you back to the hut for another detox."

I shake my head. "No. I'm not doing it."

I have to trust Al. I have to.

I hug my injured hand to my chest. It hurts so much, I want to tear it from my wrist.

"Do it." He thrusts the passport into my right hand. "Throw it in the fire. Now. Do it now!"

"No. I can't. I can't."

"Then I will."

He snatches it from my hand and throws it into the fire pit.

"No!" Johan grabs me as I reach for it. He locks me in his arms as the flames lick at the edges of the passport, then creep across the book, turning the maroon cover black. When the passport is no more than gray dust, he shoves me in the direction of the huts.

"Start walking, Emma."

44

"Where's Al?" I ask as we cross the wooden bridge, the huts in our sights. "At least let me say good-bye to her, Johan."

It's dark, and with the fires burning brightly on the patio in the distance, his face and body are in silhouette as he looms beside me.

"I know Gabe's going to kill Al tomorrow," I say. "He's going to bring her body back here afterward and tell everyone they were attacked, then she'll be cremated on the banks of the river. Just like Ruth was."

Johan says nothing.

"Convince Isaac that Gabe should take me instead. I know he trusts you; he listens to you. Tell him I tried to hurt you. Tell him I wouldn't sleep with you. Tell him—"

"I can't do that, Emma."

"You can. You can convince him."

"I can't convince Isaac to do anything. No one can."

"But you're one of the original founders. You've got power. You've—"

He laughs hollowly. "You've got no idea."

"But—"

"Emma, the passport I just threw into the fire wasn't Al's. It was Frank's."

"Frank's?" All the hairs go up on my arms, and I hug myself, suddenly icy cold.

"I took his passport from him a few days ago, before one of Isaac's sessions. You saw me. You also saw what happened to him the other night."

My heel catches on a rock as I take a step backward, but I don't gasp or cry out. "I don't know what you're talking about."

"Yes, you do." He takes a step toward me. "You saw what happened down here, by the river. You were watching from behind a lavender bush."

He saw me. He saw me watching when they killed Frank. That's why he's brought me down here. To kill me too.

"No." I turn to run, but Johan's too fast. He scoops me up off my feet and presses a hand to my mouth. His lips brush my ear.

"Don't scream."

I twist and kick, but he holds me firm.

"I'm not going to hurt you, Emma. I'm going to help you escape. Al's leaving tonight, and she wants you to come too, but I had to check that we could trust you. That's why I asked you to throw her passport into the fire. It was her idea. She knew I still had Frank's passport. She said we'd know if you'd bought Isaac's bullshit if you threw it in the fire. Leanne betrayed her, and she had to check if you would too."

"Leanne?"

"The knife, Emma. Al was the only other person in the kitchen apart from Leanne, Sally, and Raj when the knife disappeared, so they knew she must have taken it to give to you. Isaac wanted to find out if you were still loyal to Al—that's why Cera asked you where you got it from—and when it turned out you still were, that was it, the decision was made for Gabe to kill Al. Isaac thought it was too dangerous if she stayed in Ekanta Yatra."

"So why not kill me too?"

"Because he wants to break you. That's what the detox was about. If he can't seduce or manipulate people into this way of thinking, he tries to break them physically instead. There was no detox when we first started this place. There was no *law* about not being in a couple. There was no reserving the new joiners for sex. I had to pretend I wanted to have sex with you to protect you."

"From who?"

"Kane. He wanted to sleep with you. He's only a junior member of Ekanta Yatra, so he would have had to wait until after I'd slept with you."

"But you slept with Daisy after her massage. Cera said Isaac was supposed to sleep with everyone first."

"He wasn't interested in her; he was after you. I didn't want to sleep with Daisy, but I couldn't arouse suspicion, not after what happened with Ruth." He glances up toward the patio. The fire is still burning, and Paula and someone else are running around it, jumping and skipping. "Ruth came here as a visitor with Sally a couple of months before you guys. She was different from anyone who'd been here before. She was strong and feisty and opinionated and—"

"Like Daisy."

"She was nothing like Daisy. She was kind and gentle and loyal. She was loyal to me." He rubs his hands over his face. "We slept together and got closer, closer than we should have. She figured out what was going on, and we were going to leave. We were going to convince as many people as we could to leave with us. It was all going to plan until Isaac decided he wanted to sleep with her, and she refused. A couple of days later, she disappeared, and Isaac told everyone she'd gone on the Pokhara run with Gabe. When I found out, I went for him, but Kane and Jacob were with him, and they pulled me off. He said that if I so much as looked at him the wrong way, he'd kill one of you. He said he'd kill Al.

Isaac's not homophobic, but he is a control freak, and he doesn't know how to deal with her. He told Isis what Leanne had told him about Al's dead brother, but it backfired."

"Because she freaked out?"

"Exactly."

"But surely people would get suspicious if Gabe came back and said there'd been another attack."

"Not if Gabe said Al decided to leave when they got down to Pokhara. There are a hundred thousand places on the mountain where you could hide a body, and no one would ever discover it."

"We have to take more people with us. There are other people who want to leave. Raj, Sally…"

Johan shakes his head. "Do you trust them? Enough to risk Al's life? Because Ruth and I were planning on taking half a dozen people with us, but one of them betrayed us. They told Isaac. He could have killed us both, but that wouldn't have satisfied him. He wanted to see me suffer. He wanted to put me on a leash and get me to jump, roll over, beg. He enjoys it, Emma. He gets a kick out of playing with people. Leanne's the same. You know she was the one who told Frank that you liked him, don't you?"

"No!"

"Isaac asked me to check on him one night, and he told me. He said she encouraged him to make a move on you because you were too shy to initiate anything. You have to be very careful who you trust, Emma. Very careful indeed."

The sound of drumming drifts down from the patio. Other instruments too—guitars, tin whistles, and tambourines. I look for Leanne, but there are too many people dancing now, spinning and jumping and twirling one another around, blocking my view. Why would she have done that? She can't have known he would have attacked me. She probably wanted him to make a move on me in public and embarrass me—raise a cheap laugh for her and Daisy. I look back at Johan.

"I don't trust anyone."

"Do you trust me?"

"I don't know."

He looks at me for several seconds, then nods as though satisfied with my answer. "Let's go find Al."

~

We keep to the perimeter, walking single file along the fence.

"If anyone sees us"—Johan pauses to look back at me—"we tell them we're on patrol. If they insinuate we just slept together in one of the huts, we play along with it. Okay?"

I nod. The palm of my hand is burning and blistering from the fire. I couldn't speak even if I wanted to.

We move quickly as we head up toward the house. Johan strolls ahead, swinging his arms, his head up. He glances over toward the patio as we pass the party, but I keep my own gaze firmly fixed on his back.

Act natural.

Someone screams, and my heart jolts with fear, but the sound is followed by the sound of laughter and Paula swearing loudly. Johan doesn't so much as twitch. Instead, he continues his even-paced march along the curve of the fence past the main gates and around the log pile, then turns sharply and slips into the shadows by the side of the house. He draws to a halt underneath the window of Isaac's study, then glances back to check that I'm still with him.

"Okay?" he mouths, and I stand beside him, my back pressed against the wall, my heart pounding in my chest.

He doesn't wait for a reply. Instead, he gestures upward with his index finger. The main study window is closed, but the smaller window above it is open. It's eight feet up, and the opening is tiny, but it's a way in. It's the only way in.

Johan interlinks his fingers, arms straight, and nods at me, then the window.

"Is Al in there?" I whisper.

He nods, then gestures for me to put my foot in his hands. I slip off my flip-flops, put my hands on his shoulders, and place my foot in his interlocked fingers. He nods.

One.

Two.

Three.

I'm launched into the air.

I reach for the window and fasten my fingers over the sill. There's a grunt below me as Johan rearranges his grip on my right foot and pushes. My body jolts upward a couple of inches, but it's not enough for me to hook an arm over the window. I'm still too far away.

"Put your left foot on my head," Johan hisses. "Use me as a step."

He heaves me up again, and my left leg waves wildly in the air as I search for traction. It connects with something solid, then slides away. Johan swears under his breath.

"The next time I push, you need to pull, Emma. Pull yourself into the window. Ready? One, two, three."

He launches me upward again, and I reach up with my right hand. My arm goes through the window, but I slide down again before I can hook my armpit over. The sill scrapes my forearm as I slip back down.

"Fuck."

Johan wraps his arms around my legs and lowers me to the ground. He gestures for me to stay where I am, then edges along the wall and peers around the corner of the house. A couple of seconds later, he inches back to me.

"People are starting to drift away from the party. We need to hurry."

"We'll have to break the window." I glance over toward the log pile. "If we hold something soft against the window, it will help deaden the sound."

Johan follows my gaze, indecision written all over his face as the drumming increases and Kane starts singing again. I don't wait for him to reply; instead, I sprint toward the log pile, grab the biggest one I can carry, and run back to the window.

"Take off your T-shirt, then hold this. Careful, there are a couple of rusty nails sticking out of the side." I wait for him to pull off his T-shirt, then exchange it for the log and hold the thin material up to the window, just below the catch. The drumming grows louder, Kieran sings, and a woman screams with excitement. "Now!"

There's a dull thud, a cracking sound, and the tinkle of falling glass. Johan taps at the T-shirt, and more glass shatters and falls away, littering the floor of Isaac's study. I pull the T-shirt away. There's a fist-size hole in the window. Wordlessly, Johan takes the T-shirt from me, wraps it around his hand and wrist, and slips his arm through the hole. He twists his hand around so he can reach the catch. A second later, the window flies open, and he swings himself up and through it.

～

I keep one eye on what's happening through the study window, one eye on the corner of the house. Every sound from inside Isaac's study is amplified as Johan drags the desk away from the rug, the legs screeching on the wooden floor. *Come on, come on, come on.*

He rolls up the rug and opens the hatch, then disappears into the hole.

Come on, Johan. Come on.

I hear the footsteps just as Johan's blond head pops up through the hatch, and then a cloud of cigarette smoke drifts toward me, followed by Gabe.

"Gabe!" I throw myself at him as he rounds the corner and wrap my arms around his neck. The weight of my body knocks him off balance, and he stumbles backward, away from the window.

"Emma?" He pushes me away and looks me up and down. A wry smile lifts the side of his mouth. "Are you drunk?"

I put a hand on his chest, stroke my thumb over the worn material of his T-shirt, and smile. "I might be."

"I heard about you putting your hand in the fire."

"It was a dare. Seemed like a good idea at the time."

"Right." He moves to walk around me.

"I've got a better idea." I take a step in sync with him, blocking his path. I keep my hand on his chest and lean toward him so our faces are inches apart. "Why don't we go talk about it somewhere more private? Somewhere like…I don't know…the huts?"

"Why go all the way down to the huts? Why not have a conversation right here?" His hands snake around my waist, and he pulls me close, pressing his groin into me as his thick, wet tongue searches out mine.

He walks as we kiss, moving me away from the bright lights of the house and into darkness. We stop abruptly as the backs of my thighs make contact with the log pile, and he presses himself into me, forcing me to lie back against the wood. He hitches up my dress, and his hand snakes its way up my thigh. I stiffen as his fingers pluck at my underwear, and a wave of panic crashes through me.

I can't do this. I can't do this. I can't. I—

I twist from side to side, but the more I struggle, the more frantic he becomes, grabbing at my breasts with one hand, yanking down my underwear with the other.

Where are Johan and Al?

There is the sound of a zipper being pulled, a low grunt, and then a sound I've heard before. The sound of a football being kicked. Only this time, it's followed by a violent crack, like a butcher's knife cleaving through bone, and Gabe's lips slip from mine. They trail down my cheek, striping my skin with saliva as the full weight of his body collapses onto mine.

Before I can move, scream, or cry, Johan appears behind him. He grips Gabe's shoulders and hauls him off me, then tosses him roughly to one side. Gabe's body slips down the log pile and falls to the ground with a soft thump. Johan throws something at the body. It's the log we used to smash open the window. The three nails on the end are dripping with blood.

Someone leans over me. Someone with pale skin, terrified eyes, and bleach-tipped hair clinging to her forehead.

"He's dead," Al says. "Gabe's dead."

45

"Come on." Johan jabs the key at the lock. "Come on!"

I sneak a glance at Al, who's standing right beside me. Her pupils are huge black pools; her cheeks are pinched, with sweat beading above her eyebrows. She's staring at the pile of logs we rolled onto Gabe to hide his body. She steps toward the log pile, but I grab her wrist, just as the front gate squeaks open and Johan mutters something in Swedish under his breath.

"*Come on.*" He ushers us outside. "Go." He pulls it shut behind us and then gestures toward the stone steps that lead back down the mountain. "As quickly as you can."

We step into the darkness, the only light the haze of the half moon. I glance back at Ekanta Yatra—at the faded prayer flags that adorn each of the windows. They flutter and twist in the wind, but there's no escape; they're pinned in place, held tight.

"Run!" Johan hisses in my ear. "Emma, run."

⌣

We've been running for some time, stumbling down the steps two at a time, speeding around corners and jumping over buried roots, when I realize I can no longer hear Al behind me.

"Johan!"

He continues to run, a good hundred feet ahead of me, so I raise my voice. "Johan!"

He whips around, teeth gritted, and gestures for me to keep my voice down.

"Al." I gesture back up the mountain. Trees and bushes loom like dark shadows either side of the steps. "She's disappeared."

Without saying a word, Johan takes off back up the mountain, pumping his arms and leaping up the steps two at a time. I follow. I run as fast as I can after him, but my flip-flops slow me down, and the cold night air catches in my chest, making each breath tight and painful.

I see them as I round the first corner, Al standing with her back to a tree, doubled over with her hands on her knees, Johan beside her, one hand on her back.

"Asthma," he mouths as I draw closer.

"Al." I crouch beside her. Her forehead is dripping with sweat, and she's breathing shallowly. She screws up her face in discomfort each time she inhales. "Have you got your inhaler?"

She shakes her head and mouths the word "backpack."

Johan's shoulders slump, and he rubs a hand over the side of his face.

There's no way we can go back to the house for Al's inhaler. The alternative is climbing farther up the mountain to see if one of the hostels have any hikers with inhalers, but there's little chance Al could make it. We'd have to split up. One of us would have to stay here with her while the other went for help.

I make a decision and stand up. "I'm going to see if I can find a hostel nearer the top. Someone might have an inhaler."

Johan shakes his head. "The nearest hostel is half a day's walk away. By the time you got there and back, even if someone did have one…" He tails off and nods toward Al. "Our best bet is to hide and continue on in the morning, or keep going but slower.

We'll have to keep to the edges of the paths, just in case anyone comes after us, but we could do it. If we can get to the Maoist checkpoint, someone there could call for an ambulance."

"I don't need an ambulance." Al pushes up on her thighs and stands upright. "Let's go."

"No." I touch her on the arm. "Let's wait it out. We can find somewhere to hide."

"And freeze to death? I pushed myself too hard, that's all. I've got my breath back now. If I take it easy, I'll be fine. And besides"—she glances at Johan, who's rubbing his forearms with his hands—"if we wait until morning, we're more likely to be spotted."

"If you're sure, then—" Johan freezes. We all hear it: voices, men's voices, further up the mountain. Shouting, calling to each other.

"Go." Al grabs my hand. "Go!"

~

The shouts grow louder, joined by the sound of heavy footsteps scrambling down the mountain behind us, pebbles and stones crunching and crashing, and branches snapping. Al and I are still hand in hand, but she's lagging behind, and I have to drag her after me. Her face is deathly pale in the moonlight, her lips blue, but every time I glance behind to check if she's okay, she glares at me, urging me on. I know Johan could run faster than he is. Instead, he stays with us, shouting directions, pointing out broken steps and steep drops. My heart is pounding in my ears, and my lungs are burning, but my legs keep moving, carrying me further away from Ekanta Yatra and closer to safety.

A woman screams, and all the hairs on my neck stand up.

I'd know that scream anywhere. Daisy.

My ankle gives way as I twist around to check, and my hand,

sticky with sweat, slides out of Al's grasp. I slip off the step and tumble to my right toward a steep drop. With nothing to break my fall, I hurtle down the mountain, spinning over and over and over, crashing through bushes and bouncing over rocks, down, down, down. Branches and bushes, a blur of green and brown, scratch my palms as I claw at the air, desperate for something, anything, to slow my descent, but I'm going too fast. As I roll, I screw my eyes tightly shut. I'm going to die. I'm going to—

The air is thumped from my lungs, and my body jackknifes as I hit something hard: a tree stump, I realize, turning my head slightly. I lie still for several seconds as the world continues to spin, then whimper in pain. Everything hurts.

"Emma?" Johan comes crashing toward me through the undergrowth. "Are you okay?"

He skids to a halt a foot away from me, and the color drains from his face.

"Don't move. Whatever you do, don't move."

I look in the direction he's looking, but all I can see is a great, black stretch of sky.

"There's a sheer drop off the edge of the mountain. If you'd fallen ten feet farther, you'd have rolled right over the edge. Now we just—" He stiffens and glances behind him as the bushes twitch and crackle. Someone's coming.

"Oh, thank God." Al steps out from the undergrowth and doubles over to catch her breath. The air fills with wheezes and whistles.

"We need to get back to the path." Johan crouches down, then inches toward me on his bum, digging his heels into the dry soil to ground himself. "Take my hand."

I hook my left arm around the tree stump to steady myself and twist toward him, reaching out with my right hand.

"Ready?" He wraps one hand around my wrist and steadies himself with his other. "On three, I'm going to yank you toward me. I need you to dig your heels into the ground to give you leverage."

"Okay."

"On three. One, two, three!"

Johan pulls, I push, and my body jolts with pain as I'm hauled back up the slope. We collapse in a heap at the entrance to the undergrowth, both of us on our backs, sucking in air, wincing with pain. When I get my breath back, I crawl over to Al, who's sitting on the other side of the clearing, her head in her hands. I touch her gently on the knee, but she doesn't look up.

"We can't hang around here," Johan says as he forces himself up into a sitting position. "And we can't risk carrying on down the steps, because we're sitting ducks. We'll have to pick our way through the undergrowth instead. It's more dangerous because there's no path, but—"

"Dangerous?" says a voice above our heads. "Who's dangerous?"

Isaac steps through the undergrowth toward us, a dangerous smile on his face and a nine-inch kitchen knife in his hand, the blade glinting in the moonlight. A second later, Daisy appears beside him, cheeks pink, the indigo scarf wrapped around her head now askew, her eyes bright with excitement.

"Well, well, well," Isaac says, looking at each one of us in turn. His sneakers are caked in mud, and his T-shirt clings damply to his body. "Look who we have here. Are you going to come back to the house like good boys and girls, or do we have to do this the difficult way?"

"Where's Leanne?" Al asks. "Does she know you locked me in the basement?"

Daisy clutches Isaac's arm. "You locked her in the basement?"

"I did, yes." He looks at her steadily. "They colluded to try to kill me, and I had to separate them for my own safety and for the safety of everyone at Ekanta Yatra."

Daisy looks across at me and Al and squints her eyes as though she's trying to focus. I don't think I've ever seen her as drunk. "You tried to kill Isaac?"

"It wasn't like that, Daisy." I take a step toward her, but Isaac jabs the knife toward me, forcing me to stop.

"To answer your question, Al"—Isaac says the words slowly and deliberately, but he can't stop the slur that makes the words run into each other—"I told Leanne to stay at Ekanta Yatra, where she's safe."

"Don't you want *me* to be safe?" Daisy whines, but when she tries to rest her head on his shoulder, he shrugs her off.

"And yes, Al," Isaac continues, "Leanne knew I'd put you in the basement. She thought we could help you—God knows you need it—but you fought us every step of the way. That didn't stop Leanne loving you and believing in you, but you crossed the line when you gave Emma the knife."

"How about you just let us go?" Johan asks.

"How about you stop telling me what I should do? You've always been a fucking liability, but I had no idea what a sneaky bastard you actually are."

"You need to look in the mirror, Isaac."

"And you need to shut the fuck up, or I'll twist this between your girlfriend's eyes. Although," he adds, glancing at me, "that might actually be an improvement. I always thought her eyes were a little too close together."

Daisy snorts with laughter and moves to slip an arm around his waist. The dry soil shifts under her feet, and she has to cling on to him to keep her balance. She points at Al with her free hand.

"Stop being a dick and go back to the party. You can fuck off, though, Emma." She laughs again, her head rolling back on her neck, her eyes half-closed.

Al, standing beside me with her hands clenched at her sides, is still gasping for breath. The wheezing has stopped, and instead, she's making little "uh, uh" sounds as she sucks hollowly at the air.

"We're going back to Pokhara," I say. "Come with us, Daisy. I know you hate me, but you need to listen. Ekanta Yatra's more dangerous than you realize. So's Isaac. Please, you need to trust me. You need to—"

"I don't *need* to do anything." Her eyes fly open, and she squints at me. "Trust you? Ha! You're a *psychopath*, Emma." She shouts the word so loudly it seems to ring in the air. "You said you wanted to kill me."

"I didn't mean it."

"Really? Because you sounded pretty bloody convincing to me."

I catch Johan's eye as Daisy continues to rant. He flashes a look toward Isaac. He's off his guard; the knife is still in his hand, but it's hanging loosely by his side as he listens to what Daisy is saying. Johan looks from Isaac to Daisy, then at me. His gaze flicks back and forth between us, and I know instantly what he wants me to do.

"Do you know what Isaac called you?" I ask, interrupting Daisy's rant.

"What?"

"After I slept with him, do you know what he called you?"

Isaac snorts with amusement and wipes the back of one hand over his brow.

Daisy's mouth twists into a bitter grin. "How about you enlighten me, Emma?"

"He said you were cheap and that women like you are ten-a-penny. That's why he let Johan sleep with you in the massage hut. He lets the other men sleep with the sluts."

Daisy looks incredulous for a moment, and then her eyes narrow. "You fucking bitch!"

I topple sideways into Al as Daisy launches herself at me. Her nails slide down the side of my face, and she yanks at my hair as we fall, a tangle of hair, limbs, and clothes. We hit the ground with a jolt, then, before I can take a breath, we're off, slipping down the slope at speed, hurtling toward the drop. I grab at rocks, tree roots, and branches as the air whistles past me. There's a blur of movement up by the clearing where Isaac and Johan were standing, raised voices, an anguished shout, and then something tumbles past us and disappears off the edge of the cliff. And then we stop.

~

Daisy jumps to her feet first. She scrabbles away from the cliff edge and grabs at something lying on the ground a couple feet away. It's Isaac's knife.

"Get up!" she screams. "Get up!"

I tentatively raise myself onto my hands and knees, the drop just inches to my left, and slowly stand up. Al does the same. Behind her, lying on his side near the clearing, his eyes half-closed, is Johan. Even in the gloom, I can see the gaping wound in his shoulder and the dark bloody stain pooled around him.

"Daisy." I take a tentative step forward. "Johan's hurt."

"No." She extends the knife toward me, but her hand's shaking. "You're not helping him."

"Daisy. Don't do this."

"He killed Isaac!" Her face is pale in the moonlight, her eyes bloodshot and puffy in a pool of dark, smudged eye makeup. "You saw. You saw what just happened. He's down there! Isaac!" She takes a step nearer the edge and peers down into the darkness. "Isaac?"

"Come with us," Al says softly. "Come back to Pokhara. This...all this...it's fucked with our heads. You're not thinking straight. None of us are."

"I am."

"That's not true."

"Isn't it?" She takes a step back from the edge, the knife a raised barrier between her and us. "I'm being myself for the first time in my life. You don't know me, Al, not really. Do you think I like being Party Girl Daisy? Do you have any idea how tiring it is? How boring to have to entertain people all the time? Seven years we've been friends, and you still insist on keeping me in the same little 'wild, crazy Daisy' box that you put me in while we were at university."

"And I'm the one that keeps getting dumped, and Leanne's the private one, and Emma's the neurotic one. We're all in boxes, Daisy. That's what happens in friendship. It shouldn't, but it does," Al chips in.

"You do know that Leanne is Isaac's half sister?" I ask.

Al gawps at me, but a strange half smile twists Daisy's mouth. "Actually, I do. No need to look so surprised, Emma. What's the matter—disappointed that I'm not horrified? Who cares if they're related? I think it's great that they've found each other. You think you've been so bloody clever, manipulating people into feeling sorry for you, but Isaac's told me everything. He told me how you'd tried to turn him against me, how he liked me right from the start but you'd tricked him into defending you from Frank, how he's never met anyone like me before, how much he loves me—"

"It's bullshit. All of it."

"He loves me."

"He doesn't love anyone."

"Urgh." Johan groans in pain, and I take another step up the slope toward him. His skin is gray in the half-light, his eyes are closed, and the pool of blood around him has grown bigger. If we don't do something, he'll die.

"Oh, no you don't!" Daisy steps between us and raises her hand so the knife is pointed at my chest. "No one's helping him until we've found Isaac. Isaac? Can you hear me? Isaac!"

"Daisy, he's dead. You said as much yourself. That's a two-hundred-yard drop. Please." I reach for her. "You need to come with us. You need to trust me."

"Trust you!" She knocks my arm away. "After everything you've done? You told Isaac I killed my sister!"

"What?"

"He told me. He said you'd tried to convince him that she didn't die by accident, that my mom was right, that I drowned her. How could you say something so cruel when you know, you *know* how fucked up I am about it? I was five years old, Emma. I only got out of the bath for a minute. If Mommy hadn't taken my toy off me... If she... If she..." She swipes at the tears that have filled her eyes. "Fuck you, Emma. Fuck you for using that against me."

"I didn't. Daisy, I swear. Leanne told Isaac about Melody. She wrote him emails before we came over here, telling him all about us, telling him *everything* about us. They've been manipulating us since we stepped foot through the gates."

"Have you seen these emails?" Daisy looks at Al.

"No, but—"

"See! It's all lies. More lies, Emma! You've sucked Al in, but I won't let you do that to me. It's not Leanne and Isaac who've been manipulating people; it's you. Leanne knows you don't like her, she's always known, and she was scared to talk to me in case you turned on her too, but she told me everything. She told me about the conversation she overheard between you and Al when you were telling her how embarrassing I am; she told me about you pretending to be attacked by Frank; she told me about you sleeping with Isaac—"

"Because she wanted to come between us and convince you to stay at Ekanta Yatra!"

"Because she cares about me!"

"I'm not arguing with you anymore, Daisy. I need to check on Johan."

"No!" She lunges at me, the knife still clutched in her right hand, the blade aimed at my chest. As I raise my hands to protect myself, Al launches herself at me too, knocking me sideways. The air is forced from my lungs as we tumble to the ground, Daisy and Al landing on top of me. I reach out with my left arm, but my hand grasps thin air. If we'd fallen a couple of inches to my left, we'd have been pitched into the ravine. I try to anchor myself with my right hand, but my arm is trapped under Al's knee.

No one moves for a couple of seconds, and then Daisy tries to get up, but Al grabs the back of her tank top and reaches for the knife. As she wraps her hand around Daisy's wrist, Daisy twists around and swipes at her, scraping her nails along the soft flesh of Al's cheek. Al winces but doesn't let go of her wrist. They twist and grapple above me, pulling at each other's clothes, pinching, scratching, and thumping as the knife flashes through the air.

"Stop it!" I scream as Daisy grabs a handful of Al's hair and jerks her head back. At the sound of my voice, Daisy looks around. Her grip on Al loosens, and as I watch, Al lets go of her wrist and, using all her strength, pushes Daisy off me and over the cliff.

46

However hard I try, I cannot close the disconnect in my brain between what I just saw and what I feel. What I saw was my best friend of seven years plummet to her death. What I *feel* is that none of this is real. Not the icy early morning wind on my face, not the stained and torn dress fluttering around my thighs, not the burn on my hand or the whip lashes on my back.

There is a part of me, the part floundering around in the disconnect trying to make sense of it all, that believes all I need to do is take a step off the cliff, and I'll wake up in my bed back in London. My head will hurt from a wild night out clubbing, having consumed too many vodka and Cokes and not enough water, and my phone will be bleeping with half a dozen messages from Daisy, joking about the things we said and did the night before. And I'll sip at the water beside my bed and read the messages, and then I'll swing my legs from under the duvet and pad into my kitchen to make myself a cup of coffee. And while the kettle is on to boil water, I'll sigh at the thought of my regular Sunday phone call to my mother, and the pile of laundry I can't bring myself to tackle, and the prospect of another sweaty Monday morning Tube ride to the job I hate. And as the water boils, I'll fight the urge to run, to pack a bag and just go. Start again somewhere else: be myself, whoever that may be…

"Emma, stop!" Al screams, yanking me away from the edge by the back of my dress. "What the hell are you doing?"

The haze in front of my eyes clears, and her face zooms sharply into view.

"Emma!" She thumps me in the chest with her closed hand.

"I wasn't…I wasn't going to jump… I…"

"Emma! What's the matter with you?"

"I just… I can't…"

We stand on the edge of the cliff for the longest time, staring into the dark drop beneath us. For the first hundred yards, spiky flowers and straggling plants cling to the mountain, but then they too are swallowed up by the inky blackness below.

"I thought she was going to stab you," Al says, her voice no louder than a whisper. "I never meant…I can't believe…"

"I know." I should reach for her hand, I should put an arm around her, I should do something to comfort her, but I can't shake the feeling that, if I did, I'd put my arm straight through her. She isn't real; neither of us is real.

"What do we do?"

"I don't know."

"If we report it, I'll go to jail. Have you got any idea what jail's like over here?"

"It was an accident, Al."

"No one's going to believe that." She looks at me. Her skin is pinched and ashen, and her lips are chapped and blue, but it's her dull, glassy eyes that worry me the most. They are as lifeless as a doll's. "Gabe's dead. Johan's stabbed. Daisy and Isaac are gone. There will be an investigation. It'll all come out. Someone at Ekanta Yatra will ask questions. And if they don't, Leanne certainly will."

"You didn't do anything wrong," I say, but even as the words leave my mouth, I know she's right.

There's no way of reporting Isaac's and Daisy's deaths without the truth coming out. Daisy didn't deserve to die, but Al doesn't deserve to go to jail. What's going to happen if Leanne or someone at Ekanta Yatra gets in touch with the police?

"There's no proof we did anything." I lower my voice. "Johan killed Gabe, not us. We didn't kill Isaac either; and as for Daisy… there won't be any evidence that you pushed her over the cliff." I feel sick even as I say it. "Al, you said it yourself. You thought Daisy was going to stab me."

"We could try to make our way down there," she says, but there's no conviction in her voice, no feeling behind the sentiment. Daisy is dead, but neither of us wants to be the one to say the words, because then they're out there, they're real, and her death is real.

A wave of grief and regret washes over me, so huge it takes my breath away. I should have done more. I should have forced Daisy to listen to me. But I never dreamed this would happen. I thought we'd go back to the UK, separately, and Al would try to save our friendship; she'd force us to talk about what happened at Ekanta Yatra. We wouldn't go back to the friendship we'd once had—we could never do that—but we'd put it behind us and move on with our lives. Daisy didn't deserve to die. She never deserved that.

I grip Al's arm. "Johan!"

Without waiting for a reply, I climb the bank toward him, small stones flying as I scrabble on my hands and feet. Al follows me, panting and wheezing.

"Johan?" I crouch down beside his slumped body. His eyes are closed, his head resting on his outstretched arm, his fingers unfurled. A line of saliva winds its way down his chin from the corner of his parted lips. "Johan, open your eyes."

Al gently wraps her fingers around his wrist, but he doesn't so much as twitch.

"Johan?" I ask again. "Can you hear me? It's Emma and Al. Open your eyes."

Al shakes her head and lets go of his wrist.

"Open your eyes, Johan!" I press a hand to the side of his face and gently tap him. His skin is rough with stubble under my fingertips. "Johan, wake up."

"Emma!" Al says.

"Johan, wake up!"

"Emma! He's dead."

"No." I push her away. "No. No. He can't be. No. Johan! Come on. Come on, wake up."

"Emma, stop it!" She clamps a hand over my mouth and half drags, half wrestles me away from him. "You need to be quiet! There are still people looking for us. I just heard voices from the steps. We need to get out of here."

I shake my head stiffly under the weight of her hand.

"What?" She peels her hand from my mouth, her voice little more than a whisper. "What is it?"

"We can't leave him here. He wanted to go back to Sweden. We've got to find a way of getting him back down the mountain."

"He's too heavy."

"Then we hide him. We drag him into the undergrowth, and we hide him until we can get help."

Al looks at Johan and then at the bushes. She's still wheezing heavily and coughing every couple of seconds.

"It's okay," I say. "I'll do it. You catch your breath."

"No." She stands up and takes one of Johan's arms. "I can do this."

~

We are both pouring with sweat and panting as we drag Johan off the clearing and into the bushes. We work in stops and starts. One, two, three, pull! Then rest. Then one, two, three, pull as we drag him on his back, his head lolling to one side, his shoulder striping the soil with blood, into the seclusion of the undergrowth.

We work as quickly as we can, hiding his body with leaves and branches, then flop to the floor just as a man's voice echoes around us.

"They came this way."

I stare at Al in horror.

"Come on," I whisper and reach for her hand, but she shakes her head.

"Leave me here."

"No."

"Emma." She pauses to breathe, her face contorting with discomfort. "You go. Get help. I'll stay here with Johan."

"You can't." Even as I say the words, I know there's no way that Al's going anywhere. Moving Johan's body used every last bit of energy she had. Her lips are blue, and she's fighting to keep her eyes open.

"Don't tell anyone." She points toward the cliff edge. "Promise me."

"I promise." I touch her on the back of the hand. "But you need to hide. Don't move until I come back and get you. I will come back for you, Al. I promise."

~

The sky is striped with orange, pink, and scarlet. The gloom of night has lifted, and the birds are singing again, the cicadas chirping merrily in the trees, and the men, leaning on the hut, their chins tipped to the sky, are smoking, puffing on their cigarettes with their eyes shut, enjoying the warmth of the sun on their faces. They start as I draw near. One of them throws his cigarette to the ground and grinds it out with the heel of his boot. Another says something in Nepalese that I don't understand.

"Please help." I take a step toward the Maoists. "My friends have been hurt. One of them is dead. The other needs urgent medical help. You have to help me."

"Huh?" He turns and says something to his friend in Nepalese. His friend shakes his head.

"Two?" He looks back at me and holds two fingers in the air. "Two friends on the mountain?"

"Yes!" I take another step toward them. "Just two. Please, please help. We were attacked and robbed; they stabbed my friend. Please, please help!"

47

The first thing I do after I get off the phone with Al is Google the name of the hospital that Sergeant Armstrong mentioned.

A link to the Royal Cornhill Hospital immediately appears, and I click on the "About Us" link, but it doesn't tell me much, just that it's a hospital near the center of Aberdeen that provides inpatient and outpatient care to people with mental health issues as well as training medical staff who work in the field.

I click through the other links, but it's mostly about visiting times, gifts you can and can't bring into the hospital, and health records and data protection. They mention inpatients and outpatients, but there are no specific details about the types of mental health problems they deal with.

I text Al:

Leanne was in a mental health hospital in Scotland. Just Googled it.

Seconds later, my phone bleeps:

Maybe she got help for her anorexia? Why Scotland, though? Her mom lives in London.

I text back:

She's originally Scottish, though, isn't she? She was born there, then her mom moved to London with her dad. Isaac stayed. He said he grew up in care homes and foster families. Maybe she went looking for him?

Neither of us knows what happened after we left Ekanta Yatra, although we know there was a fire. After I told the Maoists what had happened, they came back up Annapurna with me to look for Johan and Al. I was scared we'd run into someone from Ekanta Yatra, but the mountain was silent, and Al and Johan were where I'd left them. Al's condition had seriously deteriorated. She was breathing so shallowly I was scared that she'd died, and when one of the Maoists picked her up, grunting as he shifted her weight into his arms, she just lay there, limp and floppy. They lifted her onto a donkey, and she clung to its neck, her face pressed into its mane as it bumped and jerked its way down the mountain. They put Johan's body on the other donkey and covered it with a blanket.

No one said a word on the way back to the Maoists' hut, and when we got there, an ambulance was waiting. There was no room for me in the back with Al, Johan, and the paramedic, so I sat in the front with the driver, staring into the darkness as we drove through the streets of Pokhara to the hospital. I spent the rest of the night in the overcrowded waiting room, too shocked to sleep, too dazed to do anything other than stare straight in front of me.

The next morning, I was allowed into the ward to see Al. We were joined by a Pokhara policeman, who questioned us at length about what had happened the night before. We told him we were returning from a hike up to the top of the mountain with a friend we'd made there when we were attacked by masked men who stole our backpacks and stabbed Johan. Al let me do most of the talking. The policeman wrote down a "description" of the men who'd attacked us and said he'd be in touch if he had any further questions.

When I inquired whether we could return to Kathmandu and fly back to the UK, he simply shrugged his shoulders, and when Al asked what would happen to Johan's body, we were told his family would have to make arrangements for it to be flown back to Sweden. We shared a look. With no passport and no surname, we knew the chances of Johan's family being found were almost nil, but we had to try. That's why, two days later, I called my mom and asked her to wire some money to me so we could fly back to Kathmandu. There was no way Al and I were up for another six-hour bus trip, but we had no money left to pay for a flight back to the Nepalese capital. I was in no state to tell Mom what had really happened, so I made up a story about a pickpocket in a bar in Pokhara. Thankfully, she didn't ask too many questions, so we got to buy fresh clothes and fly to Kathmandu, where we visited the Swedish and British embassies.

We told the Swedish embassy everything we knew about Johan, and they assured us they'd do all they could to try to find his family. I've got no idea if they did, but I can't bear the thought that Johan never found his way back home.

Neither Al nor I wanted to stay in Nepal longer than we had to, and we certainly had no interest at that point in the Chitwan jungle trek, so we brought our return flights forward a day. As they'd been booked online, it didn't matter that our physical tickets were still with our passports and visas, locked away in Isaac's study. The British embassy in Kathmandu helped us sort everything out; we just wanted to go home.

We were standing outside the airport before our flight, sucking down cigarette and after cigarette, when we overheard a middle-aged couple talking as they got out of a taxi.

"Sorry?" Al said as they walked past us, dragging their suitcases behind them. "I just heard you say something about a fire on the Annapurna range."

They paused to look us up and down. "Haven't you heard? It was some kind of lodge or religious retreat or something. Burned to the ground, and between ten and twenty people died. Nothing left but bones by the time the police got there, apparently. All of those young people with their lives ahead of them. Awful tragedy. They don't know if it was an accident or arson. Either way, it's a terrible, terrible shame."

They stared at us as though waiting for a response, then, when neither of us said a word, they simply nodded and continued on into the airport.

To this day, that's all we know. We still don't know whether the fire was deliberate or accidental. By the time we got back to the UK, it was all over the press—SEX CULT IN NEPAL BURNS DOWN. BRITISH STUDENTS DEAD. Six of the bodies that were found were identified, including the new girl Abigail and one of her friends, but the rest of the bodies were so badly burned that the police found little more than piles of bones. According to one report I read, the remains were going to be sent off to be DNA profiled, but I never read anything more about it, so Al and I will never know whether Leanne was one of the fire's victims, or, like several of the members, she fled and vanished. We don't know what happened to Raj or Sally or Isis or Cera. When we got back to the UK, we tried to trace Ruth's family, but with only a first name to go on, we drew blank after blank. Al tried to justify her decision to sell her story by saying that maybe Ruth's family would read it and get in touch. As far as I know, they never did. Sometimes people go missing for a reason.

I navigate from the hospital's website to Facebook and reread the messages sent from Daisy's account:

Help me, Emma!

It's so cold.

You never came back for me.

I don't want to die alone.

Could Leanne have sent those? It's possible, but how would she have gotten hold of my cell phone number to text me this:

Only the good die young. That'll explain why you're still alive, then.

Al told me there's some kind of website you can use to get hold of someone's details, but Leanne's never been technologically minded. If she had been, she could probably have found Isaac by searching the web instead of going to the Salvation Army. And what about the letter? I don't have it anymore, but I read it enough times that the shape of the handwriting is indelibly imprinted behind my eyelids. I have no idea if it's Leanne's handwriting or not—I don't think I've ever seen her writing—and now there's no way of comparing it with any letters or postcards Al might have.

Anyone could have written the messages. The words are all spelled correctly, and they're grammatically correct, but what does that tell me other than that they were written by someone with an education?

I enter the cell phone number that sent the anonymous text message into Google, but nothing comes up, not that I'm surprised. If anyone would be able to trace the number's account holder, it would be CSI, and they've found nothing so far. At least they're still investigating; that's the one thing that makes me feel a bit safer.

I scroll through my messages, rereading the last couple from Will:

> Am considering accidentally on purpose scratching Chloe's Frozen CD. If I have to hear these songs one more time, I'm going to walk into the nearest bloody freezer and shut the door!

> Stopped at a service station en route to Polperro. Chloe insisted we go to Burger King. She really had to twist my arm! ;)

> Got here safely. No Wi-Fi or cell phone reception in the house. Feel like I'm in 1991. Very odd. Sending this from a café. Hope you're ok. X

That'll be why he didn't answer the phone. It's late, and Chloe will be tucked up in bed. I reach for the remote control and change channels. I should be in bed too, but it's going to be another night spent wide awake on the sofa for me. I don't think I'll ever sleep again, not until the police find out who's behind all this.

～

By 6:00 a.m. on Monday, I can't bear the silence or the solitude a second more. Every creak of the cottage, every squawk from outside, even the DVD automatically turning itself off makes me jump. Even in my sleep, I toss and turn, never quite allowing myself to settle. It's not that I'm afraid of Leanne, if indeed it is her who's been sending the messages; it's the anticipation I can't bear. I can't relax, and I can't settle. No matter what I do—watch TV, read a book, listen to music—my attention is focused on my phone. I tried moving it from the arm of the sofa to the kitchen so I wouldn't keep reaching for it, but then I found myself going into the kitchen every couple of minutes, certain that the soundtrack of whatever film I was watching had masked a plaintive bleep. I've found myself willing my tormentor to send me a text message or a notification; at least then I'd be able to do something. I've taken to pacing from room to room, desperately seeking something, anything, to distract me, but my mind has constantly returned to the living room, to the phone on the arm of the sofa. It doesn't matter whether you're locked in something the size of a cupboard or the size of a house: if you're locked in, you're a prisoner—whether or not you hold the key.

It takes me several hours to work up the courage to get back on my bike. Last week, I managed to convince myself that the hit-and-run was a coincidence, but now I can't shake the feeling that something bad's going to happen. I've been jumping at shadows ever since Sergeant Armstrong called to tell me that Leanne's still alive, and I won't be able to relax until he tells me that she's been found.

I could call Green Fields and say I'm not feeling well, but I'd be landing Anne right in it. I'm scheduled to run the volunteer training sessions for the first half of the week. Plus, Sheila's not the only one away this week; two of the other girls are still off with the flu. Who would look after the dogs? With Angharad gone and Barry not due in until Thursday, Anne would have to assign one of the girls who normally look after the small animals to look after them. That wouldn't be fair on the dogs—they don't know Becky or Laura—and it wouldn't be fair on the girls either. I know neither of them is particularly comfortable with the more dangerous breeds. I should be there; it's my job.

I try Will's phone again just before I set off, but it goes straight through to voice mail. I end the call, then call him, then end the call again. I'm torn between telling him what Sergeant Armstrong told me and letting him enjoy his half term week away with Chloe. I know he's exhausted after all his inspection preparation, and the last thing I want to do is have him worry for the whole week. But then I promised him that I'd call if anything happened. He insisted. I could read the subtext beyond his concerned gaze: stop keeping secrets and share them. This isn't just about telling him about Leanne; I need to prove to him that I trust him.

"Will," I say as the phone goes to voice mail again. "It's Jane. It's nothing to worry about, but there's been a development. Sergeant Armstrong called me on Saturday evening to tell me that one of the girls I went on vacation to Nepal with has been found. It's Leanne, the one I thought had died in a fire. She's been in a psychiatric unit for the last few years, and she was discharged a couple of months or so ago. It's probably got nothing to do with what's happened, but...well...you told me to call you, so this is me calling." I laugh, but there's a hollow sound to it. "I'm guessing you don't have a very good cell phone signal, because I tried calling you over the weekend, so I'll speak to you whenever you get this. I hope you and Chloe are having an amazing break. I'm off to work now, so...um...I'll see you soon. Bye!"

I scroll through to my text messages and double check that I haven't heard from Al again. I sent her a series of texts on Sunday—starting with questions about Leanne and whether she really thought she had been hospitalized for her anorexia, and then, when those didn't get a response, inquiring about Al's new girlfriend Liz and how they met—but she didn't reply. She'd sounded pleased to hear from me on the phone, but maybe I'd confused pleased with shocked.

I unlock my bike, throw my leg over it, and settle myself on the saddle. I don't blame Al for ignoring me. Talking to me reminds her of Ekanta Yatra, and that's something we'd both rather forget.

My day at work passes without incident, other than a case of doggy diarrhea from one of our new intakes and Freddy the parrot calling me a fucking bastard as I pass his cage. Shortly after I arrived, I checked in six Jack Russell puppies and their very tired and overbred mom. One of our inspectors had rescued them from an unlicensed puppy farm in West Wales after a tip-off from a member of the public. They were being kept in cramped, dirty conditions and were forced to play, sleep, and eat in the same small space where they also had to defecate. The vet who saw them treated them for fleas, kennel cough, and ear mites, and now it's down to us to help rehabilitate them psychologically, with the help of the dog behaviorist, before we attempt to find them new homes. I hate puppy mills with a passion, and the irony is that some of the worst ones are licensed and sell the dogs on to pet shops, who in turn sell them on to unsuspecting members of the public.

"You okay?" Anne hovers beside me in the doorway to the staff room, a jug of orange juice in one hand, a pile of plastic cups in the other. "Not nervous about the volunteer evening, are you?"

"God no." I manage a laugh. "Sorry, I was just thinking about those Jack Russell pups. They were absolutely caked in crap. I had to wash them twice to get them clean."

"I know." She shakes her head. "The breeders should be bloody strung up. Still"—she glances at the sea of nervous and excited faces in front of us—"at least you'll be getting some help. Shame about Angharad leaving; she seemed lovely."

I make a suitably positive sound, and Anne scurries off to set out the juice and plastic cups on the trestle table on the opposite side of the room. Green Fields doesn't have the budget to add cookies to the refreshment table.

"Okay." I take a step into the center of the room and clap my hands together. Seven expectant faces stare back at me. A man in a blue polo-neck sweater on the left of the room sits up a little straighter in his seat. "First of all, welcome and thank you all so much for coming along this evening. As you know, Green Fields is run solely on donations, and we couldn't keep the place going without the help of our lovely volunteers. My name is Jane Hughes, and I'm responsible for looking after the dogs that come into Green Fields, but I've had experience of working in all the different areas of the shelter. I'd like to begin by giving you a little bit of history about Green Fields and..."

As I continue the welcome speech, I become aware that something in the left pocket of my gray work pants is vibrating. My phone is turned to vibrate only, but the eyes of several of the volunteers are trained on my pocket, so I have no choice but to pause.

"I'm sorry." I reach into my pocket. "I'll just turn this off, and then..."

Al calling, says the display.

"I'm so sorry." I make an apologetic face at my audience. "I really need to get this. Talk among yourselves, and I'll be right back."

I slip out of the room, pulling the door closed behind me, and hold the phone to my ear.

"Al? Everything okay?"

There's a pause, then a rustling sound, then the roar of traffic.

"Emma, what's your address?" Al sounds breathless.

"Honeysuckle Cottage, Bude. I'll text you my postcode. Why?"

"I'm in my car. I should get to you about 9:00 p.m. We need to talk. You were right. Daisy's not dead."

"What?"

"I'll tell you everything when I see you. Don't tell the police. Promise me. Promise me you won't contact them, Emma."

"But—"

"Promise me, Emma. Please."

"Okay, but you can't just... Al? Hello, Al? Can you hear me? Al!"

The phone goes dead, and when I try to call her back, it goes straight to voice mail. I text her my postcode anyway and then look at the time: 8:15 p.m.

"Anne?" I sprint down the corridor toward reception, desperately hoping she hasn't already left. "Anne?"

"Yes?" She pauses in the door to reception, holding it open with a gloved hand, her duffle coat buttoned up to her neck. She's clutching her car keys in her free hand.

"I need to go. There's been an emergency. I wouldn't ask you unless it was really important, but please could you talk to the volunteers for me and then lock up?"

"But I was just—" She gestures toward the dark yard. We've been waiting for Derek to install a security light since the break-in, but he discovered some kind of problem with the electrical system that confounded him.

"I know." I grip the reception counter with both hands. "I know you were just leaving, but this is so important. I'll make it up to you, I promise."

Anne looks me up and down, then purses her lips and sighs.

"Okay, but if there isn't some kind of chocolate or cake-type affair on my desk first thing tomorrow," she says as she unbuttons her coats and slips it off her shoulders, "you won't hear the last of it. I promise you that!"

48

t's 8:40 p.m. when I arrive at my cottage, breathing heavily, sweat rolling down my cheeks. There are no cars in the drive and no sign of Al, so I prop my bike up against the side wall and let myself into the cottage. The door catches on a pile of mail, and I stoop to pick it up, then double lock the front door. I move through the house, checking all the windows are locked and all the curtains are closed, then head for the kitchen and perch on a chair as I flick through the mail. It reveals nothing—just junk mail and bills. I trash the junk mail, put the bills on the china hutch, and check the time on the kitchen clock: 8:50 p.m. Ten minutes until Al arrives. I sit down again and check my phone, but there are no missed calls, no texts, no Facebook notifications.

I rest my elbows on the table and clasp my hands together in front of my face, my thumbs pressed to my lips as I watch the door. Underneath the table, my foot *tap-tap-taps* on the tiles. I look at the clock again—8:52 p.m.—and get up to turn the kettle on. I put a tea bag in a mug, then take it out and reach for a bottle of red wine from the rack instead. The corkscrew is halfway through the cork when I abandon that too. 8:57 p.m. Three minutes to go.

I scroll through my phone until I reach Sergeant Armstrong's number. Al said not to call the police, but she didn't say why. Is it because she's scared Daisy will press attempted murder charges? But Daisy's not coming here. Al said she was coming alone. Or did she? She said Daisy was alive, that I shouldn't tell the police, and that she'll explain everything when she gets here. She didn't say Daisy wasn't with her. I stand up, walk to the sink, and peer through the blinds. My reflection peers back at me. It's so dark outside, I can't even see the end of the drive.

Daisy must have sent me the messages. But why now? Why wait five years? That doesn't make sense, even if she did manage to survive the fall. Unless Al's lying. She lied about talking to the press, and she told me she wasn't the one who put my antianxiety pills in her bag. She said Leanne must have done it to try to turn me against her, and I'd believed her, but what if I was wrong?

I glance at the clock. 9:02 p.m.

～

I give it until 9:10 p.m., then I call Al's phone. It goes straight to voice mail.

"Hi, Al, it's Emma. I just wanted to check that you're not lost. Give me a call if you are."

I place the phone on the table, then walk to the sink and peep between the blinds. My own worried face peers back.

At 9:30 p.m., I open the front door and walk to the bottom of my drive. The lane is silent apart from the rustle of wind in the leaves and the faint hooting of a wood pigeon. I stand by the wall for several minutes, shivering in my short-sleeved polo shirt, staring into the darkness, waiting for the flash of headlights in the distance, then turn and walk back to the cottage. I'm halfway up the drive when I notice the plume of gray steam, puffing up from the ground and twirling in the night sky, obliterating the stars. For a second, I'm confused: the railway tracks run south of my cottage, not north. But then it hits me. It's not steam from an old engine gusting into the air; it's smoke. The thick, dense, choking smoke that billows from a burning building. And it's coming from the direction of Green Fields.

~

The acrid smell of burning straw, wood, and plastic grows stronger as I approach the peak of the hill, my palms clammy and my thighs burning as I grip the handlebars and transfer my weight from left to right, left to right. The frenzied barking I heard halfway up the hill becomes a cacophony as I skid around the corner into Green Fields, but despite my frantic 911 call before I left home, there are no flashing lights awaiting me, no fire engine sailing over the brow of the hill, sirens wailing. The shelter parking lot is empty, apart from a single Fiat Uno, parked at a strange angle just outside the doors to reception. Whoever is responsible for the fire has either abandoned the car or they're still here. Instinctively, I glance up toward Sheila's house, but it's shrouded in darkness. She won't be back from her vacation for another five days.

The yelps, barks, and howls from the dog compound increase, almost as though the dogs know I have arrived. I throw my bike to the ground and run toward the car parked outside reception. It isn't until I'm ten feet away that I realize it hasn't been abandoned. Someone is sitting in the passenger seat, their head pressed against the window as though they fell asleep during the journey and the driver left them to slumber. I don't want to risk waking them, so I run around the car and push at the doors to reception. They're locked. Whoever started the fire must have found an alternative way in. I reach into my pocket for my keys and then pause. Something prickles at my spine—uncertainty, confusion, recognition—and I duck down and peer through the driver-side window at the person slumped inside. It's a woman. A heavyset woman with strong arms, a generous gut, and a double chin cushioning her jaw against the glass. Her hair is longer than the last time I saw her, swept across her forehead rather than spiked up to the sky, and she's got a new tattoo on her right forearm.

"Al!" I yank open the passenger door and try to catch her, but she's too heavy. She slips from her seat and through my fingers, landing on the gravel with a thump, her sneakered feet still in the seat well, half in the car, half out.

"Al!" I push the hair from her face and tap her lightly on her cheek. She's breathing, and there are no marks on her body, no evidence she's been hurt. She doesn't smell of alcohol either.

"Al?" I slap her harder. "Al, wake up! What happened? Where's Daisy?" I glance toward the shelter as the sound of Freddy squawking and Bill and Ben squealing is carried on a gust of black smoke so thick and acrid I start to cough. "Al?"

Her eyes stay closed, but the quietest of groans escapes from her parted lips.

"What was that?" I lower my head so my ear is near her mouth. "Al, say that again."

I feel her breath in my ear, and then, so quiet I can barely hear it, she says, "Leanne."

"Leanne? What about Leanne?"

Her lips move silently, and then her head lolls to one side.

"Al? Al?" I grab her shoulders and shake her, but she's fallen back to sleep. "Al!"

I cradle her in my arms, rocking her back and forth as the fire rages beyond the fence, a continuous, roaring bass note playing below the higher pitched barks, squawks, and squeals that tear at my heart. I can't leave Al alone, but I can't let the animals die. I can't. I can't let them die.

~

The food sheds have become huge crackling bonfires spitting black smoke into the air and showering the surrounding compounds with white-hot embers and flaming straw. Smaller fires burn near each of the dogs' pens where someone has dragged bales of straw to the end and set them alight, then pushed flaming torches through the gaps in the fence, setting light to toys and bedding. The dogs have all retreated inside, scratching at the doors, pacing back and forth and barking, or else pressed into a corner, their eyes huge and fearful.

I fumble my keys into the lock, then run down the corridor, the hem of my polo shirt pressed to my mouth as I open door after door. The dogs knock at my legs as I free them, barking, yelping, jumping on each other in their desperation to reach cool, fresh air. I gather two of the smaller dogs into my arms, then shoo the larger stragglers through the corridor and toward the open doorway. We spill out of the building and into the yard. I head for the cat compound, farther away from the food sheds and not on fire, but the dogs are still confused and scared, circling this way and that, barking at the fire and jumping up at me, so I change my mind and run toward the field. It's secure, and there's no danger of them running into the road. Freddy squawks at me as I run past the small animal enclosure and pecks desperately at the sides of his cage.

"I'll come back for you," I shout as I speed past him. It's only fifty or so yards to the field. I can still get him; there's still time to get him out. He screams as I disappear around the corner, and I falter. Is there? Is there enough time? The air is thick with smoke. If I'm struggling to breathe, how will he—

He screams again, and I stop in my tracks. I turn to go back to him.

And all the hairs on my arms stand up as the scream continues—a terrified, piercing screech.

That wasn't Freddy. That was human.

~

The heat of the fire hits me the second I turn the corner. The boars' shed is alight, the right side and the roof engulfed by flames, and Bill and Ben are squealing and running back and forth in their pen, smashing against the fence and nudging the bolt with their snouts. The dogs reach them before I do, jumping up at the pen, barking and scratching, whining to be allowed in. If I let the boars free, Jack and Tyson will attack them, but it's not the boars' well-being I'm worried about. They'll gore the dogs in a heartbeat. Most of the dogs come with me as I run up to the top field and throw the gate wide. They bound away into the long grass, delighted with their unexpected freedom.

By the time I get back to Bill and Ben, only Willow, Vinny, and Stella are still with me. There's a creaking noise as I fiddle with the bolt to the pen, then a crashing sound as part of the shed roof collapses. Then there's another scream, a scream that goes right through me, as a small dark figure, cloaked in smoke, appears inside the door to the shed and throws itself at it. The door holds firm. The latch at the bottom has been flipped over.

"Leanne!" I pull at the bolt to the pen, but it's stiff and rusty, and I'm shaking so much I can't get a good grip on it. "Leanne!"

Willow and Vinny jump at my legs, and Bill and Ben squeal with fear inside the pen.

"Leanne!"

There's another crash, and the side of the shed crumples as flames leap into the air. The trapped figure screams again, and the sound goes through me. It's a scream of anger, of terror, of despair. I wiggle the bolt back and forth, back and forth, never taking my eyes off the dark shape reaching for me from the shed.

Come on, come on, come on.

The boars bowl into me as I finally yank open the gate, and I have to cling to the fence to stay upright.

The world goes very quiet as I raise an arm to my eyes, shielding my face from the intense heat, and take a step toward the shed. The dogs stop barking, the pigs stop snorting, Leanne stops screaming, and I stop walking.

Leanne tried to run me over. She sent me threatening messages. She set fire to Green Fields. She doesn't care if the animals die. All she cares about is hurting me. I take a step backward, and the flames on the shed leap and dance, painting it red, orange, blue, yellow, white. It's almost beautiful, like a living wash of color. Leanne, almost hidden in a cloud of smoke, reaches a hand toward me. Why should I save her? She turned Daisy against me. She encouraged Frank to come after me. She pushed my hand into a fire. I take another step back. If Leanne hadn't convinced us to go to Nepal, Daisy would still be alive. But Daisy's dead because Leanne manipulated us. She and Isaac used our greatest fears, our deepest regrets, and our biggest insecurities against us. They tried to break us down and then turn us against one another.

The roof of the shed creaks, Leanne screams, and the world speeds up again. I can't walk away and let her burn. If I let her die, I'm no better than her.

I crouch down and reach for a sturdy branch I saw the boars playing with what feels like a lifetime ago. There is a part of my brain that knows there's no way I'll be able to get close enough to open the latch, but there's another part that won't listen to reason, a part that believes that, if I can do it, if I can open the latch, the scales will tip. I couldn't save Daisy, but I can save Leanne.

There is a moment, as I draw closer to the burning building and the heat is so intense I am forced to shut my eyes, that I convince myself that I just saw her. There was a gap in the smoke, a brief moment when our eyes locked, and then she was gone again. But in that brief moment, just before I screwed my eyes tightly shut, I let myself believe that she knew. She knew I was trying to rescue her.

I twist away and take a step back, my eyes streaming with tears as I try to force them open again. There's a crack, like a tree being felled, and the shed—and Leanne—collapse to the ground.

49

There's a woman I don't recognize sitting beside the empty hospital bed. She's got dark brown hair, cut into a neat bob, rosy cheeks, and an engagement ring on the third finger of her left hand. She twists it idly as she watches Jerry Springer stride back and forth on the television. She jolts when I clear my throat and angles the TV away.

The base of her throat blushes a deep magenta. "Can I help you?"

"I was told this was Al's room."

"She's in the bathroom."

"Right."

We stare at each other for a couple of seconds, then I clear my throat again. The paramedic told me the smoke inhalation is unlikely to have done any lasting damage, but I might have a cough for some time.

"Are you Liz?"

"Emma?"

"Yes."

The anxiety on her face fades instantly, but it's replaced by another emotion—anger. A porter with a cart shouts "Beep, beep!" and I'm forced to step into the room. I keep a hand on the door frame.

"I'm sorry, Liz."

The fingers of her right hand return to her engagement ring. She twiddles it back and forth as though it's a talisman warding off evil spirits as she gives me a long, lingering look—a look that says *You abandoned her, again.* "She could have died."

"She was breathing when I left her. I knew the ambulance and fire trucks wouldn't be far away."

"No, you didn't."

I look down at the shiny, speckled floor. "No, I didn't."

Neither of us says anything more. On the TV, Jerry Springer makes a big song and dance about reading out the results of a lie detector test. He's got the audience in the palm of his hand.

"What happened to the animals?" Liz asks.

"They've been moved to neighboring sanctuaries while we try to fix the damage. We managed to round up all of the dogs apart from Tyson. The boars are long gone, and we lost three of the older, sicker cats to smoke inhalation, as well as all the hamsters, rodents, and Freddy the parrot." I stare up at the ceiling and blink back the tears that are pricking at my lower lashes.

"I'm sorry," Liz says softly.

"All the staff at Green Fields are very upset."

"No, not about that, though I am very sorry about the animals. I'm sorry for having a go at you, Emma. You had an impossible choice to make."

I bite down on the inside of my cheek and shake my head. If I speak, I'll cry.

"Emma." I hear the squeak of a chair leg on linoleum as Liz stands up. I tense as she approaches, but she doesn't touch me. Instead, she stands over me, her hands knotted in front of her. "What happened wasn't your fault."

I shake my head again. I shouldn't have come. I should have stayed with Will and called the ward to check that Al was okay.

He told me not to come. He said I was too shaken up, that I had to let him take care of me, but I refused. He was right, again.

"She's right, Emma. It wasn't your fault."

Al is standing in the doorway in her bare feet, a fluffy baby blue dressing gown wrapped over her hospital gown, her hands in the pockets. Her face is still wan, but it's lost its deathly pale pallor. Liz takes a step back as Al pads across the floor toward me.

"Al." I force myself to look her in the eye. "I'm so sorry. I'm so incredibly—"

She pulls me into her arms before I can finish my sentence and holds me as I cry into her shoulder.

"I'll give you some time," Liz says softly. Her shoes squeak on the linoleum as she leaves the room.

~

"A Valium overdose?"

"Yeah." Al reaches for the jug of water beside the bed and pours herself a glass. "The doctors think she must have crumpled some pills into the flask of tea she gave me when we arrived at Green Fields. They don't think she meant to kill me..." She pauses to take a sip of water. "She was a mess, Emma. She told me that she started the fire at Ekanta Yatra. She waited two days for Isaac and Daisy to come back, and when they didn't, she became convinced that something was going on and everyone was keeping it from her. Isis and Cera tried to calm her down—they said Isaac and Daisy had probably gone to Pokhara together—but Kane, who was drunk, started winding her up. He told her that Isaac and Daisy had run off together and left her behind. She believed him; I don't know why. She said she was the happiest she'd ever been at Ekanta Yatra, that she'd finally found her home, but maybe a part of her believed that would only ever be transitory. Anyway"—she shrugs—"she got really drunk and really angry that Isaac had used her just so he could sleep with her friends. She set fire to his study when everyone was asleep. She walked out of the gate with her passport in one hand and all Isaac's money in the other."

"Oh my God. Was she in Pokhara when you were still in the hospital?"

Al nods. "Apparently so. We could have ended up on the same flight back to Kathmandu as her, but she said she decided to stay in Pokhara for a bit. She said she thought that Isaac and Daisy were hiding out from her, and she was determined to find them."

"How long did she stay there?"

"About three months, she said. Then she met someone in a bar who told her that they'd heard about Ekanta Yatra burning down, and there was a rumor going about that Isaac was starting up a new one back in the UK."

"So she came back?"

"Yeah. Emma, she was obsessed with him. She really wasn't well. That's why she was hospitalized. She used the last of Isaac's money to fly to Aberdeen, then she started hassling his best friend, some guy the Salvation Army had put her in touch with."

"I read about him in one of her emails."

"Yeah, so she started hassling him and was arrested for putting a brick through the window of his car when he wouldn't tell her where Isaac was. She was in such a state when the police interviewed her—hearing voices, threatening suicide, seeing things, that sort of thing—that they called in a doctor. And he had her committed. She said she liked the hospital. Everyone was nice to her, and no one judged her, and she made some nice friends, but then they decided she was well enough to leave, and she felt like it was Ekanta Yatra all over again."

"Her happiness taken away?"

"Yeah, and she convinced herself that you were the reason why. I didn't realize that until we got in the car. She'd convinced me that Daisy was alive and she knew where she was. She started ranting the second we hit the highway; it was as though she'd kept it all corked up inside her until then. She threatened to throw herself out of the car if I didn't help her. She opened the door twice on the highway. I nearly crashed trying to yank her back in."

"That's why you called me?"

"Yeah. She told me what to say to you. I was planning on pulling into a service station to call you from the bathroom, but she grabbed my phone and threw it out of the window. I had no choice but to keep driving. I thought that, once we got to your house, we could call for a doctor or something, but she convinced me to go to Green Fields. She said there was a volunteer evening, that you'd be there."

"And when she realized I wasn't…"

"She set light to it anyway. She wanted to destroy everything you love." Al pulled the dressing gown more tightly around her. "She knew a lot about you, Emma. She knew about your boyfriend and your little girl."

"Chloe is my boyfriend Will's daughter."

"Right, well, she didn't know that, but she was ranting about how you had the perfect family life and the perfect job and how it was so unfair that everything had turned out okay for you while she had nothing. She blamed it all on you, Emma—Isaac and Daisy disappearing, Ekanta Yatra burning down, her hospitalization. She was convinced that you were behind it all, that you'd single-handedly destroyed her life. That's why she got in touch with me, I think. I think she thought I'd believe her when no one else would." She looks at me steadily. "What I don't get is how she managed to find me."

"Same way she managed to find me, I guess. She just asked someone."

"What do you mean?"

"She called my mum. She still had my home phone number

from back in university, and she just called up, said she was some-one I went to school with—Mom can't even remember the name she used—and said she was trying to organize a school reunion and did Mom have a contact number and an address for me?"

"And your mom just told her? Even though she knows you changed your name?"

I shrug. "Mom never understood why I did it. She told me I was being melodramatic and that I was insulting her and Dad by changing my name. I honestly don't think she'll have given it a second thought. I wouldn't have found out at all if she hadn't called the night of the fire. She saw it on the news and called up to check that I was okay, then casually said, 'Did someone get in touch with you about your school reunion?'"

"Shit."

"Once Leanne had my name and address, all she had to do was type it into Google, and then she found out where I work. All the press stuff I've done for Green Fields is up there; there are photos and everything. Don't forget how quickly I found you on Facebook, Al. It literally took me seconds."

"God." She leans back on the pillow and gazes listlessly at the TV. Jerry Springer has been replaced by *This Morning*, and the hosts are perched on the sofa, laughing uproariously at something their guest is saying.

"So what happens now?" Al asks, still looking at the screen.

"CSI have got Leanne's cell phone and laptop—they were in the bag she put in your car—and they've gained access to her bank account. Sergeant Armstrong called yesterday to say that she rented a car in Bristol the day before my hit-and-run. If it matches the car they found abandoned in the pull off, that'll prove she was responsible. They just need a bit more information, and then they'll close the case."

"No, that's not what I meant." Al looks me straight in the eye. "What do *we* do now?"

"What do you want to do, Al?"

"Tell the truth."

~

The inquiry lasted six months. CSI worked with the Nepalese police, and there was a second sweep of the Annapurna range, but there was no sign of Daisy's and Isaac's remains. The undergrowth was too thick, the range too expansive. Al got angry. She accused the Nepalese police of doing a cover-up so that tourism wouldn't suffer and threatened to fly over there and look for them herself if they couldn't do it properly, but Liz talked her out of it. The case was dropped a month later, and Isaac and Daisy are still officially classed as missing persons. Al's still beating herself up about it. I think she was hoping she'd be tried for Daisy's murder, even though it was an accident, just to rid herself of the terrible weight she's been carrying around for the last five years.

If only it were that easy. There are still times when I wake up in the middle of the night, choking on black smoke and crying out Leanne's name, only for Will to wrap his arms around me and Jack to bound into the bedroom and push his furry head between us. I adopted him after the fire. The court case against Gary Fullerton, prosecuting him for animal neglect as well as his involvement in the break-in, had been successfully concluded, and Jack was free to find a new home. I knew he'd struggle to settle into a new shelter, and he'd already had enough trauma to last a lifetime.

When Sheila returned from her vacation three days early and surveyed the blackened remains of Green Fields, I handed her my notice, but instead of accepting it, she sat me down at her kitchen table and listened for three long hours as I told her the truth about who I really am. The only time she showed a flicker of disapproval was when I told her the real reason Angharad had quit as a volunteer, but she seemed unperturbed when I warned her that Green Fields might suffer if Angharad kept to her word and ran a piece on me.

"So people will come to stare at you instead of the animals for a change. If you can deal with that, Jane, then so can I."

And they did—stare—for a while. And it wasn't just the visitors. The staff kept a wary distance for a couple of days, and the staff room fell silent every time I walked in to get my lunch, but gradually, over time, talk returned to normal topics—like who'd be voted off *Dancing with the Stars*, and who had tickets to see Elton John, and whether Jenny Craig or Weight Watchers is better for weight loss—and the ugly shadow that the article had cast over me slowly faded away. I'm pretty sure Angharad was responsible for stealing the first letter Leanne had sent to me. She never admitted it, but she speculated in her article that the fire had been started by someone who had a grudge against me, and she mentioned that she'd seen evidence to prove it.

There's still a shadow hanging over me, but it's not one that others see. The ghosts of Daisy and Leanne still haunt me. Neither of them deserved to die. Leanne was mentally ill, and Daisy was drunk, blinded by love, and manipulated into turning against me. I got in touch with Daisy's dad after the CSI closed their investigation and asked if we could meet. I expected him to refuse or scream abuse at me down the phone. Instead, he said yes and drove to Bude to see me. He sat at my kitchen table and listened as I told him what had happened in Nepal. I didn't mention the knife when I described how Daisy and Al had tussled on the clifftop. I didn't want his last image of Daisy to be of her with a knife in her hand, threatening her friends. As I ended the story, I expected him to cry or shout or run from the room. Instead, he sat very still, his hands on his thighs, and raised his eyes to the ceiling. Pain was etched on his face, not just from Daisy's death, but also from the two other deaths—of his wife and younger daughter—that he'd had to mourn many years earlier. When he said good-bye at the front door, he hugged me tightly and told me he'd be in touch, but I knew he wouldn't.

I tried to phone Leanne's mom, but she slammed the phone down. I tried a couple more times, and then Will told me to stop. It wasn't helping her, and it wasn't helping me. However Leanne's mom felt about her daughter and Isaac, she didn't want to share it with a stranger.

A couple of weeks ago, I found a photo of the four of us taken in a bar in Soho two days before we left for Kathmandu. We all look so fresh-faced and hopeful in the photo, and we were. It was supposed to be the vacation of a lifetime. I was escaping from a job I hated, Al was escaping from a failed relationship, Daisy was tagging along for the adventure, and Leanne…well, she was looking for somewhere to call home. I often wonder what would have happened if Daisy had won the argument back in Leanne's tiny studio flat in East London about where to take Al on vacation. Daisy would still be alive if we'd gone to Ibiza instead of Nepal, I'm sure of that. I'm not sure our friendship would have survived, though. Our relationship was too cracked and splintered, worn thin from years of petty arguments and hidden resentments. Would I have had the strength of character to call time on it? I'll never know. I was a very different person back then.

"Jane!" Chloe skips into the kitchen with Jack padding along beside her and Will trailing behind. He locks eyes with me and smiles warmly. "Can we take Jack for a walk? Please! He's ever so keen to go out."

"Jack? Or you?" I look from Chloe's hopeful expression to the openmouthed smile on the face of the happy, sweet-natured, loyal dog at her feet. There are people who believe that a fighting dog should be put down, that it's too physically and psychologically damaged to ever live a normal life, but I know differently. Jack's strong, stronger than the things that happened to him, and he's surrounded by people who love and care for him. Your past doesn't have to define your future, not if you won't let it.

"Jane?" Chloe asks again. "Can we, please?"

I stand and reach for the leash hanging from a hook on the china hutch. "Of course we can, sweetheart."

READING GROUP GUIDE

1. One of the themes of the book is whether your past defines your future. At the end of the book, Emma says that it doesn't if you surround yourself with people who love and care for you. Do you agree?

2. What did you think of the character Al? Was she sympathetic or unsympathetic?

3. Emma tries to rescue Leanne from the fire. Would you have done the same?

4. After Emma has told Will about who she really is, she tells him she'd rather he still called her Jane. Why do you think she did that?

5. At what point in the story do you think Daisy's death could have been prevented?

6. When Emma reads Leanne's emails, she finds out that Leanne thinks she's a pessimistic person who uses what happened to her in the past for her own gain. Do you agree with this?

7. How do you think Emma changes over the course of the book (both as Emma and as Jane)?

8. What did you think of the ending? Should it have ended differently?

9. The book explores female friendships and the fact that some friendships have undercurrents of jealously, competitiveness, and resentment running through them. Is this true of any of your friendships?

10. What other similar books would you recommend to people who enjoyed *The Lie*?

A CONVERSATION
WITH THE AUTHOR

What inspired you to write _The Lie_?

I wrote _The Lie_ because I've always been fascinated by the nature of female friendships, in particular the dynamics of close-knit groups of friends. Most of the time, female friendships are healthy and supportive—you literally trust them "with your life"—but sometimes they're not. Sometimes they're much more toxic than they appear, with possessiveness, resentment, bitterness, competitiveness, and envy lurking under the surface.

I wanted to write a story about a group of women who appear to get along well but whose friendship is riddled with issues that none of them are willing to confront. I was curious as to what would happen if I put those friends in a dangerous, crucible-type situation where they're forced to trust one another to survive. Would they support or turn on one another instead?

Did you include any of your own real life experiences in the novel?

Like the women in the novel, I went to Nepal on a vacation of a lifetime. Unlike Emma and her friends, I had the most amazing time, and, if anything, stronger bonds were formed among my friendship circle as a result of our experience.

But I have also experienced friendships that weren't healthy—friends who were effervescent, generous, spontaneous, and fun, but also unpredictable, competitive, possessive, and argumentative. When someone like that is at the center of your friendship group, they can get away with antisocial behavior, because everyone is aware that if they call them on it, they'll be frozen out. That can make for a lot of tension, isolation, and mistrust—sensations I hope my readers experience when they read *The Lie*.

Your characters are so authentic. As a writer, how do you get into their psyches?

My characters are an amalgamation of me, people I've known, people I've observed, and my imagination. I always make sure I know what each character desires—something they want more than anything else in the world—and also what they fear most. I also look to their childhoods to discover how their pasts have shaped them into the people they are now. As well as obvious things like the way they look and the things they wear, I also spend a lot of time thinking about my characters' mannerisms, the way they hold themselves, the way they walk, and the way they speak. Sometimes I know everything about a character before I start to write the novel; sometimes it's not until I've written the first draft that I've fully gotten to know them.

Why did you decide that Emma should work in an animal shelter?

Emma always wanted to be a vet, and after her experience at Ekanta Yatra, I felt it made sense to give her a new start that was centered on animals rather than people. Even though she's still quite isolated socially (she still doesn't trust people enough to let them get close), I wanted to make her content so that when the letters and messages start arriving, she's got a lot to lose. I also liked the similarity between Emma and the animals she cares for. Like Jack, she's been hurt and mistreated and needs patience and gentleness to teach her to trust and love again.

Did you know the ending when you started writing the book?

Actually, it changed several times. Originally, Daisy was going to fall off the cliff by accident, and Al was going to die of an asthma attack (or die in the car after Leanne had attacked her), but I felt it would be too bleak to completely destroy Emma's friendship group. I needed there to be one friendship that survived, one person who Emma could trust, despite everything. I don't imagine that Emma and Al will remain close for the rest of their lives. I think they've both been through so much that spending time together will bring back bad memories, but they'll both move on to happier times, and in part, they have their trust in each other to thank for that.

The Lie **has so many unexpected twists and turns. Do you sometimes even surprise yourself when you are writing?**

Absolutely! When I was writing the first draft, I had a pretty good idea what was going to happen, but new twists occurred to me as I was writing it. That sometimes meant I had to veer off in a completely different direction from the one I was planning, but that's one of the magical things about writing: the way your mind can surprise you. It keeps you entertained as a writer, and hopefully, it means some unpredictable twists for the reader too.

Read on for an excerpt from C. L. Taylor's

BEFORE I WAKE

April 22, 2012

C oma. There's something innocuous about the word, soothing almost in the way it conjures up the image of a dreamless sleep. Only Charlotte doesn't look to me as though she's sleeping. There's no soft heaviness to her closed eyelids. No curled fist pressed up against her temple. No warm breath escaping from her slightly parted lips. There is nothing peaceful at all about the way her body lies, prostrate, on the duvetless bed, a tracheostomy tube snaking its way out of her neck, her chest polka-dotted with multicolored electrodes.

The heart monitor in the corner of the room bleep-bleep-bleeps, marking the passage of time like a medical metronome, and I close my eyes. If I concentrate hard enough, I can transform the unnatural chirping into the reassuring tick-tick-tick of the grandfather clock in our living room. Fifteen years fall away in an instant, and I am twenty-eight again, cradling baby Charlotte to my shoulder, her slumbering face pressed into the nook of my neck, her tiny heart outbeating mine, even in sleep. Back then, it was so much easier to keep her safe.

"Sue?" There is a hand on my shoulder, heavy, dragging me

back into the stark hospital room, and my arms are empty again, save the handbag I clutch to my chest. "Would you like a cup of tea?"

I shake my head, then instantly change my mind. "Actually, yes." I open my eyes. "Do you know what else would be nice?"

Brian shakes his head.

"One of those lovely tea cakes from M&S."

My husband looks confused. "I don't think they sell them in the canteen."

"Oh." I look away, feigning disappointment, and instantly hate myself. It isn't in my nature to be manipulative. At least I don't think it is. There's a lot I don't know anymore.

"It's okay." There's that hand again. This time it adds a reassuring squeeze to its repertoire. "I can pop into town." He smiles at Charlotte. "You don't mind if I leave you alone with your mum for a bit?"

If our daughter heard the question, she doesn't let on. I reply for her by forcing a smile.

"She'll be fine," I say.

Brian looks from me to Charlotte and back again. There's no mistaking the look on his face—it's the same wretched expression I've worn for the last six weeks whenever I've left Charlotte's side. Terror she might die the second we leave the room.

"She'll be fine," I repeat, more gently this time. "I'll be here."

Brian's rigid posture relaxes, ever so slightly, and he nods. "Back soon."

I watch as he crosses the room, gently shutting the door with a click as he leaves, then release my handbag from my chest and rest it on my lap. I keep my eyes fixed on the door for what seems like an eternity. Brian has never been able to leave the house without rushing back in seconds later to retrieve his keys, his phone, or his sunglasses or to ask a "quick question." When I am sure he has gone, I turn back to Charlotte. I half expect to see her eyelids flutter or her fingers twitch, some sign that she realizes what I am about to say, but nothing has changed. She is still "asleep." The doctors have no idea when, or even if, Charlotte will ever wake up. She's been subjected to a whole battery of tests—CAT scans, MRIs, the works—with more to come, and her brain function appears normal. There's no medical reason why she shouldn't come around.

"Darling." I take Charlotte's diary out of my handbag, fumble it open, and turn to the page I've already memorized. "Please don't be angry with me but…" I glance at my daughter to monitor her expression. "I found your diary when I was tidying your room yesterday."

Nothing. Not a sound, not a flicker, not a tic or a twinge. And the heart monitor continues its relentless bleep-bleep-bleeping. It is a lie of course, the confession about finding her diary. I found it years ago when I was changing her sheets. She'd hidden it under her mattress, exactly where I'd hidden my own teenaged journal so many years before. I didn't read it though, back then; I had no reason to. Yesterday I did.

"In the last entry," I say, pausing to lick my lips, my mouth suddenly dry, "you mention a secret."

Charlotte says nothing.

"You said keeping it was killing you."

Bleep-bleep-bleep.

"Is that why…"

Bleep-bleep-bleep.

"…you stepped in front of the bus?"

Still nothing.

Brian calls what happened an accident and has invented several theories to support this belief: she saw a friend on the other side of the street and didn't look both ways as she ran across the road, she tried to help an injured animal, she stumbled and tripped when she was texting, or maybe she was just in her own little world and didn't look where she was walking.

Plausible, all of them. Apart from the fact the bus driver told the police she caught his eye and then deliberately stepped into the road, straight into his path. Brian thinks he's lying, covering his own back because he'll lose his job if he gets convicted of dangerous driving. I don't.

Yesterday, when Brian was at work and I was on bed watch, I asked the doctor if she had carried out a pregnancy test on Charlotte. She looked at me suspiciously and asked why, did I have any reason to think she might be? I replied that I didn't know but I thought it might explain a thing or two. I waited as she checked the notes. No, she said, she wasn't.

"Charlotte." I shuffle my chair forward so it's pressed up against the bed and wrap my fingers around my daughter's. "Nothing you say or do could ever stop me from loving you. You can tell me anything. Anything at all."

Charlotte says nothing.

"It doesn't matter if it's about you, one of your friends, me, or your dad." I pause. "Is the secret something to do with your dad? Squeeze my fingers if it is."

I hold my breath, praying she doesn't.

Friday, September 7, 1990

It's 5:41 a.m. and I'm sitting in the living room, a glass of red wine in one hand, a cigarette in the other, wondering if the last eight hours of my life really happened.

I finally rang James on Wednesday evening, after an hour's worth of abortive attempts and several glasses of wine. The phone rang and rang, and I started to think that maybe he was out when it suddenly stopped.

"Hello?"

I could barely say hello back, I was so nervous but then...

"Susan, is that you? Gosh. You actually called."

His voice sounded different, thinner, breathy, like he was nervous too, and I joked that he sounded relieved to hear from me.

"*Of course,*" *he replied.* "*I thought there was no way you'd call after what I did. Sorry, I'm not normally such a twat, but I was so pleased to run into you alone backstage that I... Anyway, sorry. It was a stupid thing to do. I should have just asked you out like a normal person...*"

He tailed off, embarrassed.

"*Actually,*" *I said, feeling a sudden rush of affection toward him,* "*I thought it was funny. No one's ever thrown a business card at me and shouted 'call me' before. I was almost flattered.*"

"*Flattered? I'm the one who should be flattered. You called! Oh god.*" *He paused.* "*You are calling to arrange a drink, aren't you? You're not ringing to tell me I'm an absolute jerk?*"

"*I did consider that option.*" *I laughed.* "*But no, I happen to be unusually thirsty today, so if you'd like to take me out for a drink, that could be arranged.*"

"*God, of course. Whenever and wherever you want to go. All drinks on me, even the expensive ones.*" *He laughed.* "*I want to prove to you that I'm not...well, I'll let you make your own mind up. When are you free?*"

I was tempted to say NOW but played it cool instead, as Hels had ordered me to do, and suggested Friday (tonight). James immediately agreed, and we arranged to meet in the Dublin Castle.

I tried on dozens of different outfits before I went out, immediately discarding anything that made me look, or feel, fat and frumpy, but I needn't have worried. The second I was within grabbing distance, James pulled me against him and whispered, "*You look beautiful,*" *in my ear. I was just about to reply when he abruptly released me, grabbed my hand, and said,* "*I've got something amazing to show you,*" *and led me out of the pub, through the throng of Camden revelers, down a side street, and into a kebab shop. I gave him a questioning look, but he said,* "*Trust me,*" *and shepherded me through the shop and out a door at the back. I expected to end up in the kitchen or the toilets. Instead I stumbled into a cacophony of sound and blinked as my eyes adjusted to the smoky darkness. James pointed out a four-piece jazz band in the corner of the room and shouted,* "*They're the Grey Notes—London's best kept secret,*" then led me to a table in the corner and held out a battered wooden chair for me to sit down.

"Whiskey," he said. "I can't listen to jazz without it. You want one?"

I nodded, even though I'm not a fan, then lit up a cigarette as James made his way to the bar. There was something so self-assured and masculine about the way he moved, it was almost hypnotic. I'd noticed it the first time I'd seen him on stage.

James couldn't be more different from my ex Nathan. While Nathan was slight, baby-faced, and only a couple of inches taller than me, James was six-foot-four with a solidity to him that made me feel small and delicate. He had a cleft in his chin like Kirk Douglas, but his nose was too large to make him classically good-looking. His dirty blond hair continually flopped into his eyes, but there was something mercurial about them that reminded me of Ralph Fiennes; one minute they were cool and detached, the next they were crinkled at the corners, dancing with excitement.

I knew something was wrong the second James returned from the bar. He didn't say anything, but as he set the whiskey tumblers down on the table, his eyes flicked toward the cigarette in my hand and I instantly understood.

"You don't smoke."

He shook his head. "My father died of lung cancer."

He tried to object, to tell me that whether I smoked or not was none of his business, but his frown evaporated the second I put my cigarette out, and the atmosphere immediately lightened. The band was so loud it was hard to hear each other over the squeal of the trumpet and the scatting of the lead singer, so James moved his chair closer to mine so we could whisper into each other's ears. Whenever he leaned in, his leg rested against mine, and I'd feel his breath against my ear and neck. It was torturous, feeling his body against mine and smelling the warm spiciness of his aftershave and not touching him. When I didn't think I could bear it a second longer, James cupped his hand over mine.

"Let's go somewhere else. I know the most magical place."

I barely had a chance to say "okay" when he bounced out of his seat and crossed the room to the bar. A second later, he was back, a bottle of champagne in one hand and two glasses and a threadbare rug in the other. I raised an eyebrow, but he just laughed and said, "You'll see."

We walked for what felt like forever, weaving our way through the Camden crowds until we passed Chalk Farm. I kept asking where we were going, but James, striding alongside me, only laughed in reply. Finally we stopped walking at an entrance to a park, and he laid a hand on my shoulder. I thought he was going to kiss me. Instead he told me to shut my eyes because he had a surprise for me.

I wasn't sure what could be quite so astonishing in a dark park at silly o'clock in the morning, but I closed my eyes anyway. Then I felt something heavy and woolen being draped over my shoulders, and warm spiciness enveloped me. James had noticed I was shivering and lent me his coat. I let him lead me through the entrance and up the hill. It was scary, putting my trust in someone I barely knew, but it was exhilarating too and strangely sensual. When we finally stopped walking, he told me to stand still and wait. A couple of seconds later, I felt the softness of the worn cotton rug under my fingers as he helped me to sit down.

"Ready?" I felt him move so he was crouched behind me, then his fingers touched my face, lightly brushing my cheekbones as they moved to cover my eyes. A tingle ran down my spine and I shivered, despite the coat.

"I'm ready," I said.

James removed his fingers and I opened my eyes. "Isn't it beautiful?"

I could only nod. At the base of the hill, the park was a checkerboard of black squares of unlit grass and illuminated pools of yellow-green light cast by glowing street lamps. It was like a magical patchwork of light and dark. Beyond the park stretched the city, windows twinkling and buildings sparkling. The sky above was the darkest navy, shot with dirty orange clouds. It was the most breathtaking vista I'd ever seen.

"Your reaction when you opened your eyes..." James was staring at me. "I've never seen anything so beautiful."

"Stop it!" I tried to laugh but it caught in my throat.

"You looked so young, Suzy, so enchanted—like a child on Christmas day." He shook his head. "How is someone like you single? How is that even possible?"

I opened my mouth to reply, but he wasn't finished.

"You're the most amazing woman I've ever met." He reached for my hand. "You're funny, kind, intelligent, and beautiful. What on earth are you doing here with me?"

I wanted to make a joke, to ask if he was so drunk he didn't remember leading me up the hill, but I found I couldn't.

"I wanted to be here," I said. "And I wouldn't want to be anywhere else."

James's face lit up as though I'd just given him the most wonderful compliment, and he cupped my face with his hands. He looked at me for the longest time and then he kissed me.

I'm not sure how long we kissed for, lying there on a rug on the top of Primrose Hill, our bodies entwined, our hands everywhere, grasping, pulling, clutching. We didn't remove our clothes and we didn't have sex, yet it was still the single most erotic moment of my life. I couldn't let go of James for more than a second without pulling him toward me again.

It grew darker and colder, and I suggested we leave the park and go back to his flat.

James shook his head. "Let me put you in a taxi home instead."

"But—"

He pulled his coat tighter around my shoulders. "There's time for that, Suzy. Plenty of time."

ACKNOWLEDGMENTS

A big thank-you to my editor, Shana Drehs, and the team at Sourcebooks for their tireless support and hard work. It is thanks to them that I am able to share my books with U.S. readers, and for that, I am incredibly grateful. Thank you to Alex and Jo at LightBrigade PR, for doing such a good job promoting my books, and a big hug to my wonderful agent, Madeleine Milburn, for being my constant cheerleader and for doing her best to keep me sane in what's been quite a stressful year. Thank you too to Cara Lee Simpson, for all her hard work.

I couldn't have written the present-day thread of *The Lie* without the kindness of Anna James and Little Valley Animal Shelter, Exeter (RSPCA). Little Valley does a wonderful job caring for unwanted, abandoned, and cruelly treated animals in the South, East, and West Devon areas, and Anna very kindly gave me a guided tour of the shelter, answered my million-and-one questions about procedures and practices, and responded to the countless texts and emails I sent her afterward. I can't thank you enough, Anna.

Thank you also to Dr. Charlotte McCreadie for her medical knowledge, Paul Finch and Sharon Birch for answering my police procedural questions, and to Fionnuala Kearney, who won the

Authors for the Philippines online auction to name a "baddie" in this book. She named Frank.

A huge thank-you to my family for their never-ending love and support: Reg and Jenny Taylor, Bec, Dave, Suz, Sophie, Rose, Steve, Guinevere, Nan, Granddad, Angela, and Ana. And my wonderful friends: Joe Rotheram, Becky Harries, Bex Butterworth, Laura Barclay, Kimberley Mills, Claire Bagnall, Rowan Coleman, Julie Cohen, Kellie Turner, Tamsyn Murray, Miranda Dickinson, Kate Harrison, and Scott James. I love you girls (and boy) to bits. Thank you for putting up with me.

This book is dedicated to Laura B., Georgie D., and Minal S., the friends I went to Nepal with in 2006. Unlike the girls in *The Lie*, we really did have the vacation of a lifetime, and for all the right reasons. Thanks for making it an amazing vacation, girls— and for not killing me! (I promise none of the characters are based on you.)

Finally, I'd like to thank my amazing, supportive partner, Chris, and our beautiful, funny son, Seth. None of this would mean anything without you two.

ABOUT THE AUTHOR

Photo credit: Jim Ross

C. L. Taylor lives in Bristol with her partner and son. She started writing fiction in 2005, and her short stories have won several awards and have been published by a variety of literary and women's magazines. C. L. Taylor was voted as one of the Bestselling Adult Fiction Debut Authors of 2014 in *The Bookseller*. She is also the author of *Before I Wake*.